THE QUIET ROOM

THE QUIET ROOM

A JOURNEY OUT OF THE TORMENT OF MADNESS

Lori Schiller AND
Amanda Bennett

WARNER BOOKS

A Time Warner Company

Grateful acknowledgment is given to reprint excerpts from the following songs:
"Easy" (Lionel Richie) © 1977 Jobete Music Co., Inc./Libren Music. Reprinted by permission. All rights reserved.

"Winchester Cathedral" (Graham Nash) © Nash Notes. Reprinted by permission. All rights reserved.

"Song for Adam" (Jackson Browne) Reprinted by permission of Atlantic Music Corp./Open Window Music. All rights reserved.

"The Needle and the Damage Done" (Neil Young) © 1971 Broken Fiddle. Reprinted by permission. All rights reserved.

Warner Books, Inc., 1271 Avenue of the Americas, New York, NY 10020
Visit our Web site at http://warnerbooks.com

 A Time Warner Company

Printed in the United States of America

Originally published in hardcover by Warner Books, Inc.

First Trade Printing: January 1996

10 9 8 7 6

Library of Congress Cataloging-in-Publication Data

Schiller, Lori.
   The quiet room : a journey out of the torment of madness / Lori Schiller and Amanda Bennett.
      p.   cm
   ISBN 0-446-67133-9
      1. Schiller, Lori—Mental health. 2. Schizophrenics—United States—Biography.
   I. Bennett, Amanda.   II. Title.
   RC514.S332A3   1994
   616.89'82'0092—dc20
   [B]   94-7693
                                                            CIP

Book design by Giorgetta Bell McRee
Cover design by Rachel McClain
Cover photograph by Sally Boon

For my
Mom and Dad . . .
Who never gave up hope.

I thank you . . .
I admire you . . .
and I love you.

Author's Note and Acknowledgments

Although this is my life story, I have chosen to tell it not only in my own voice, but also in the voices of others whose lives are interwoven with mine.

The others who speak in this book, from my college roommate, Lori Winters, to my psychiatrist, Dr. Jane Doller, to my parents and two brothers, are among the many people besides me who were affected by my illness. In telling my story, I tried to do the best job I could to show what the experience of schizophrenia is like for the person who is in its grip; in letting the others tell their stories, I want to show what the experience is like for friends and family.

In many ways too these people serve as my memory. My illness and, I believe, some of the treatments I went through have wiped out big chunks of my recollections of some periods of my life. I have turned the telling of those periods over to people whose memories are clearer than mine.

As I get better, my ability to remember accurately and to distinguish fact from fantasy improves. In writing this book Amanda Bennett and I have done the best job we could to make sure that we rendered events as accurately as possible. All the people, places and events in this book are real, and are portrayed exactly as I recall them. With a few minor exceptions all names in the book are real too. Because of their deep involvement with cocaine, however, I have changed the names and other identifying details of Raymond and Nicole. I also changed the names and descriptions of Robin, Carla and Claire to protect their privacy as fellow psychiatric patients.

In the interests of accuracy, we tried to interview as many people involved with my life, my illness and my treatment as possible. We tried to take their perspectives into account in the telling of this book. Ultimately, however, the final viewpoint is mine.

The only place where my memory still conflicts in any substantial way with external evidence is in my recollections of the events at Lincoln Farm, in the early months of my illness. Chapter 1, therefore, was written from a combination of my best possible recollection of those events; records from Lincoln Farm; and the memories of several fellow camp counselors, my parents and friends of the family. We would like to thank fellow counselor Jackie Pashkes for her special help in enabling us to unearth camp records; Mrs. Beatrice Loren, owner of the former Lincoln Farm, for making them available to us; and Amy Potozkin, another fellow counselor who shared her memories.

A number of people helped us fill in my recollections of the years before my hospitalizations. These include: Lori Winters Samuels, Michele Crames, Dr. Richard Dolins, Janey and Louis Klein, Dr. Philip Moscowitz, Bonnie Smith, Barbara A. Kobre, Tara Sonenshine Friend and Bradford A. Winters. I would especially like to thank Gail Kobre Lazarus for her help and for her friendship, then and now.

Amanda and I would like to thank New York Hospital—Cornell Medical Center, Payne Whitney Clinic, and New York Hospital—Cornell Medical Center, Westchester Division, for making my medical records available to us. Those records helped me to pinpoint dates of events, medications and procedures. They also gave me insight into how other people perceived the events I was experiencing.

We would also like to thank Dr. Otto Kernberg, medical director of New York Hospital Cornell Medical Center, Westchester Division, for making his busy staff available to us for interviews.

Many people contributed their recollections either to this book or earlier during the reporting for the October 14, 1992, *Wall Street Journal* article that launched this project. For help in remembering the periods of my earliest hospitalization, I would like to thank Dr. Eugenia Kotsis. At New York Hospital, I would like to thank Jody Shachnow, Dr. Richard Munich, Dr. Michael Selzer, Dr. Kenneth Turkelson, Kay Dinoff, and Ronald Inskeep.

For memories of other periods in my life, I would like to thank Eddie Mae Barnes and Rochelle Forehand.

Many people read this book's manuscript and offered valuable suggestions. They include: Lisa Ames, Janet Bennett, Nancy Ehle, Deborah Gobble, Betsy Julien, Shelly Benerofe and Sidney Rittenberg. My kindest thanks go to Anne Schiff, who not only read my earliest manuscript versions, but also painstakingly transcribed them.

For technical assistance and professional help, Amanda and I would also like to thank Mark Berman; Dr. Frederick Goodwin, director of the National Institute of Mental Health; Dr. John Kane, chairman of the department of psychiatry at Long Island Jewish Medical Center; Dr. Carmela Perri; Dr. Daniel Weinberger of the National Institutes of Health; and Dr. Richard Weiner, associate professor of psychiatry at Duke University Medical Center.

At *The Wall Street Journal*, we thank managing editor Paul Steiger and editors Jane Berentson, Roger Ricklefs and David Sanford.

Our thanks too to our agent, Michael Cohn, and to our wonderful editor, Jamie Raab.

I would like to offer my thanks to the doctors, nurses, social workers and friends who made my recovery possible: Janet Levkoff; Nancy, Carol and Glady; Penny and Michael Horgan, Phyllis Mossberg, Kathleen McDermott, Ron Kavanaugh, Andrew and Susan Sklarz; Nathaniel Goldberg; Maria Tivey; Myrt Armstrong; Julie Alkaitis Hall Houston; a special thank-you to Jacquie Aamodt for helping me out of the quicksand while I was sinking; Debbie, Jeannine, and Rosemary from Sandoz, Deanna at Futura House; Michael Rustin at the Mamaroneck unit of Search for Change and all of his staff; Beth Harris and Luba Spikula from New York Hospital Patient Education, who taught me how to give hope to others through teaching; the special members of the nursing staff at New York Hospital, including J.J., Gladys, Danny, Jean, Margo, Barbara, Cathy, Debbie, Rose, Peter, John, Glen, and especially Sorin Weiss, who kept on believing in me even when I didn't.

Dr. Diane Fischer will always have a very special place in my heart. She opened avenues that I didn't even know were around the corner. Her help in putting together this book—and my life—will always be appreciated.

And to Dr. Jane Doller, of course, my thanks to one of the most wonderful, dedicated, genuine, tuned-in and helpful psychiatrists I have ever worked with. You've taught me the meaning of partnership. Whatever we do, we do together.

I owe a special thanks to Dr. Lawrence Rockland, for the five years of dedication and the care and attention he gave me. If it weren't for him, I probably wouldn't be alive today. We also owe Dr. Rockland an enormous debt for the hours of time he gave in the preparation of this book.

And we would like to thank our families. Our thanks to Amanda's husband Terence Bryan Foley and son Terence Bennett Foley for their patience and understanding.

My most important thank-you is to my mother and father and brothers. They all lived beside me for years while my world was infested by hell. Thank you to Steven and to Mark; and now to their wives, Ann and Sally, for their friendship; and also to my three nephews, Mason, Jake and Austin. To Mom and Dad—just plain thank you. You're incredibly special. Love and many hugs.

—Lori Schiller and
Amanda Bennett
March 1, 1994

Foreword

I first met Lori Schiller when she was a patient and I was a staff psychiatrist at New York Hospital. I was her case administrator while she was in the throes of the worst of her illness. I followed her through her depths into recovery. Today I am her therapist.

Even knowing Lori as well as I do, I was both surprised and moved by her account of her battle with schizophrenia. For, in this very personal book, Lori Schiller becomes our eyes and ears into a strange and terrifying world. Hers is one of the most compelling looks inside that world we have ever been able to take.

Back in the early parts of the century, such personal accounts of mental illness were more common in medical literature. Back when psychiatrists knew little about the workings of the brain or about the causes of mental illness, they pored over case studies looking for clues. Back then the anguished accounts of mental patients were an important window—if only for medical professionals—into what the subjective experience of mental illness was like.

Today, the whole psychiatric field has become much more scientific. Our focus has shifted to the study of the biological causes of mental illnesses like schizophrenia. Our treatments today turn increasingly to medications. Our hope for the future of many mentally ill patients lies largely in a whole range of new drugs now under development.

These new drugs have already changed the lives of hundreds of thousands—if not millions—of people who suffer from mental illness. Lori herself received her final, major push back into the real world from a then-experimental drug, clozapine. In the years since Lori first took the drug, we have learned that the dangers we had at first feared are much more controllable than we had understood. The benefits of clozapine can thus be made available to a much wider range of patients than we had initially expected. Other, newer drugs will expand that range even further.

Physicians, families, friends and the mentally ill themselves can only be grateful for these enormous medical developments. But Lori Schiller's story helps remind us of something we may have lost in our rush to embrace science: Mental illness is not just about drugs and biology. It is about people. It is clozapine that made Lori's final recovery possible. What made her recovery so successful is Lori herself.

I believe that the turning point for Lori occurred long before clozapine came on the scene. It happened during the early months of her final hospitalization when she finally began to face the illness head-on, when she finally became able to say: "I'm very sick. I need help." It was only then that she was able to take the risk of becoming truly involved in her treatment, of opening up to others about what she was feeling, and of beginning to connect with other people.

Lori's experiences with schizophrenia are at the same time very typical and very unusual. The course the illness took was extremely typical: The onset in late adolescence after an apparently normal childhood; the initial difficulty in finding a correct diagnosis; her own denial, and that of her parents, and their refusal at first to recognize her illness for what it was. The initial failure of treatment is also, unfortunately, fairly typical. The average young person with schizophrenia has, as did Lori, repeated hospitalizations, numerous medication trials and several separate courses of treatment with several different doctors before the illness is finally correctly identified and treated appropriately. Like Lori, many of these people turn in the meantime to illicit drug use in an effort to manage the frightening symptoms.

Her story is unusual, however, in the enormous personal courage she brought to her illness. She didn't fall victim to the prison of repeated substance abuse. Instead, she was able to recognize her problem, and then to stop it. When she finally was able to recognize that she was sick, she let nothing stand in the way of getting well.

She had a lot of support—loving parents, good hospital care, the best possible treatments available. But she would never have been able to return to the kind of life she is living now if it had not been for her own willpower and determination. In a very real way she herself helped conquer her own illness.

Lori's story offers important messages for all of us. For psychiatrists and medical professionals, it is a look at the inner world of a psychiatric patient, a world that we sometimes forget to take into account. It is a reminder that our traditional therapies that aim to reach past the illness to the person inside should not be thrown out even in this era of high-tech medication. In my own experience a connection with another person is a powerful tool for healing in a curing arsenal that also includes drugs.

For the mentally ill themselves, Lori's story offers a glimpse at the possibility that this medication or some other can offer them the same chance at a new life that Lori has had and that they too have a chance of overcoming their illnesses as she did.

For all the rest of us, Lori's story is a moving account of a very personal journey. It is a story not just of mental illness, but of a human being. It is a story of personal determination, courage and hope.

—Jane Doller, M.D.
Clinical Assistant Professor of Psychiatry
Cornell University Medical College
New York Hospital, Westchester Division

THE QUIET
ROOM

Part I

I Hear Something You Can't Hear

1

Lori
Roscoe, New York, August 1976

It was a hot night in August 1976, the summer of my seventeenth year, when, uninvited and unannounced, the Voices took over my life.

I was going into my senior year in high school, so this was to be my last time at summer camp. College, a job, adulthood, responsibility—they were all just around the corner. But for the moment I wasn't prepared for anything more than a summer of fun. I certainly wasn't prepared to have my life change forever.

I had been coming to Lincoln Farm for several years, first as a camper, later as a counselor. By day, I shepherded the nine- and ten-year-olds through sailing, canoeing and archery.

At night after the little kids were safely in bed, the counselors would hang out together in the long, low wooden bungalows we called "motels," playing cards, eating cookies and drinking a Kool-Aid type of concoction we called bug juice. Some nights the older counselors drove us into town to the Roscoe diner. We laughed, told jokes and fooled around.

It was just an ordinary summer, and I was just an ordinary girl. Except that sometime during that summer things began to change.

At first, the change was pleasant. Somehow, without my quite knowing why, everything seemed much nicer than it had been before. The lake seemed more blue, the paddlewheels bigger and the sailboats more graceful than ever before. The trees of the Catskill Mountains that ringed our camp took on a deeper green than I remembered, and all at once the whole camp seemed to be the most wonderful place in the world.

I was overwhelmed by what life had to offer. It seemed that I could not run fast enough, could not swim far enough, could not stay up late enough into the night to take in everything I wanted to experience. I was energetic and active, happy and bubbly, a friend to everyone. Everything around me was bright, clean and clear. And as for me, it seemed that I too was a part of this beauty. I was strong and attractive, powerful and exciting. It seemed that everyone around me had only to look at me to love me the way I loved them.

What's more, my memories became more vivid than ever before. It had been here at Lincoln Farm two years earlier that I had fallen in love. As I thought back to that summer, it too seemed wild and bright and wonderful. I had been in love as no one had been in love before. And the man I fell for was like no one I had ever met before.

He had been an exchange student that year, the summer I was fifteen. He was gorgeous, a real hunk, blond and lanky with bright blue eyes, and a cute little accent. Since I was short and dark, he seemed especially exotic. I really liked him, and could scarcely take my eyes off him. What's more, at twenty-three years old, he was my first older man. I admired him for his courage to come all the way over here alone for a summer, and I was charmed by his sense of humor.

We really enjoyed each other's company. My memories of those evenings became sweetly sad as I recalled talking about being in love, and how terrible it was going to be when he finally had to return home. We even made up an absurd little song to the tune of the Beatles' "Ticket to Ride":

> *He's got a ticket for home.*
> *He's got a ticket for home.*
> *He's got a ticket for home,*
> *And won't be back . . .*

But several weeks later, after camp was over and I had returned home to Scarsdale, he showed up at my house—with a pretty woman whom he introduced to my parents as his fiancée.

As the days went by, I found myself obsessing on that moment two years ago. Gradually, my mood began to shift, and the brightness of the world began to darken. As I remembered the past, the feelings began to blur the present. Then came the dreadful thoughts. Why had he left me that summer? Why hadn't I been good enough? Maybe it was because I really wasn't beautiful, exquisite and passionate. Maybe I was really ugly. Maybe more than ugly. Maybe I was fat and disgusting, an object not of romance but of ridicule. Yes, that was it. Maybe everyone around me, far from loving me, was instead laughing at me, mocking me to my face.

My mood began to turn black. A dark haze settled around me. The beautiful camp turned foul, a thing of evil, not of beauty. All around me were shadows, and I was wrapped in a dark haze.

My memories became so vivid that at night as I lay in my bunk wracked by unhappy thoughts and unable to sleep, it seemed as if I really were back in that summer. In my memory we were again down by the huge, dark, romantic lake. Over to the dockside we could hear the water lapping up against the sailboats and giant waterwheels the kids played on during the day. Late at night, the fireflies were gone, but we could still hear frogs croaking along the banks. The sky was heavy with stars I felt I had never seen before. We sat in the thick grass that ran right down to the water's edge and laughed and talked together.

In my memory, we snuggled and kissed. And then he became more insistent. We lay down together on the top of one of the picnic tables that ringed the lake. His hands began to roam, under my T-shirt, into my shorts. I was excited and worried, terrified and thrilled all at the same time. I wanted more, and I wanted him to stop. We were pushing the limits of my experience and I didn't know how to handle it. In my mind I was back there, rolling and caressing in the darkness, and I was washed over with complicated feelings from past and present—love, embarrassment, rejection, fear.

Then, in the middle of this chaos, a huge Voice boomed out through the darkness.

"You must die!" Other Voices joined in. "You must die! You will die!"

At first I didn't realize where I was. Was I at the lake? Was I asleep? Was I awake? Then I snapped back to the present. I was here at camp, alone. My summertime fling was long gone, two years gone. That long-ago scene was being played out in my mind, and in my mind alone. But as soon as I realized that I was in my bunk, and awake—and that my roommate was still sleeping peacefully—I knew I had to run. I had to get away from these terrible, evil Voices.

I leaped from my bed and ran barefoot out into the grass. I had to find someplace to hide. I thought if I ran fast enough and far enough, I could outrun the Voices. "You must die!" they chanted. "You will die."

Frantically, I ran out to the wide, open center lawn. The grass was wet under my feet. I raced for the huge trampoline where the kids practiced backflips and somersaults.

I climbed on. My head was filled with wild, strange thoughts. If I could jump fast enough and high enough, I thought, perhaps I could jump the Voices away. So I jumped and I jumped, all the while hearing the tormenting Voices ringing in my ears. "You must die. You will die." I jumped for hours, till I began to see the sun peeking over the hills. I jumped until I was out of breath, exhausted. I jumped until I really was ready to die.

Yet still they continued, commanding me, pounding into my head. They began to curse and revile me: "You whore bitch who isn't worth a piece of crap!" they yelled at me. I tried to answer them, to make them stop.

"It's not true," I pleaded. "Leave me alone. It's not true." Eventually, both I and the Voices collapsed in exhaustion.

In the nights that followed this torture continued. In the morning, I was exhausted, drawn and white from fear and lack of sleep. In the dead of night I jumped, pursued by the vicious Voices. Night after night I jumped, unable to sleep, either because of the screaming Voices, or my fear they would return.

As best I could during the day, I kept a calm but distant front. I spent as much time as I could in my bunk. But gradually people began to notice that something was wrong. My cheerful banter vanished, and I could sense that increasingly people were beginning to wonder what was the matter with me.

Finally at 9:30 A.M. on August 12 the camp owner, worried about my health, instructed a staff member to drive me home to Scarsdale.

Since that time, I have never been completely free of those Voices. At the beginning of that summer, I felt well, a happy healthy girl—I thought—with a normal head and heart. By summer's end, I was sick, without any clear idea of what was happening to me or why. And as the Voices evolved into a full-scale illness, one that I only later learned was called schizophrenia, it snatched from me my tranquillity, sometimes my self-possession, and very nearly my life.

Along the way I have lost many things: the career I might have pursued, the husband I might have married, the children I might have had. During the years when my friends were marrying, having their babies and moving into the houses I once dreamed of living in, I have been behind locked doors, battling the Voices who took over my life without even asking my permission.

Sometimes these Voices have been dormant. Sometimes they have been overwhelming. At times over the years they have nearly destroyed me. Many times over the years I was ready to give up, believing they had won.

Today this illness, these Voices, are still part of my life. But it is I who have won, not they. A wonderful new drug, caring therapists, the support and love of my family and my own fierce battle—that I know now will never end—have all combined in a nearly miraculous way to enable me to master the illness that once mastered me.

Today, nearly eighteen years after that terrifying summer, I have a job, a car, an apartment of my own. I am making friends and dating. I am teaching classes at the very hospital at which I was once a patient.

Still, I have been to a place where all too many people are forced to live. Like all too few, I have been permitted to return. I want to tell others about my journey so that those who have never experienced it will know what life inside of my schizophrenic brain has been like, and so that those who are still left behind will have hope that they too will find a path out.

2

Lori
Scarsdale, New York,
August 1970–August 1977

As I look back on my childhood, one memory plagues me. It is the memory of the afternoon of the dog.

I remember that when I was young my family had a medium-sized black mongrel. He was kept chained to a door, unable to move very far in one direction or another. One day as I was in the kitchen with him I suddenly grew very angry.

In a burst of rage, I grabbed a nearby golf club and began beating the dog furiously. At first he barked hysterically. But because of the chain, he could not escape. He began to foam at the mouth. As I beat him, one by one his legs collapsed. He kept struggling to rise, but I wouldn't let him. I kept hitting him, and hitting him, and hitting him. He fell to the ground. Then he stopped barking. His body writhed in horrible spasms, blood dribbling from his ears and mouth. After a while he stopped moving. Dead.

To this day I do not know why I did it. I try to imagine the evil impulses and anger that must have led to such a crime. In my thoughts over the years, I have punished myself over and over again for having committed such a terrible sin against an innocent creature.

But there is one big problem with this memory: It isn't true. It never happened.

My mom and dad say we never had such a dog. They say that the incident I remember so clearly never took place. My younger brothers, Mark and Steven, agree. We had only one family dog when I was growing up—not medium-sized and black, but a tiny gray miniature schnauzer. She died, not a brutal death, but a poignantly normal one when Steven took her to the vet to be put to sleep in her old age after a long, comfortable life. The vivid memory of the dog I murdered, my family tells me, is something my troubled mind conjured up years later, long after I became ill.

My increasingly healthy mind tells me they are right. The further I progress toward sanity, the more such dark images are fading, letting my real memories of my real childhood peep through.

Instead of such horrors, when I look back today on my childhood I find few signs of the illness that was secretly growing within me. I don't find a past filled with fear and violence and conflict. I don't find a troubled childhood of abuse and rage.

What I find instead is an exceptionally happy childhood, filled with love and comfort, fun and friendship. And the most compelling images of my past are not those of rage and hurt, but are instead of a girlhood of the most ordinary and tranquil sort.

"Ninety-nine bottles of beer on the wall, ninety-nine bottles of beer . . . you take one down and pass it around, ninety-eight bottles of beer on the wall. Ninety-eight bottles . . ."

It was the summer of 1970, we were driving across the country, and I thought we would drive my father crazy. Between our endless singing and our endless demands for bathroom stops, we kids were being wickedly, deliberately, irritating.

"Daddy, I have to go to the bathroom again."

"I'm hungry."

"I'm Yugoslavia."

"That's stupid."

"You're stupid."

"Mommy, Mark called me stupid."

"Daddy, I have to go to the bathroom."

My father threatened, my mother suggested car-spotting games. But still we persisted. "I have to go to the bathroom,

Daddy. I have to go to the bathroom." Finally, after a couple of hours of this, Daddy snapped.

"I don't want anyone to mention bathroom to me for the rest of the trip," he announced in exasperation. Well, that held us—for about two minutes. Then in somber tones one of us shouted over the front seat: "I have to go to the bathroom—Bob," and collapsed in fits of giggles. And for the rest of the trip we made our bathroom requests, not to our dad, but to our new imaginary friend. "I have to go to the bathroom, Bob," we shouted, knowing from the look on our parents' faces as they tried to stifle laughter that we had won. "I have to go to the bathroom, Bob."

I was eleven years old, Mark was eight, Steven was five, and the whole Schiller family was on the move again. I had been born in Michigan where my father, a graduate student from the Bronx finishing up his Ph.D. in psychology at Michigan State had met and married my mother, the daughter of a prosperous department store owner. When my dad graduated and got his first job, the three of us moved to Chicago where Mark was born. When I was six, my father was promoted, and we all moved to Los Angeles, where Steven was born.

Now, five years later, Daddy was being promoted again and we were all moving east. For us kids, this trip was great fun. For two weeks, we were trekking past the Petrified Forest, to the Grand Canyon, through Indian reservations in New Mexico and the seemingly endless drive across Texas. We saw men in cowboy hats, had our pictures taken with oxen in reconstructed villages, played the license plate game, and—despite my father's warnings—continued to beg Bob for bathroom stops, especially when they could be combined with forays for hamburgers and fries at McDonald's.

But underneath, we were all a little uneasy. We had loved California. Our house had been modern and bright and airy, and we had a big yard and swimming pool.

New York seemed so foreign, and far away. Even my normally confident mother and father seemed a little unsure. They had decided Dad should accept the new job, had flown to New York, bought a house and returned in just a few days. So it was only partly a game when they began pointing out the most outlandish, tumbledown houses, teasing us and each other.

"Is that it, honey?" my father asked my mother, pointing at one old farmhouse with a sagging front porch. "Is that what our new house is like?"

And then a few miles later, my mother caught sight of a broken-down trailer. "Marvin! Marvin! That's it! That's it!" she cried excitedly to my father. And then, twisting around to address us kids in the back seat: "That's what our new house is like." Later, they lapsed into stand-up comedy-type routines.

"Did we buy the house with the bathroom?" my mother asked my father.

"Yes, I think there's a bathroom," he answered, deadpan.

All the way across the country, they bantered on like this until, as we neared New York, none of us was quite sure what to expect. We all knew they were joking, of course. But all the same, we almost collapsed with relief when we pulled into the driveway of the beautiful old white Colonial with black trim and a big backyard.

I ran through the house, eagerly inspecting the stairs up to the second floor, the family rooms downstairs and the bright bedroom that was going to be mine. "This is a cool house," I told Mom and Dad.

As it turned out, we were very happy in Scarsdale, the New York suburb where we settled. Mom and Dad made friends. I settled in at school, sometimes walking there, sometimes biking. Little Steven took to kindergarten as if he had been going there all his life. And even Mark, who at first felt awkward and shy in his new neighborhood, eventually began to feel comfortable. The house really began to feel like home to us, with its big yard for snowmen and leaf piles, and even a kid's playhouse out back.

My mom and I made excursions to museums in the city, both dressed alike in red and white checked blouses and wire-rimmed sunglasses. We ate foot-long hot dogs and chocolate milk shakes, and laughed at people's outfits on the train on the way home. Dad played paddle tennis or shot hoops with Mark and Steven. On Sundays he played golf, and he often let me come along to drive the golf cart or walk the course with him and keep score.

Of course, I think our family could have been happy just about anywhere. Maybe it was because we moved so often that we never really got to know our other relatives. For us, the word "family" meant the five of us. We were all very close. One day when Daddy was taking pictures around the fireplace, he got irritated and raised his voice at me. I started to cry. And then, because I was crying, Steven started crying. Then Mark began sobbing, and pretty soon the whole family was in tears. No one of us could even feel anything without everyone else feeling it too.

We had a whole private language, that only we could understand. When someone was sick, we'd call the sick person Ill-ke Sommer. A Telly was a short haircut, as in Telly Savalas. If someone yelled "GPY," it meant "God is Punishing You." That was what happened when someone, say, Mark, stole the biggest French fry off my tray, and then burned the roof of his mouth.

After we moved to New York, Dad came home from work every night at 6:30. We were always so hungry that by 6:31 we were already seated on the wicker chairs around the butcher block table in the kitchen. We each had our own places, but because it was a kitchen set for four, the kids rotated the extra spot on the step stool.

No matter how busy Daddy had been during the day, at night at dinner he was completely ours. We talked about politics. We talked about current events. Then Daddy went around the table asking us each one by one what we had done during the day. On Thanksgiving, Dad had another ritual: He went around the table again, only this time he asked us each to tell the family about the things we were thankful for. We kids always hooted and hollered, and cut up in embarrassment, but at bottom, we liked it. We all knew just how lucky we were.

Growing up, I had always felt special. I was the oldest. I was the only girl. And I always liked having the center stage.

I loved attention. To get it, I usually chose achievement. I was the kid in the Spanish class with the best accent. I was always vying for the lead in the school play. When I was only picked literary editor—and not editor-in-chief—of the school publication, I was really upset. Whatever I did had to be done all the way.

Sometimes, though, I got my attention through pranks. I was always a show-off, and once I got myself kicked out of math class for stuffing a dissected frog into the light socket of the overhead projector where my teacher could find it when she went to see why it didn't work.

From when I was a little girl, I loved performing. I remember my favorite toy wasn't a Barbie or a bicycle. It was a Jerry Mahoney dummy that I got for Christmas one year. I learned to throw my voice, and I loved entertaining my parents with my little skits. I decided that when I grew up I would be a ventriloquist.

Scarsdale was filled with successful people—lawyers, doctors, stockbrokers—all of whom wanted their kids to be successful too. So demanding parents and competitive kids were nothing unusual. There was no question about whether you were going to college. Everyone went. The question was how good a school you could get into. Everyone was very aware of where they ranked in class, what activities they participated in, and what their SAT scores were.

Even in Scarsdale, though, other kids could occasionally goof off and come home with Bs and Cs. Not the Schiller kids. My parents were upset with anything less than an A. Other kids could hang out, listen to music and just fool around. My parents demanded that we play sports, get involved in school activities,

I suppose it was because they were both so successful themselves at whatever they did. My mom was beautiful, tall and slender with dark curly hair. Everything she did, she did well, from decorating the house to cooking dinner for fifty people, to being a room mother for the PTA.

And my dad—well, we were all so proud of my dad. He had come from a poor family in the Bronx, and had been the first person in his family to graduate from college. Now he had a Ph.D. My parents expected big things from themselves, and they expected big things from us too.

Mom and Dad drilled us endlessly in proper behavior. Keep your napkin in your lap. No elbows on the table. Spoon your soup away from yourself and don't snarf your food down faster than you can swallow.

They encouraged us in all our accomplishments, and loved to show us off. Whenever they had parties, they paid me and Mark and Steven to serve hors d'oeuvres for them. And when supper was over, Mom and Dad used to ask me to sing.

Actually, I had a voice like a crow, and I could barely carry a tune. If I sang alone in my room, I could almost always count on some smart aleck shouting up the stairs: "Lori, are you all right?" my father would call. "Is there a wounded animal in your room?" my mother would chime in. I was no great shakes on the guitar either. I had taught myself to play from a book, but I had such a bad sense of pitch that I had to keep going back to the music store where, laughing, they would retune the strings for me.

But still, I did what my folks wanted. With the guitar as my support, I played John Denver and James Taylor songs, because they were the easiest, and somehow managed to stay in tune. Even though it was hard, it was something I prided myself on. If I had to do something—even something difficult—somehow I found a way to do it. I so much wanted my mommy and daddy to be proud of me.

But after I came home early from camp that summer, I suddenly had a new task: keeping my terrible secret. It took all of my determination, and all of my drive. I was putting on a super performance nearly every day. I was pretending that nothing had changed, even though nothing at all was the same.

When the camp staffer dropped me off at my house, my parents weren't home. With all of us away at camp, my parents had driven back to Michigan to visit relatives. Some friends of my parents were staying at our house. By the time I arrived home, I had pulled myself together enough that I only looked a little drained. That was easy enough to explain.

"I have a bad flu," I told them. "I just want to go to bed."

They called my parents, and reassured them that I was fine, with nothing wrong that a few days' bed rest wouldn't fix right up. So nobody seemed surprised when, armed with this excuse, I went into my room and stayed there, sleeping most of the day . . . and the next.

By the time my parents returned, the worst seemed over. I must have seemed more myself, because they didn't seem unduly concerned. The only person who was concerned was my best friend, Gail. And she was only worried that I was mad at her. Quite by accident she had dropped by and found me home from camp three weeks before she had expected me.

"You didn't even call me!" I could hear the hurt in her voice.

She had stayed up late before I had left, sewing my name tags into my clothes, just laughing and being with me before we were to be separated for the summer.

It was the first time I ever kept anything from Gail. We had been as close as sisters. We did everything together. We got our hair cut together, we slept over at each other's houses, we studied together, we got kicked out of the library together for talking. When she had troubles in high school, it was me she confided in. When her parents got a divorce, she cried on my shoulder. When I hit my teens, and began feeling gawky and awkward, it was she who reassured me. I told her everything.

But this time, I told her nothing. I was evasive. I mumbled something noncommittal, and she left, the hurt still clearly showing on her face. But what could I do? How could I tell her, or even my parents, about the Voices, about what was happening to me?

As time went on, sometimes I thought I was mentally ill, but I only vaguely knew about mental illness. What I did know I had only learned from whispered conversations. There was one girl in school who—the rumor had it—had gone crazy and torn her room apart. She vanished from school for two weeks. I was very disturbed by her experience. When she came back to school, I wanted to help her. I wanted to know what had happened to her. But I didn't want to tell her what was happening to me. I was afraid of how she would react. I was afraid of how others would react. I watched them shying away from her, treating her almost as if she were now a time bomb ready to go off at any moment.

Her experience made me doubly sure I wanted to keep my own secret. I didn't want to be a crazy person. People shunned crazy people. They feared them. Worse, they called the men in the white coats to come put them in straitjackets and take them away to an insane asylum. I couldn't let that happen to me.

Sometimes I thought I was possessed. The Stephen King horror movie *Carrie* came out that year. The psychedelic feeling, the crazy sense of being in touch with the occult, the images of blood, and of speaking to God and to the devil—that was what I was like, I decided. I saw *Helter Skelter* that year too, the movie about Charles Manson and the murder of Sharon Tate. It stirred up old recollections: We had been in Los Angeles the year of the murder:

I remember going to the driveway every day and picking u
the newspaper emblazoned with headlines about the gruesome
murder. Demonic cults, possession, insanity—it all rang bells
with me. I didn't need a doctor, I needed an exorcist.

In school one day, I found myself especially disturbed by one
literature assignment. I confided to my journal what I could confide to no one else:

> *We're reading* The Bell Jar *in English. I absolutely hate it! I
> have never been so emotionally upset about a book before. The
> symptoms of the crack-upped Sylvia Plath-Esther Greenwood
> are me. Of course not everything, but enough. Maybe I'm
> descending into madness myself. Especially with the wounds of
> this past wonderful summer being remembered. I'm so upset. I
> didn't sleep for 23 nights. Esther G. only didn't for 21. I
> always put myself down, note the bad and not the good, am
> paranoid, am the A student who would seem least likely to
> . . . am afraid to commit myself to relationships, have an alias
> for all sorts of weird things (at least I don't have to worry about
> not eating or washing my hair) and don't know who or what
> I really am. I'm scared and afraid. I want so badly for [my
> teacher] to understand my fears and set me at ease, but she
> can't and doesn't. We will be finishing discussing the book next
> week . . .*

I had always wanted my parents to be so proud of me. It was
so important to me that I reflect well on them. So how could I
destroy my parents by letting them know their daughter was
possessed? At all cost, I had to keep it from them.

So for my last year of high school, as the Voices came and went
without warning, I played a game of cat-and-mouse. I kept on
going to school, I kept on studying. I went to the prom, applied
to college, went skiing with my friends, listened to music or talked
about guys with Gail. But always I had to be on my guard. When
the Voices began to shriek, I had to stay composed.

I had to conceal the fact that objects around me were beginning
to feel hostile. Once I was in my bedroom alone when the phone
rang. I picked it up and no one was there. A strange feeling settled
over me. It rang again. Again no one. And then again, and again,

...ays that same vacant feeling at the other end of the ...my mind knew that there was a classmate at the ...the line, playing tricks on me. And finally, I picked ...the phone and screamed into it: "I know it's you! I know it's you!" But to the other part of my mind, the empty line took on the same eerie quality as my Voices. Why was this happening? What did the phone want of me?

From then on, I became terrified of using the telephone. But I couldn't tell anyone why. So sometimes I hid behind a cloak of shyness. Sometimes I pretended I just didn't want to speak to the person at the other end of the line. Sometimes I just couldn't avoid it, and at those times I gingerly took the receiver, never knowing what horrors were going to slide down the telephone line to my brain.

In the evenings, the television became fearsome. Steven and Mark and I could watch *Gilligan's Island* or *The Brady Bunch* or *The Flintstones*. Those were okay, and I even enjoyed them. But in the evening, my parents would put on the evening news. When Walter Cronkite appeared on the screen, he began talking directly to me. As he spoke, he gave me great responsibility. He told me of the problems of the world, and what I must do to fix them. I couldn't handle it. I would immediately leave the family room, and head for my bedroom.

Mom and Dad never let me go without a fight. They wanted to have all of us together in the evening, and didn't like to feel that any of their kids were cut off from the family. So often, reluctantly I came back. I lay on the couch with my face to the wall, and pulled a blanket over my head. I had to block out Walter Cronkite's face and voice. He was telling me that it was my job to save the world, and that if I didn't, I would be killed.

I couldn't listen to him. I just couldn't. He was giving me responsibilities that belonged to God and to no one else. How was I, a seventeen-year-old girl, able to complete a task as overwhelming as saving the world?

3

Lori
Tufts University, Medford, Massachusetts,
September 1977–June 1981

For a long time relief came more often than torment. The Voices and sounds left me alone enough to let me finish high school and apply to college. My choices were reasonable ones: Harvard, because it was the best, and I always wanted to be the best; Northwestern, because it had a good journalism program, and I was interested in writing; Tufts for its prestige; and Bucknell because it was a middle-of-the-road safety school. I thought I had a pretty good chance of getting into any of my choices since my high school grade point average despite my troubles was 3.9.

The previous fall Daddy drove me up to Boston for interviews. While I was at Tufts, I stuck a wad of chewing gum on the back wall of the bookstore. If I'm accepted here, I told him, next year I'll come back and see if the gum is still there. All winter I waited, and all spring I ran to the mailbox. I was accepted at Bucknell and Tufts, wait-listed at Harvard and rejected at Northwestern. That fall, I enrolled at Tufts. As my parents were helping me move into my dorm, I walked over to the bookstore. The gum was still there. It was fate.

At first college life was wonderful. In fact, everything I did had a kind of sheen to it, an exciting biting edge. And academically it seemed I could do anything, even though I decided right from the outset that I had no intention of chaining myself to a seat in the library.

In the middle of my first year, I moved in with Tara Sonenshine from Long Island. Tara and I were really tight buddies. Later we met another Lori, Lori Winters from St. Louis, and the three of us became inseparable.

Back home, I was a big shot, a college girl. My brother Mark seemed to feel depressed a lot, and when I came home on weekends or for vacations I tried to cheer him up, and give him advice on how to handle the problems he felt he had. Sometimes I would squire him around in my car, because he didn't have his license yet. Life seemed exhilarating.

Although the Voices still hovered around from time to time, fading in and out, disturbing my peace, they were much softer than they had been at camp, and in high school. They were more like chatterboxes in the back of my brain, talking to each other about me, narrating my every move. Most of the time I could retreat into sleep, and they wouldn't follow. If I couldn't sleep, I would close my eyes and take a series of deep breaths. "You're not crazy," I would chant to myself. "You're not possessed by the devil." Then I would silently address the Voices: "Please," I would beg, "please leave me alone."

Back at school that spring I decided on a whim to go skydiving. Some friends and I drove out to Turners Falls for a course on how to jump out of an airplane. It all happened so quickly. In the morning, they taught us how to drop the streamer to test the wind, to jump backward from the plane, to pull the emergency cord if the chute didn't open, and to drop gently, with bent legs. In the afternoon, we went up.

Standing on the little step just outside the plane, clutching on to the wing supports, I looked down at the little streamer drifting to earth as we circled the jump site, and I froze with fear. We circled once, circled twice. I wouldn't let go. Finally the instructor peeled my hands off, and pulled me back in the plane.

I knew I had to do it. The next time around I forgot everything they had told me, and just jumped, praying to God the chute would open. For the first few seconds, all I saw was black. I felt sick to my stomach. Then a pop, a tug, and there I was soaring through the air.

"I can fly! I can fly!" I shrieked to the big quiet sky.

The next fall, Tara and I moved into Wren Hall, the dorm right on the Quad where everything happened. We could lean right out of our windows and shout down to our friends passing below. We had upper-class friends who helped us get parking passes, and we were set.

I had lots of friends, both men and women. I was always the one who found things to do off campus. Disco was big then and I found fun places to go dance. I would find the neatest guys in bars, and arrange parties for everyone.

I dated a lot. There was a big, good-looking medical student football player from Harvard. There was a teaching assistant in a computer class I took at Tufts. One sweet guy from Boston University was serious enough to want to marry me.

On the surface, things seemed great. Underneath, though, they were beginning to come apart. The Voices were coming louder and faster, startling me with their surprise visits to my brain. Only I didn't know they were in my brain. I heard them coming at me from the outside, as real as the sound of the telephone ringing.

They popped up when I least expected them. Occasionally they were friendly, but mostly they reviled me, shouting in their hoarse, harsh tones: "You must die, you bitch," they shrieked. "Die! Die! Die!" They filled me with anxiety. I'd turn around thinking somebody was in back of me, and no one would be there. On several occasions I tried beating through the bushes to flush out whatever or whoever it was that was taunting me. Of course I was a bloody-fisted loser every time.

I grew increasingly tense and nervous. I was always afraid I really was going to die, because that's what the Voices said would be my fate.

Once again hiding the Voices began to take up much of my time and energy. When the Voices began to screech and cackle, I looked to the floor. Sometimes I held my breath, hoping, some-how, to outlast them. Sometimes they got so bad that I had to make up some excuse—having to go to the bathroom, or suddenly feeling sick to my stomach—and leave the room.

The most important thing was to keep from looking around to see where they were coming from. If I did get caught whirling my head around, I would try to cover up.

"Oh, I just thought I heard a noise," I would say, acting nonchalant. I often found myself laughing out of nervousness, but for the most part, people didn't seem to catch on.

Still, the pressure was building.

My fear of the Voices was beginning to spill over into the rest of my life. I was always terribly anxious, because I never knew if those around me could hear them too. I watched my friends' faces expecting to see their expressions turn to horror when they heard these Voices calling me "whore." When the Voices called me a "fucking bitch" I watched my professors to see if they would throw me out of class.

When I heard the Voices yelling such terrible things, I grew afraid to make eye contact with the people I was with. I was afraid they had heard the Voices and now knew the terrible secrets about me that they were revealing. What tortured me more than anything was when the Voices laughed at me. It was a kind of hysterical laughter, as if I was the target of everyone's jokes. I didn't know why they were making fun of me so viciously but I hated myself for being the sitting duck for ridicule. I became extremely self-conscious in front of everyone for fear they too would nail me to a taunting cross.

I began to feel that my friends hated me. That's what the Voices said. I felt they regarded me as scum. That's what the Voices said too. I kept on seeing my friends, kept on partying with them, kept on laughing and joking, driving around and dancing with them. But in little ways, I began to act on my strange feelings.

One weekend, Tara threw a big birthday party for Lori Winters, and invited a lot of her own friends from home. As they began arriving, I began feeling pressured. These people didn't like me. They were talking about me. They were going to start making fun of me. I didn't want to be around, so I jumped into my car and drove four hours home to New York. Then, I turned right around and drove back to Boston.

I took a class in abnormal psychology, and pored over big fat books with teeny tiny print. Every atypical symptom in the lectures and the textbooks seemed to apply to me. I felt overwhelmed by the material, but at the same time a little comforted. At last I didn't feel so alone. There were people out there who felt the same way I did. In fact, I decided, it was really possible that everyone experienced Voices as a young adult, but, like me, chose not to discuss them.

I spent my junior year abroad. While I was in Spain my first semester, the Voices were softer, but I was so revved up, my motor seemed to be working overtime. When the Voices did speak to me, sometimes they did so in Spanish: "Puta! Puta!" they yelled. "Vaya con el diablo." Go to hell, whore.

In London during the second semester, I grew increasingly depressed. The Voices were back in force. There almost never seemed to be a time when the Voices left me alone. Still I kept forging on. I had to keep going. I couldn't let go.

Gail Kobre was in London with me, on her own junior year program from Skidmore College. We wrote reports together on Disraeli and Gladstone. We studied British history, painting and sculpture. We stopped in Trafalgar Square to have our pictures taken with the lions. We went to pubs and drank beer, ate tea and crumpets and tried to make the Queen's Guards laugh. At one time during the semester we cut our fingers and smooshed our blood together. We'll be friends forever, we said. Blood sisters. Nothing will come between us.

Of course it wasn't true. The Voices were already between us.

Keeping my secret grew harder and harder. When I got back to Tufts, Lori and Tara and I had moved in together along with another girl. We lived in a big house off campus. We shopped for food, piling up cookies, cakes, candy and donuts. Sometimes in the supermarket we tore into boxes of chocolate chip cookies and polished them off before we hit the checkout counter. We were always dieting, though. We switched to eating Twinkies, reasoning that since they weren't chocolate, they weren't fattening, like Ring Dings. We starved ourselves all day, and stuffed ourselves like pigs at dinner, finally pushing ourselves away from the table, moaning our secret code: ISF—I'm So Fat.

I kept up with them. I had to. I kept laughing with them, joking with them, rising at 5:00 A.M. with them for our part-time job waitressing at Mug 'N Muffin, a coffee shop in Harvard Square. But my hands had begun to tremble. I had begun smoking in Europe, a chic thing to do, I thought. Now I had trouble lighting up without a steady hand.

My highs were higher, my lows lower. In my high moods, I spent money wildly, recklessly. Sweaters, books, candy, tapes, records—I bought more than I could ever need, more than I could ever use, more than a college student could ever afford. My thoughts would race, speeding faster than I could talk so no one understood me. I loved everything in life, from the gripping winter weather to the power of a slamming door, to laughing back at the Voices.

The Voices were with me nearly constantly these days. Where once I could retreat in sleep, now not even that refuge was left. They followed me into the night, and followed into my dreams. I went for days without sleeping.

In my low moods, I kept to my room, refusing to go to class. Partly, it was the blackness of the depression that was making it impossible for me to move. Partly it was dread: The Voices were beginning to command me to hurt people, and I was starting to fear I might obey. If I stayed in my room, I was safe.

Lori Winters began to see that I was upset.

"Come into my room, if you can't sleep," she said. So night after night, long into the night, I sat in her room, smoking cigarettes and shaking, while she tried to coax from me my secret. But I could tell no one. I thought increasingly about hurting myself. I sat in the library, up all those flights of stairs, and considered jumping.

The problem was here, it was here at Tufts. I had known it all along. I should never have come. I would leave here, I would leave the problems behind. So I drove across the river to Boston University, wrote them a check, and told them I was transferring. The next day I transferred back. Something was about to snap.

Finally I called my parents. I told them as little as possible.

"I'm having some problems," I told them. "I think I need to talk to someone." They were already perplexed by my decision to leave Tufts in my senior year. I was just about to graduate, they said. Tufts was so much better a school, they said. What was I thinking? They could see I was upset, so they readily agreed to my consulting a therapist.

I met first with a counselor at Tufts, and then with a psychiatrist in private practice. Week after week I met with him, yet I couldn't speak. I couldn't talk about the Voices. It was too dangerous. The Voices were twisting themselves around me. It was hard to tell where they left off and I began. They threatened me, and I believed them. If I squealed on the Voices, they might kill me. If I ratted on them, the person I told would have to die.

My thoughts grew increasingly confused and poisonous. Session after session I sat in the psychiatrist's office wondering: Who the hell is this guy? What is he going to do to me? Send the white coats for me? Send me to Rikers Island? Was he going to take a scalpel and dissect the wrinkles of my brain? Do a lobotomy? What could he do about the stuff rotting there in my head? He gave me Valium for my anxiety. I took it, and grew steadily more anxious.

Things began to spin out of control. Trying to flee the Voices, I took to my car, racing up the old Hutchinson River Parkway, and the narrow Merritt Parkway. I wanted to see how fast I could go without being killed. Yet I half wanted to get myself killed.

Driving up the Mass Pike on the way back to school, I was pulled over by a cop for speeding. I rolled down my window. He asked for my license and registration.

"You are going to kill yourself driving like that," he said. I began to laugh hysterically. Right before my very eyes, the state trooper with his hat and sunglasses and uniform had changed into a fantastic creature with bugged-out eyes and hair standing up wildly on end.

On Saturday, April 25, in honor of my twenty-second birthday the following day Tara and Lori woke me up at 5:00 A.M. and handed me a scroll. "Congratulations," it read. "You have won an all-expense-paid vacation in the company of two people who love you very much." They hustled me into my clothes, handed me my overnight bag all packed, and carried me off to Provincetown. We stayed at an inn, ate lobster and curled up at night under striped sheets eating Oreos.

Six weeks later we all graduated and headed to New York City, Tara to Columbia University's School of International Affairs, Lori and I to live together and work. My last memory of college is of graduation day, caps flying in the air, mellow music playing, a frantic round of goodbye parties, and the Quad filled with parents, relatives and friends, all gathered around to wish us well in our new lives.

Part II

I Can Fly

4

Lori Winters
New York City,
July 1981–March 1982

Lori Schiller and I loved being roommates when we were together at Tufts. So we should have been perfect roommates in New York the year after our graduation. We were both just starting out in the big city. We both had interesting jobs: I had been accepted into a training program at Manufacturers Hanover Trust; Lori had a job as a Spanish translator at the Miss Universe Pageant. We were the same age, came from the same sort of background, and we enjoyed each other's company. We even shared the same first name.

And at first glance, Lori and I both thought the renovated McAlpin Hotel was an ideal place for two recently graduated college girls like us to make our first home. It was right in the heart of midtown Manhattan. It had a doorman. It was near the subway, and right across from Macy's huge department store. By day, the streets teemed with people, busy commuters and shoppers going about their business. The price was right too—about $500 for a one-bedroom, which in New York was downright cheap.

Still, there was a lot of fretting when we moved in together that summer. Lori's parents hated the idea of our moving into an apartment building located in a commercial, rather than a residential, neighborhood.

And to tell the truth, I wasn't too crazy about living there with Lori either—but it wasn't the building I was worried about. It was Lori. I kept quiet about my concerns, but they were growing every day. Lori had been such fun. She was bubbly and creative and lively and energetic. I loved her like a sister. But during the last year at school, she had just become too weird. I really didn't want to live with her anymore.

None of us at college could put our fingers on what was wrong. At first, it simply seemed as if she was depressed because she was so fun-loving and we were all such grinds. Often it seemed she would get into scrapes just to get our goats. That business about jumping out of the airplane, for example. Here we were—a bunch of girls who were scared to go up in glass elevators and she pulled a stunt like that. We just thought she was trying to get our attention.

By senior year, though, a secret side of Lori began to emerge. Some of us suspected she might be doing drugs. She just seemed so up sometimes, and so down other times, and we never could predict which it would be. When she refused to come out of her room, and refused to go to class some days, Tara and I got a little concerned. "What should we do about Lori?" Tara and I asked each other.

Still, we were just college kids and college kids were melodramatic. It was even a bit fashionable for people to talk about being neurotic, and about having nervous breakdowns from stress. Surely there were other people—people in authority, grownups—who must be more aware than we. We knew she was seeing a psychiatrist, so obviously the problems were being handled.

The best thing we could do, we thought, was to try to make her cheerful. So we bought her chocolate chip cookies, went out late at night to Dunkin' Donuts, took her to Provincetown on her birthday, and generally tried to jolly her out of her funks.

Some of our friends weren't sympathetic at all. In fact, a lot of the guys thought she was just bullshitting us. There was a group of eight men and eight women who all went out dancing or to dinner together. One night Lori refused to leave her room to come with us and one of the guys exploded.

"What is the matter with that girl, anyway?" he complained to me. "It's not like she's got some big problem."

"Yeah," chimed in his friend. "She's cute, she's smart, her parents have all this money, people like her—what's she got to be depressed about?"

All around me I could feel people nodding silently. Lori should just snap out of it, they felt. I tried to be supportive. When I heard her up pacing at night I invited her into my room. There she would sit in the middle of the night, smoking and shaking and looking glum. But by the time we graduated, I was getting impatient too. I was getting tired of her funks. I didn't want to be her caretaker, and I didn't want to spend my first months out of college making excuses for her.

Still, I didn't feel like I had much choice. I had promised to live with her in New York back at a time when I thought what I was really going to do was go back home to St. Louis to work for IBM. When those plans changed, I felt I had to honor my commitment to Lori.

I tried to look on the positive side. When Lori was up she was great. And as for her problems, I knew that her parents had found her another therapist in New York, so there were responsible people who were aware of her condition. Too, I honestly thought a lot of the problem might have been Tufts. Now that we were away from that grind, and out in the real world, things would improve with Lori I was sure. What's more, we weren't very far from her home and her parents. There was a lot of support around. Nothing really bad would happen, I reasoned. Everything would be just fine.

And for a long time, it was fine. In the early part of the summer, we lived with her parents while we waited for our apartment to be ready. I knew Dr. and Mrs. Schiller well, and I had always liked them. Because I was from St. Louis and didn't always want to go home for short vacations, I often went to Lori's house. It was fun being there. Her mother was always warm and outgoing. She and Lori's father were always teasing each other and their children, and Lori always seemed to have such a nice, close relationship with her parents and brothers.

In August, we moved into the McAlpin. True to Dr. and Mrs. Schiller's predictions, the location turned out to be a nightmare. It was noisy and dangerous and not very convenient. There was no grocery store or dry cleaners within walking distance. And at night, once the stores closed and the commuters had gone home, the streets were deserted, the cheerfulness vanished, and the area began to seem creepy.

In the beginning, we didn't care. Moving in together was an adventure. We bought unfinished furniture and painted it ourselves. We bought a wall unit with mirrors, where Lori put her stereo and tapes, and a big glass and chrome coffee table. My grandfather bought us a king-sized sleeper bed.

Most of the furniture wasn't delivered for six weeks or so, so in the meantime we slept in sleeping bags on the floor. Sleeping on the floor gave Lori an idea: We would all have a slumber party. So one weekend, we invited all the girls we knew over and a dozen or so of us rolled out our sleeping bags on the floor like teenagers.

We also began meeting a lot of nice guys. A couple of guys would always just happen by to see if Lori was there. Her job was fun too, helping the Spanish-speaking Miss Universe contestants find their way around the city. One day she came home with Miss Colombia's banner, which had been given her as a thank-you. All my fears melted away.

But the good times didn't last.

Before too long, Lori's moods began to swing again. At times, she would take to her bed, refusing to leave, refusing to go to work. Bringing people home became a problem.

The guys she was dating began drifting away, without saying much to me. When Lori did leave her room, she became hostile and aggressive. I had been set up to date my sister-in-law's cousin. The guy was nothing great to look at, but I liked him all right, and had him over a couple of times. One day when I brought him home, Lori was there.

"What is that thing on your face?" she said to him, with a not-quite-joking air. He had a mustache. "That is the ugliest thing I've ever seen, and you're pretty creepy too." I was taken aback. I tried to pass it off as a gag, and we left quickly.

Soon, however, it became hard to have people over at all, Lori was so belligerent. You are ugly. You are fat. Why did you come over here anyway? We don't want you around.

Tara was living in her own apartment up by Columbia, and I found myself calling her all the time, wondering what I should do. I tried to talk to Lori's parents too, but it was hard to explain what was happening. Lori's parents had never seen her get really bad. She always wanted them to be so proud of her that she would never admit she had problems. Often she said she didn't want to bother them. What's more, just being with them seemed to make her happy. When they were around she always seemed more normal and the vivacious, funny, lovable Lori would just seem to take over for a while. So they never knew about the days she wouldn't get out of bed. But sometimes I got so concerned myself that I called them. Lori's mother would listen to my stories, and in a very friendly motherly way, brush them aside.

"Oh, don't worry about that," Mrs. Schiller would say. "Lori is just in one of her moods. It will pass."

I always felt better after talking with her mother. Her parents knew her a lot better than I did and they didn't think her problems were such a big deal. I was just getting all upset over nothing.

Wintertime in New York is wonderful. And wintertime in New York around Herald Square where we lived is especially magical. Every street corner has its Salvation Army Santa with his bell and brass bucket for change. People with kids and strollers crowd around Macy's to see windows filled with moving figures, ice skaters, ballet dancers and reindeer. Just as the song says, there really are hot chestnut vendors, filling the air with the smell of roasting.

And on every street corner, there are the three-card monte games. One eye out for the police, their games perched precariously on cardboard boxes, these con men prey on passersby. Nearly every New Yorker knows, or quickly learns, that no matter how easy it seems to turn over the right card, no matter how many times the dealer lets you win when the bets are small, no matter how fervently you believe that you are the one who can beat the system, you will never, ever win. The games are completely crooked, and anyone who falls for them is a dope.

One evening in December around early twilight Lori came in. Her eyes were bright and there was a wildness about her, a kind of new energy.

)st my bracelet," she said, distressed.

"Your new bracelet? The one your parents gave you?" Her parents had recently given her a beautiful, and very expensive, diamond bracelet.

"Yes. I lost it," she repeated.

I thought she had dropped it somewhere, and we would have to go look for it. But that wasn't it at all.

"I lost it at three-card monte. I thought I had them. I thought I could beat them." She was excited, frightened, overheated. "I used some twenties. I lost them. Then I put down everything in my wallet. I lost it all. I was out of money so I put down my bracelet, and lost that too." It was clear she was worried. She was upset about losing the bracelet, and she didn't want to tell her parents. But she was also upset that she had lost. She felt invincible. She felt like she should not have lost, could not have lost.

Her funk had turned. Her agitation had begun.

A few days later, she called me. A group of people from work were getting together for holiday drinks in a bar in midtown. Could I join them?

After the Miss Universe Pageant ended, Lori had begun working in the personnel department of a big real estate company. I had wanted to meet the people she worked with, so I was glad to come. Besides, I felt I should keep an eye on her. I just didn't know what she was likely to do.

There were over a dozen people crowded into a small area by the bar, and the mood was jolly by the time I got there. But when I saw the look in Lori's eyes, I knew there was going to be trouble. They had that bright, out-of-control look that came just before she got wild. And it wasn't long before she started lashing out. Because of her job, she had access to confidential personnel files. In a loud voice, she began telling the group just what was in those files.

"You're on probation, and you're probably going to get fired," she announced to one co-worker, while the others listened on, stunned.

"You asked for a raise, but you're not going to get one because your boss thinks you goof off too much," she told another.

One by one, she went around the room, dishing up dirt on each person present. Everyone was too astounded to stop her, and in fact, no one knew how. As everyone grew angrier and angrier, I tried futilely to brush it off.

"Lori's such a kidder," I said to one, before grabbing Lori's arm and making for the door.

On the way home, she grew calmer.

"Maybe I shouldn't have said all those things," she said to me, looking abashed.

"Lori, you can't do stuff like that," I said. "You are going to get fired."

And the next day, she was.

A few weeks later, she got a job selling insurance. She seemed fearless, venturing out into neighborhoods where no other sales-people dared go, into immigrant neighborhoods where she couldn't understand her customers, and they couldn't understand her.

One day she came home with an engagement ring. A Chinese man she had met—or maybe he was Filipino—was in love with her and wanted to marry her. Her father was flabbergasted.

"We've never even met this man," Lori told me he said. "How can you be thinking of marrying him?" The ring vanished, and the subject was dropped.

I began to think of marrying myself. I wasn't in love with the guy I was dating. But I began thinking: Why don't I just marry him? That way I can get out of here without hurting Lori's feel-ings. It was crazy. We had signed a two-year lease and I began thinking: There's only nineteen months to go, there's only eigh-teen months to go . . . It was like a marathon.

My parents were upset. I was in an intense training program, and having a tough enough time getting through that without worrying about Lori. I was starting to resent her.

The next time she dropped into a funk, it was March, and my brother Brad was there. He had just graduated from law school, and was on his first trip to New York for his firm. He had met Lori before when he came to visit us at Tufts, and at first he acted as if she were the old Lori, joking and laughing. But I could see that he thought there was something a bit odd. For one thing, she wouldn't look him in the eye. And when she did, she seemed so angry.

"I hope it's not an inconvenience my staying here tonight," he said.

Lori twisted her face up into a grimace. "Life is horrible," she said. "It wouldn't matter if it ended tomorrow. What's a little inconvenience?"

He laughed. I think he thought she was joking. I didn't. She was dead serious.

Lori began to pace. Down the hall to the bedroom. Back through the living room. Out into the hall. Brad began to realize something serious was up.

"Have I come at a bad time?" he said, during one of her swings out of the room.

"Brad," I said, exasperated. "She's talking about killing herself."

"Killing herself?" he asked. "What do you mean killing herself?"

I was so frantic I was almost rude myself. "I mean killing herself like in killing herself."

He turned worried. "Is she violent?"

"I don't know anymore," I said.

He took me seriously. The next morning, he told me that he had hidden all our big knives and heavy objects. He didn't sleep though. He was out on our big sleeper sofa, and all through the night, Lori had walked back and forth past the bed, pacing from room to room.

I was getting more and more worried, but not that Lori would hurt me. I was worried she was going to hurt herself. Her highs were getting higher, her lows lower. I asked her how she was doing with her psychiatrist.

"I just talk to him," she said. "And he gives me medication. But it doesn't help." We never talked about what it was that needed helping. I never knew. I don't think she knew. And it was beginning to seem to me that the psychiatrist didn't know either.

A few days after my brother left, Lori came in from work. She was upset.

"What's wrong?" I asked. "Did something happen at work?"

She looked different. She was agitated, but at the same time she seemed down, defeated. She pushed by me and went into the bedroom. Leaving the door open, she made for the telephone. She began talking in a loud voice. She was clearly distraught, but at the same time, I couldn't help thinking that she wanted me to hear. After a minute or two I realized she was talking to her psychiatrist.

"I have to see you," she said. "I'm really, really bad." It was the first time I had ever heard her talk like that. I couldn't hear the other end of the conversation of course, but it was clear he was trying to reassure her. It wasn't working.

"Please, you have to help me." She was begging this guy, but he didn't seem to be responding. Her voice got higher, and more and more strident. "You don't understand," she said. "I'm telling you I'm really bad. I'm not going to make it through the night. Please help me. Please."

I don't know what he said, but he clearly wasn't going to see her. She was in tears when she hung up. She walked out in the living room where I was standing, and she mumbled something I thought was goodbye.

"I have to go take my pills now," she said dully. She went into the bathroom and closed the door.

What should I do? I stood outside frozen with indecision. "Lori? Lori?" I shouted through the door. I could hear her moving around inside, and water running. Was she going to slash her wrists? What was she going to do? Then the door opened, and she walked out.

I looked into the bathroom. For weeks I had been keeping my eye on the bottles of pills that her psychiatrist had given her, just checking their levels every day. I didn't know what they were, but I was pretty sure they were tranquilizers, and pretty powerful ones. Up until yesterday, the bottles were nearly full. Now as I looked past her, I saw empty bottles on the sink. I stood right in front of her.

"You took all those pills!"

She nodded. I was stupid with fear. "You took all those pills!" I repeated.

I heard the doorbell ring, and without knowing why, I went to answer it. It was a girl from down the hall, and I shooed her away.

"I'll talk with you later," I said. I had never been so scared in my life. Lori was looking groggy. Was she going to die right here in front of me? What should I do? Who should I call? Who could get here the fastest?

My hands trembling with terror, I picked up the phone and dialed 911.

5

Marvin Schiller
Scarsdale, New York,
March 1982–June 1982

It was late at night when the phone rang. Nancy and I were just getting ready for bed. It was Lori Winters, our daughter's roommate. She was so upset that at first it was hard to understand what she wanted. It was something about our daughter, and the police.

"Calm down, Lori," I said, trying to reassure her. "Calm down. Everything is going to be okay. Tell me what the problem is." There was a lot of commotion in the background, and she could barely get the story out. Our Lori had taken an overdose, she said. The police were there. So were the paramedics. They were taking Lori to the hospital. She had tried to commit suicide.

"I'll be there as fast as I can," I said.

Nancy was already sobbing, and shaking. I didn't want to upset her unnecessarily. I played down the news.

"Lori's fine," I said. "She's going to be fine. She's taken too many pills and she's going to the hospital." Lori was in no real danger, I assured Nancy. She's just made a little mistake with her medication. Everything will be fine in the morning. Nancy, I could see, was eager to believe me.

Driving with Nancy through the dark of the Hutchinson River Parkway, I more than half believed it myself. There was some misunderstanding, I thought. Lori Winters was just a kid herself.

She was getting herself riled up over nothing. My daughter kill
herself? That was impossible. Nothing ever happened to her that
she couldn't handle. She had just had some little upset, and made
a mistake, that was all. All this business about police and paramedics—well, Lori Winters must have been frightened and over-
reacted.

I had known that our Lori had had problems, of course. She
had told us about them in college. She had felt some stress at
school, it seemed, and she felt the need for counseling. That was
nothing unusual in Westchester. Many of our friends' children
had troubles of one kind or another. Seeing a counselor was just
a normal part of life in many families. Lori had seen someone at
the university and I understood that she found those sessions to
be helpful. She had told me that herself.

She was our oldest child and only daughter. We didn't have any
standards to compare her with. It seemed like her problems were
just what might have been expected from any moody teenager.

After she graduated, I felt she was in good hands with the
psychiatrist we had chosen, a man we knew to be a respected
member of our large circle of friends. She would sort out her
problems with him, get herself together, and go on with her life,
I was certain.

If Lori had been in any danger, by the time Nancy and I arrived
at Bellevue Hospital in Manhattan it was long past. In the ambulance, the paramedics had given her medicine to make her throw
up, and in the emergency room she had had her stomach pumped.
When she saw us, she started to cry.

"I'm sorry," she said. "I didn't mean it. I didn't mean to do
it." She was sobbing, and contrite. "I didn't mean to make all this
trouble." She turned to me. "Take me home, Daddy. I want to
go home. I won't ever do it again."

Lori Winters was with her, looking shaken. She pulled me aside
to tell me the whole story. The policemen had arrived quickly,
before the paramedics. But when they tried to take Lori out of the
apartment, she became violent.

"It was awful," Lori Winters said. "She was struggling with
them, and trying to hit them. She said if they came near her, she
would take their gun. Then she tried to grab for it."

Looking at my Lori sitting hunched over in her hospital gown, it was hard for me to believe Lori Winters's story. My Lori looked so tiny and harmless, and so frightened by the horrors surrounding us.

Bellevue Hospital Medical Center is a big public hospital that, in the middle of the night, is a magnet for society's outcasts, the homeless, the pushers, the addicts, the prostitutes. While we were sitting there, a man was carried in on a stretcher, blood oozing from a knife wound in his side. He lay there screaming, his cries nearly drowning out the shrieks from a woman in labor—a teenager, it seemed—lying in the crowded corridor.

It didn't feel real. It felt like a scene from a bad movie. This was no place for my daughter, who was cowering there whimpering for shame and fear.

Just then Lori's psychiatrist arrived. Lori Winters had called him too, and he had driven down from his home to see what needed to be done. He apparently was familiar with hospital bureaucracy, and had come prepared for a long night: He had a pillow under his arm.

When Lori Winters saw him, her face darkened in anger. "How could you do that," she lashed out. "How could you turn your back on her like that?"

She was speaking so loudly that I think she wanted me to hear, and to step in. But I didn't think quarreling was going to do us any good right then. The important thing was to get Lori the help she needed. I wanted to put the whole thing behind us as quickly as possible.

In my mind, the most important help she needed was to make sure that nothing of this incident ever came to light. As a psychologist, I knew she could carry a psychiatric label for a long time—if not forever. I didn't want my daughter to be stigmatized by some temporary rash act. I thought that whatever had been bothering her had passed, and that she could leave the hospital now and come home with me right away. But the hospital personnel refused to let her go. Attempting suicide was a serious act, they said, and they wanted her to stay for a few days in the psychiatric ward for observation. That was absolutely out of the question. I didn't want anything on Lori's record that could come back to haunt her in her later life.

We needed to negotiate, and fast. Nancy and I left Lori in the care of Lori Winters and went out to talk with the hospital people. If she had to stay in the hospital, I wanted them to let her stay overnight in the medical unit, not the psychiatric ward. We were out in the hall arguing with the staff when a friend of mine just happened by, a physician I knew from my country club in Scarsdale.

"What are you doing here?" Nancy called to him. Actually, he seemed more surprised to see us than we him. He had an office at New York University Medical Center, and had just finished up with some of his own patients. But what reason could I have for being in a city hospital emergency room in the middle of the night? Hurriedly I explained to him the situation. He left me and went off to talk to the physician on duty. I don't know what he told her, or what strings he pulled, but soon after, the paperwork arrived for me and Lori to sign, admitting her overnight to a medical ward.

"It's better this way, lovey," I said. "This way you can put this whole thing behind you, and no one will ever need to know you were here. It will all be over."

I didn't see Lori's problems as serious. She didn't need to stay in a psychiatric ward. She wasn't mentally ill. She just had a few problems. She was having a difficult transition out of her teens into womanhood, making the complex and stressful leap out of college into business, from the security of her college campus into the hustle and bustle of midtown Manhattan. She was just having some trouble dealing with those changes. I didn't want to believe it was anything more than that. This was no more serious than other phases in her life she had gone through—like being a vegetarian, or losing too much weight, or getting depressed over her date to the prom. Those things had passed, this one would too.

When our kids were growing up I pushed them. I always told them that although they would never reach perfection, they should always be reaching for it. I reviewed their report cards, and urged them to take advanced placement courses and tutorials. Good was never good enough. I wanted them to stretch the limits of their abilities in whatever they did.

Everything in my own life taught me this lesson, that education and striving and initiative were the ways to success. Both my parents were born in Europe. My father was born in 1901 in territory that was sometimes Poland and sometimes Russia. He fled a brutal military service, and found passage to America on a cattle ship.

My mother was born in Austria, but because she was only six months old when she arrived here she grew up speaking English without an accent. From childhood, she worked in a sweatshop making ladies' millinery. As the oldest girl in a family of nine, she became a second mother to her siblings.

When I was born, my father didn't have the money to pay the hospital bill and take me home, so he pawned a silver candlestick his mother had sent him from the old country.

I learned early that my brains and my determination were my tickets out. I graduated from high school when I was fifteen and started college at sixteen. I wanted to go to Cornell, but my parents didn't have the money, so I went to Queens College, a New York City school instead, where my first semester cost only $87, including books.

After my military service interrupted my studies, I returned to school, graduated with honors, and went on to graduate school. I zoomed through. I started my studies—in clinical psychology— at Michigan State University in 1956. Three years later, I had my master's degree and my Ph.D., and was beginning to work.

When I started to work at A.T. Kearney as a management consultant to business, I knew I had made it. In very short order, I began climbing the ranks of the firm. When we moved to Los Angeles, I headed that office. When we moved back to New York, I was coming back as head of that major office. On the day we shook hands to buy our big beautiful house in Scarsdale, Nancy and I drove back to the Bronx tenement where I had grown up. I didn't want us to forget where I had come from. Although it had taken a long time for me to really feel secure financially, by the late 1970s, money was no longer a problem in our family.

But by the spring of 1982, when Lori was having her problems, I was playing a high-stakes game of bet-your-job. The country was in a recession, and our consulting business was being restructured. After twenty-two years, several of my old colleagues and I felt as if we were being pushed aside.

It was a tremendously traumatic time. Those of us being shunted aside decided to stage a coup, to gain control of our company. My days were filled with tension, clandestine meetings, caucusing, polling the partners, trying to get enough votes to reconfigure the current management so that we could take control. If we won, I would be in the new senior leadership. If we lost, I would be out of work. I told no one at the office about Lori's troubles, and instructed Nancy to do the same at her job. Our work and our personal lives were separate, and no good could come from letting our minor problems leak out into the public eye. They were nobody's business but our own.

When she left the hospital, Lori was still contrite, still apologetic, still giving every sign that she realized what she had done had been wrong.

"I just flipped out, Daddy," she said. "I won't do it again."

Nancy and I tried to reassure her. We didn't want to put any more pressure on her than we had to. So we brought her back home to Scarsdale for a few days. I called her boss at the insurance company and explained that she had been taken ill, and would like a leave of absence for a while, but that she would definitely be back at work soon. He was very nice about it. Lori was a productive salesperson, he said. They would be happy to have her back whenever she was ready.

But Lori's problems didn't go away.

Although she returned to her apartment, she didn't seem willing or able to go back to work. And she began to seem alternately more agitated and more depressed. Sometimes she seemed nearly frantic, at other times she seemed nearly rigidly, profoundly down. Her appearance began to change too. She had once been meticulous about her grooming, and, while she never shared Nancy's love of ultra-feminine things and high fashion, she was always nicely dressed, with attractive clothes, and flattering haircuts. Now she was more slovenly. Her clothes seemed like she had slept in them. Her hair, once shiny and bouncy, stuck together in oily strands, looking as if she hadn't washed it in weeks.

Lori Winters had moved out, so Nancy went down to the city often to check on our Lori. She began to report to me with growing dismay the increasing disorder of Lori's apartment, and her agitation. It was hard to be in the same room with her some-times, she was so stirred up, pacing back and forth, pulling on one cigarette after another until the room was filled with the foul smoke.

In the meantime, she had stopped seeing her psychiatrist. Shortly after she was released from the hospital, we got a call from him. Lori's problems were more serious than he was prepared to handle, he told us. Lori needed more help than he could give, so he was recommending that we find another doctor. He was saying that Lori was really sick—much sicker than we had thought at first. But I couldn't hear him. I didn't want to hear him.

Partly it was my love for Lori that blinded me: I didn't want to see what was happening before my eyes. My daughter Lori was pretty and smart and talented. She was a model student and a model teenager. Everyone loved her. She was supposed to go to college, meet a wonderful man, get married, have children and live a long and happy life. I couldn't accept anything that got in the way of that picture.

But partly it was my own professional background, my training in psychology, that—rather than helping me—made it almost impossible for me to face what was happening. Back when I studied psychology in the 1950s, there was only one cause for all mental illnesses, even the most severe: a faulty upbringing. Everything was tied to the way you were raised. There were different schools of thought, of course. Some practitioners fol-lowed a Freudian model where understanding the id, the ego and the superego gave the answer to everything. Some followed Jung, with his emphasis on unconscious myths. But everyone believed that it was early life experiences that were behind mental disorders. A patient with serious mental problems had been subject at an early age to unacceptable pressures, to confusing messages, or to some destructive behavior on the part of the parents.

If Lori were really sick, my training told me, then I was to blame. I couldn't believe it. I didn't want to believe it. So I refused to believe that Lori was really sick.

Nonetheless, Nancy and I were both ready to try anything that would help our little girl. When her psychiatrist suggested that rather than psychotherapy we try drug therapy, we were more than willing to listen. There was a man in New York, a Dr.

Nathan Kline, who was experimenting in the field of psychophar-
macology. He had established quite a reputation already for treating young people's psychological problems with drugs. There
was even a whole clinic named after him. After reading some
clippings that described all the good he was doing for young
people like our daughter, we sent Lori over to his clinic on the
east side of Manhattan.

After several weeks of treatment it seemed to me that Lori
was much better. Her depressions didn't seem as severe, and she
seemed much calmer. She seemed more in control, more relaxed.
I thought the drug therapy was doing her good. Nancy disagreed.

"Marvin, that's not Lori," she said to me one night. "That's
not who Lori is. Look at her eyes. She's just drugged, she's in a
stupor. He's giving her way too much medicine. She's taking ten
or twenty pills a day."

I knew he was giving her medicine, but I didn't know what it
was, or how much she was taking, or why he was giving it to
her. To resolve the argument, I told Nancy I'd go see Dr. Kline
in his office, which wasn't far from my own office in midtown.
I called and made an appointment.

But when I arrived at the clinic, I did more talking than asking
questions. Dr. Kline was a pleasant man in his fifties with a beard.
His office was full of impressive African art. His whole setup, in
fact, was impressive. He was clearly well regarded for his work.
I spent my time in his office thanking him for the help he had
given Lori. He seemed glad to hear my comments.

But then the phone rang again.

It was New York Hospital calling. Lori was in the emergency
room. Again. Once again she had tried to commit suicide. Once
again they wanted to admit her to a psychiatric unit. This time
Nancy was too terrified to come with me. So I asked our older
son, Mark, who was home for the summer from college in New
Orleans.

Mark and I didn't talk much in the car on the way down. I was
too consumed with my own thoughts. It was mid-June, just three
months after she had come out of Bellevue, and here she was in
 hospital again. What was going wrong? What was happening to
 ughter?

When we got to the emergency room, it was like a repeat of the time before, only this time it was much worse. She apparently had had an appointment with Dr. Kline in the afternoon. En route to his office, she had swallowed a handful of Ativan, the tranquilizer that Dr. Kline was prescribing for her, and then walked thirty blocks to the office. When she arrived she was incoherent and rambling so the nurses didn't even wait for her appointment. They felt she had taken an intentional overdose in a suicide attempt. They called an ambulance right away to take her to New York Hospital, just a few blocks away.

Again, by the time I arrived Lori had had her stomach pumped. Again she was contrite.

"I wasn't trying to kill myself, Daddy, really I wasn't," she cried. "I was just feeling hyper and I took that stuff to calm down." She seemed in a partial stupor. I left Mark with Lori while I went out to discuss the situation with the doctors. They already knew her history at Bellevue. I was trying to convince them that what Lori was saying was true: She wasn't trying to kill herself, but just trying to calm down.

But when I returned to Lori's bedside, I found Mark white and stunned.

"Dad, she's cursing me out," the stricken twenty-year-old told me. "She's telling me to get the hell out of here, that she hates me, that she's always hated me." Mark idolized Lori, from the time they were kids. He looked shocked. "She's been trying to take off her clothes and leave, Dad. I've been having to hold her down."

And just at that moment she tried to do it again. She was lying in a hospital bed, dressed only in a cotton gown open at the back. When she saw me enter the room, she began to shout. "There's nothing wrong with me. I'm not sick. I'm not staying here." And then, just as if her brother and I were not in the room, she began to take off her gown.

That was when I finally realized her problems were serious. Lori was the most modest of girls, shy and private. When she was well, she would never ever have considered disrobing before me or her brother. But now, shrieking and yelling, she was preparing to walk—naked and without shoes—into the pouring rain outside the hospital.

I have always tried to stay in control. It is simply part of my nature. But that night at New York Hospital, I lost it. I pleaded with her. I begged her. I did everything I could to try to get her to sign herself into the hospital. Over the next hour Mark and I struggled to get her back into her clothes, and tried to calm her down. I tried to reason with her. Then I tried to threaten her. She was hostile. She was unmoving.

"I'm not sick, Daddy. I want to go home. I want to get out of here."

I tried to get her to see the reality of the situation. Matters had spiraled out of our hands. If she didn't sign herself in, chances were good they would commit her involuntarily.

"If you sign yourself in," I told her, "you will stay in control of the situation. You will be able to sign yourself back out when you want. If you don't, they can force you to stay."

Still, I kept giving her a hopeful picture, one that I myself was aching to believe. The Payne Whitney Clinic of New York Hospital, where she was to be sent, was a well-known acute-care facility. That was where people were sent with short-term psychiatric problems. It never occurred to me that people left such short-term care facilities and went on to long-term hospitals. I simply thought she would go in, get some rest, and leave.

"It will only be for a few days, Lori," I told her.

Lori trusted me. Lori had always trusted me. So after about an hour, tired and tearful, she capitulated. The paperwork had already been prepared. She signed it. She looked very small and very helpless as they wheeled her away to be transferred to the psychiatric unit.

In the car on the way home, I knew that Mark was hurting. He hadn't been able to understand what was happening to his sister and was frightened and shocked by the night's events. But I couldn't find anything in myself to comfort him. I was too caught up in the battle raging within my own mind. Lori's problems were only temporary, I kept saying to myself. It was just an acute problem that was going to be over quickly. She would snap out of it in the hospital and be home soon.

But then the dark thoughts I had been trying to hide began pummeling at my hopeful barricade: It's all your fault, I thought. Lori is very sick, and you caused it. You weren't affectionate

enough. You didn't pay enough attention to her. You pushed
too hard. You were too demanding. It's you who have caused
problems. You. You. You. My mind reeled over Lori's enti
childhood, looking for answers.

What had I done? What had I done?

New York Hospital is a white, cold-looking building overlooking Manhattan's East River. Because it is perched right atop the
FDR Drive where cars zoom down the east side of the city, I must
have driven by it hundreds of times in my life, and never given it
a second look. This time, when Nancy and I drove together to
the Payne Whitney Clinic at New York Hospital, I looked closely.
I knew that behind one of those dark, anonymous windows was
Lori.

The hospital had made some attempt at cheer: There was a
small rotunda containing a pleasant garden with scarlet maples
and a scraggly tulip or two in front of the main entrance. But
from the moment we entered the hospital, it was clear that this
was no ordinary place where ordinary people came to get well.
This was a locked-door psychiatric facility. The people inside
couldn't just walk on out. And we couldn't just walk on in. After
taking the elevator up to Lori's floor, we buzzed and waited to be
scrutinized through a window in the door and admitted.

I didn't know what to expect. After her first suicide attempt,
at least she had seemed fairly normal. Apologetic, yes, and afraid
that we would be angry. But we had talked things over coherently,
and she had explained herself. What would she be like this time?

As it turned out, it was worse than anything I could have
imagined. We were admitted to a corridor filled with blank-faced
people, muttering strange things to themselves, or knitting jittery
patterns in the air with restless fingers, or pacing or rocking inces-
santly in their chairs. And there, in a visiting room, where thousands of devastated parents must have looked with horror on
thousands of distraught children, I saw my daughter. But it was
not my daughter. The Lori I knew was gone. And in her place
was a stranger, a person who seemed to be living only partly in
this world, and partly in some faraway world of her own making.
There were no more apologies, no more pleas to let her out. The
illness had captured her, and was part of her.

l talked briefly of home, of her brothers, of
ner and how much we hoped she would be
ne things we said weren't registering. She was
ith thoughts that seemed to perplex and amaze her
same time.

aned over, and in a hushed, confidential tone, whispered

"I know you aren't going to believe this, Daddy, but I can fly."

"What?" The hairs in my arm stood out. I wasn't sure I had heard her correctly, but I was afraid that I had.

"I can fly. Really, Daddy. I can."

It was not a boast, or a challenge. She herself, I could see, found this state of affairs incredible. She was very soft-spoken and focused, deliberate and serious.

"Why don't you show me, Lori."

She scanned the hallway until she spotted a nearby sofa. She climbed up on the pillows. I saw the soft cushions of the sofa sink under her weight. She stood up straight, with a deliberate, almost practiced motion, and then spread her arms as if ready to take flight. She looked down, first at her feet and then at the floor. And then she paused.

"It's not high enough. I can't fly from here." She looked around her. "If you could take me to that window there, I could show you. I can fly."

And she believed it. There was no doubt about it. If we had taken her to an open window, she would have plunged, arms outstretched in flight, to the ground.

We didn't know what to say, so we changed the subject, and left the hospital soon afterward. As we left, her words rang in my ears. "I can fly, Daddy. I can fly."

6

Payne Whitney Clinic, New York City, June 1982

MEDICAL RECORDS

6/17/82 Primary Therapist Note

Patient describes her day of admission as one where she heard voices. "I was afraid I would take my hammer and smash my apartment."

6/17/82 Nursing Note

At 8 p.m., patient had episode of severe auditory hallucinations coupled with intense psychomotor agitation: She was writhing, forcefully grimacing, holding her hands to her ears, shaking her feet repeatedly, and seemed nearly oblivious to external stimuli. This episode lasted about ten minutes. After it subsided, she was initially guarded about what had happened, but later did admit to auditory hallucinations, to feeling ashamed and hopeless about the hallucinations, and to feeling that she must "fight" the voices when they occur, and that discussing them makes them more difficult to "fight."

atient appeared quite preoccupied and angry earlier this morning. Patient refused to discuss what was the matter and stated she was fine! She stated she knows what to tell the doctors in order to let them discharge her. She wants very much to leave Payne Whitney Clinic and was able to say her parents brought her here and that was the only reason she remains here.

6/23/82 Primary Therapist Note

Patient remains agitated and intermittently actively hallucinating. It became clearly evident in discussion how tormented she is by these voices and how hard she is fighting to resist their commands. Much of her treatment resistance appears to stem from fear of the repercussions of revealing these hallucinations to staff. "They'll kill me if I tell."

7

---·◆◆·---

Steven Schiller
Scarsdale, New York, July 1982

I was sixteen years old when Lori was committed for the first time. When my parents told me what they had done, I lost it. I stood there in the kitchen, my hands shaking with rage.

"You're wrong!" I shouted at my parents. "You're wrong! This is no way to treat one of your kids."

My father sat at the butcher block table. My mother was nervously fluttering through the kitchen, compulsively arranging and rearranging her kitchen that was already spotless.

"Steven," my father began, "Lori is sick." There was a pause. "We are doing what is best for her . . ."

"Sure you're doing what's best for her," I said sarcastically. "You just don't know how to handle her. You're doing what's best for you."

"We're trying to get help for her," my mother began.

"You're trying to sweep her under the carpet," I shouted. There was another long silence. There wasn't anything left to say. I started crying.

I really believed they were trying to sweep her away. At my age, everything looked black and white. There was right and there was wrong, and putting Lori in the hospital was wrong. This seemed like typical stupid Scarsdale stuff. I knew how people around here hushed up divorces, and kids on drugs, and jobs lost and other unpleasant things. To me, putting Lori in a psychiatric hospital was just like that. It was something that had to be whispered about.

"Let's put her where we can't see her, so we don't have to confront this every single day," I mocked. "Let's put her where no one else can see her, where no one else will know she has problems."

To be honest, I didn't really have any idea what was wrong with Lori. Because I am six and a half years younger than her, I was still just a kid when she began having difficulties in college. My parents didn't seem to understand much of Lori's problems. What they did understand, they weren't passing on to me. I was only vaguely aware of talk of Lori having troubles in school.

And when Lori graduated and moved back to New York, all I heard was more talk, again vague, about her seeing a doctor. Even her suicide attempt a few months before didn't really register. I was lying in bed at night when I heard the phone ring. There was the scuffle of someone dressing, and then my father poked his head in my bedroom door.

"We have to go get your sister in the hospital," he said. "She's tried to kill herself."

It was out of the blue. I didn't understand it, and no one took me aside to explain what had happened. Now Lori was suddenly a major problem—bigger than anyone knew how to deal with. Since there were no answers, nobody talked about the questions. I felt isolated in the silence and confusion.

When my parents put Lori in the hospital, it reopened an old wound for me. It was loneliness. I was still resentful that my mom had gone back to work many years earlier. I was still feeling abandoned.

So when Lori went in the hospital at the end of my junior year in high school, I just felt it was more of the same. Mom started coming home later and later. Both Mom and Dad were more and more preoccupied. They both had even less time for me than they had before.

That summer, they left me more on my own to do things than they ever had with the other kids. My summer job that year was working at Cherry Lawn Farm, helping bag produce and wait on customers. In the evenings I sometimes started dinner. My mom had always done all the cooking, and somehow the fact that she wasn't doing it all the time anymore seemed to signal the end of a happy era to me. We used to start dinner together. Now I was doing it alone. I would start the burgers, or chicken or steak, and cut up vegetables for a salad.

Then once they got home in the evening there we were, just the three of us around the dinner table. Mark was away at college. Lori was put away someplace. My parents were silent and tense. We were hardly even a family anymore.

So when Mom started coming home crying, I wasn't exactly sympathetic. She never talked about Lori. I thought she was upset about work. She always talked about work. She was upset, she said, because someone had said something mean to her. Or because someone had taken credit for something she had done. Or because of some bit of office politics. It never really registered that she was coming home late and always crying because she had gone to visit Lori.

Had I been older, I might have thought that all the stress in my mother's life was making it hard for her to deal with things that otherwise she might have taken in stride. But I didn't think that at all. I thought she wasn't cut out for business. I thought she was finally finding out that she had no business leaving home—and me. Lori had nothing to do with it.

And when my mother started smoking again after seven years without a cigarette, I wouldn't buy her explanation. Is smoking the solution? You and Dad are just using Lori as an excuse for everything bad that is going on in our family. I was harsh. I knew I was being harsh, but I didn't care. I didn't know what was going on, and I was very confused.

Underneath my complaints and my criticisms, though, there lurked something much deeper.

It was fear.

Was whatever it was that had happened to Lori going to happen to me? Was there going to be a day down the road when my parents would lock me away? If it had happened to Lori, why couldn't it happen to me? They said this was a genetic problem, and I had the same genes she did.

My fear was all the more acute because for as long as I could
remember Lori was what I was going to be when I grew up.
When I was little, one of the first things I remember thinking was
that I wanted to be older like Lori. When I was in grade school,
she was already in high school, which seemed like the place to be.
When I went to camp, she was already a counselor, and that meant
power and authority. When I was eleven, all I wanted to be was
seventeen, because Lori was seventeen and she had it all. Lori's
life looked so glamorous that I often enjoyed fantasizing about the
day when I would be able to do the things she was doing.

That was especially true when I got into high school and she
was in college. I was having a miserable adolescent time of it. But
Lori gave me a break. She invited me up for a weekend at college
with her friends. She and her roommates Tara and Lori Winters
took me to do all the fun things that college kids do in Boston.
We walked around the Common and looked at the sights of the
city. We went to the original Steve's and made our own sundaes
from homemade ice cream. Lori filled her pockets with M&Ms
when the guy behind the counter wasn't looking. We even went
to the top of the Hyatt and watched the city from the rotating
bar. We picked the raisins from the trail mix on the tables near
where we were sitting. We made jokes when the waiter threw us
out because I was underage. To me, a miserable gawky high
school sophomore, it all seemed unbelievably exciting. I left Boston thinking: In a few years this will be me. What's happening to
Lori now will happen to me soon.

So now, a year later, I worried that in illness too, Lori's fate
would be mine.

My dad's behavior was troubling. After Lori became ill, Dad
suddenly changed the way he behaved toward me. For years he
had pushed us all to achieve, to do the hardest things possible.
But this summer, as I was preparing to enter my senior year in
high school, he began to urge me to take the easiest classes possible, even perhaps remedial classes. I thought Lori's illness was a
result of the way my parents treated her. I began to feel that he
thought the same thing I did—that he had caused Lori's illness,
and that he was afraid of causing it in me.

Finally I summoned up enough courage to talk to my dad.

"Dad, I'm having problems, and I think I need to see a psychiatrist," I said. Then I held my breath and waited.

He looked at me for a very long time. Finally, he spoke very seriously.

"If you think you need to see a psychiatrist, of course you can go see one," he said very slowly. "But, Steven—I don't think you need one." He paused. "Why do you think you do?"

I didn't really have an answer. And I never did see a psychiatrist. I guess I just wanted to see how he'd react. To see if he'd laugh, or look scared, or agree that I needed help.

My fears had one other powerful side effect: I refused to visit Lori in the hospital. Partly I was just being selfish. I didn't know what I'd say. I didn't know how to act. But partly, I was thinking about myself. When I had visited Lori at Tufts it had been like I was looking into a mirror at my own future. I couldn't go visit her at Payne Whitney and look into that mirror.

8

Nancy Schiller
*Payne Whitney Clinic, New York,
August 1982–September 1982*

Click. Click. Click. Click.

Every night the tap of my high heels on the steaming pavement sounded a drumbeat as I walked from the subway to the hospital. One. Two. Three. Four. Shoulders back. Chin up. Head high. "If you can keep up a good front for your co-workers and clients, you can do it for Lori," I told myself. I had to keep control. I couldn't let her see me cry. I had to be cheerful, and upbeat and smiling and supportive. I had to play the role.

All the way on that long hot walk I rehearsed as if for a sales pitch—the hardest one of my life. I had to convince my sick little girl that everything was going to be all right. I had to convince her that life was worth living. But first I had to convince myself.

Every step of the way was a battle. First I stopped at Peppermint Park at the corner of 66th Street and First Avenue to buy ice cream. Lori loved ice cream. How many times when she was a teen had we looked at our thighs and laughed. "Who better deserves?" we would say. "Let's have a hot fudge sundae."

So what was I hoping for? Did I think I could bring her back with a pint of rocky road? I felt like a jerk. How could I hope ice cream would cheer Lori up when even buying it made me dizzy with disbelief. The pink and green store awnings, ice cream parlor chairs and fake Tiffany windows infuriated me.

"Don't you know my daughter is on a locked ward at Payne Whitney, and she thinks she can fly?" I wanted to scream at the silly laughing clerks. "How dare you laugh? How can you be happy when there is so much misery in the world?" And at the back of my head, the ugly thought lurked: "How dare you be well when my Lori is so sick?"

From the ice cream store, I walked over to York Avenue. There I stopped at a flower cart between 66th Street and the hospital entrance on 69th. Buying Lori flowers was extravagant and stupid. She had retreated into her own world, and was barely noticing the room around her. What did she care about flowers? But every day I bought some just the same. I had to do something. Anything.

As I headed up to the locked ward on the third floor, I checked my reflection in the mirrored elevator doors, and gave myself one last pep talk: "Okay, Miss Sparkle Plenty, get your act together," I ordered myself. "All right, Stella Stunning—it's show time!"

Lori was more than just my daughter. She was everything I had ever wanted. When she was a baby, she was my doll; when she got older, we were playmates. She was my friend, my confidante, my soul mate. She was the childhood I never had.

When I was a little girl, I would sit in the lilac tree in our backyard and dream of my future. I would be slim and beautiful. I would have a doctor for a husband. I would have a little daughter to hold in my arms. I would sing to her, laugh with her, dress her, cuddle her, play with her and shower her with all the love that I craved so much.

When I was growing up my parents rarely hugged me, or held me on their laps, or told me they loved me. Instead, they fought and argued constantly. My father was a shrewd businessman, cold and calculating. My sister thought he worshipped my mother. I thought he was an opportunist. I think he married my mother—who was very beautiful, very wealthy and very scattered—for her money.

In any case, they were terribly mismatched. My father was orderly, disciplined and focused. My mother was an artist, flighty, disorganized and indecisive. She always seemed overwhelmed by life, unable to cope, to discipline me and my sister, or to handle running a household.

Late at night, when I would hear them screaming and quarreling, I would run crying to my German nanny's bedroom for the only comfort I could get. In the morning, my mother would scream at me: "You are the cause of all my unhappiness." She never wanted children, and didn't know how to handle them. "You're too loud" was all I ever heard. "You're too fat." "Stand up straight!"

And as for my father, I adored him, and did everything I could to have him love me—including trying to be the son he wished he had had. I washed his cars, climbed trees, asked about his business. Of course, I was a complete failure, for in reality I was a terribly feminine child, caught up in my dolls and my dreams. When my father asked me to dance at the synagogue, I felt like a princess as we whirled and twirled. But he was a sadistic man, and to him it was a joke. He purposely tripped me and laughed as I lay, humiliated, on the floor in front of everyone.

Was it any wonder, then, that I married the first man who was good to me? I knew I was going to marry Marvin from the moment I spotted him across the room at a fraternity dance. He was dark, sophisticated and older—a graduate student, and an adviser to the fraternity. When I saw him head across the room to me, I almost fainted. By the time the dance was finished, I was madly in love. We were married on December 14, 1957, just a month short of my nineteenth birthday.

With his Ph.D. in psychology, he would be the doctor of my childhood lilac tree dreams. And with his help, I would become the slim beautiful wife I wanted to be. I was terribly lucky. Such an impulsive match could have turned out so differently. But it didn't. We loved each other and together we became a team. From the beginning, we taught each other things. I was a small-town girl; he was from the big city. He introduced me to a more cerebral, sophisticated world. His family had been poor. Mine had lacked for nothing. I had dancing lessons, piano lessons, singing lessons. I taught him which fork to use, how to make small talk, how to write thank-you notes. I taught him how to be less aloof and more diplomatic.

And when, nine months later I became pregnant, all I could think of was fulfilling the rest of my old dream from the lilac tree. Let it be a girl, I thought. Let me have a daughter.

★ ★ ★

Lori Jo didn't disappoint me. She was born when I was twenty, and I loved her more than anything on the face of the earth. My every waking moment was spent with her. I would dress her up in crinolines and little dresses. She was a very precocious child. She walked early, she talked early. We showed her off at every chance we got. She wasn't a cuddly snugly child, which did frustrate me. Instead, she was a little tomboy, off and running and doing. She was terribly stubborn too, a little girl who knew her own mind, and got her own way however she could.

But how could I help loving her so much? She was the perfect child. She was bright, funny, alive, beautiful, giving and warm and loving. A friend once said that Lori just climbed into your bones.

When she got older, my friends would call and complain that they and their teenagers had all these problems. They were fighting. There were secrets, and suspicions, and testing. Not between Lori and me. We went to movies together. We went shopping, tried on hats and got hysterical together. We lay in the backyard and sunned ourselves together. We never argued. There was none of the head-butting and distrust that my friends and their teenage daughters went through. We were as close as a mother and daughter could be.

Where had she gone?

When the hospital elevator let me out on the third floor, I had to ring the bell. A nurse peeked through the window and let me in, closing the door carefully behind lest someone escape. It was a dreary, bleak place with scuffed paint and institutional furniture. Sometimes Lori and I visited in her room. Sometimes she would take me to a visiting room at the end of the hall. It never made much difference to me. There I was with this shell of my daughter. Half the time she sat as if in a fog, as if a veil had been drawn between us. Half the time she was incoherent and rambling, full of a peculiar energy.

How could I talk to this stranger? What could I say that would make a difference? But still I put on the show. "Don't worry, Lulubelle," I said, using my childhood pet name for her. "You'll get better. You'll be well soon. Everything will turn out all right."

Half the time I didn't know what I was saying, murmuring reassuring nonsense. But I did it anyway. I had to. For her sake.

Leaving her every evening was torture for me. As the door swung locked behind me when I left, her parting pleas were like razors.

"Don't go, Mommy," she cried. "Don't leave me in here. I don't belong in here, Mommy. Please take me home. I'll be good, I promise."

For the longest time, I told no one where Lori was. The boys knew, of course, but no one else in the family did. I didn't tell my sister. I didn't tell my mother. I didn't tell a soul. Marvin wouldn't let me.

When we left the hospital for the first time, his face was grim.

"I forbid you to tell anyone about this."

I was taken aback. Forbid? We had been married for twenty-five years. Never once had I heard him utter a word like that. Forbid?

"If we let people know about this, no one will ever let her forget it," he said. "It will put a terrible stigma on her. When she gets out, she will have to put this behind her. It will be impossible if people know where she has been."

"But, Marvin, they said . . ." The people in the hospital had been hinting that Lori was sicker even than we knew.

"I don't care what they said."

"How are we going to keep a secret like that? She may be in here for a while." In truth, neither of us knew how long she'd be there.

"I thought of that. From now on, the story is that Lori has gone back to Boston to study. It's a logical thing to have happen."

It didn't make any sense to me. "We still have her apartment. Her roommate knows . . ."

He wouldn't budge.

"I can't keep this inside. You know I'm no good at keeping secrets. I have to talk about it with someone. I need to talk."

"We'll talk about it together," he said.

And that was that.

The deception made everything ten times worse for me. I

needed to talk, to vent, to get sympathy and support from my friends. Instead, I could confide in no one. What was worse, I was lying to them. I hated lying to my friends. I hated pretending everything was all right when it wasn't.

I began to see how marriages could break up. The strain was more than we had ever experienced. We were still friends. We still enjoyed each other's company. But our traditional roles were jarred. I had always been the wife and mother. He was the bread-winner. He was precise and methodical, the kind of man a family could lean on.

But this was different.

One evening leaving the hospital, we held hands and looked at each other.

"Is everything going to be all right?" I asked.

"I don't know," he said.

It was a terrible moment. I had never heard him say "I don't know" before. He had always been so positive and take-charge. He always thought everything was going to come out all right. I had never heard him express any doubt. How could he say he didn't know? I needed him to know.

For all those years I had depended on Marvin. Now, suddenly he was helpless. Helpless in the face of something dreadful happening to the little girl he adored. Helpless in the face of something he couldn't manipulate. He couldn't buy it. He couldn't pull strings and make it go away. He couldn't make it all better.

Lori's illness was something over which he had no power. He felt impotent. And so he did everything he could to deny what was happening. He made up ridiculous stories. He threw himself even more into his work.

I never thought he was making up excuses to travel away from home. Traveling was part of every management consultant's job. And as one of the senior people, he was forever having to spend days and nights at the firm's head office in Chicago. Still, I was brutally angry with him for going away and leaving me alone. "You're never here when I need you," I thought. It was unfair of me, I realized, but I thought it all the same. I couldn't help myself. When I returned to an empty house at night after visiting Lori, it was the loneliest I had ever been. Marvin called every night, and we talked. Even though he was tired, and had worked a long day, we talked as long as I needed to. He was very loving and caring, but he was seven hundred fifty miles away, and I was alone.

When he came home, we talked endlessly. He blamed himself, and I didn't argue.

I was thinking the same thing. He *had* been too demanding. He *had* been too hard on her. While she was growing up, he had been away from home too much. He had been insensitive to her needs. When she had been under pressure, wanted to switch schools, why hadn't he let her?

Through long, sleepless nights, he tortured himself. "It's all my fault," he said.

And I didn't say no.

Unlike Marvin, though, I didn't blame myself.

I thought I was a wonderful mother. I was working now, and doing very well, selling advertising space for a fashion magazine. But when the kids were growing up, I was home and always there for them. I was the mother with the PTA, and the milk and cookies and the carpool. I had so much time for my children when they were growing up, and I loved them so much.

No. What I tortured myself with were questions. If I had loved her so much, why hadn't I seen this coming? How could I have been so blind?

I combed through my memories of her childhood. Everything had seemed so normal to me, but now in the cold light of this illness, I wondered. Lori had always been moody, especially as she got into her teens. Sometimes she would say she was depressed and fat and had no friends. But then I would talk to my own friends, and they would say their daughters said the same thing. We all chalked it up to hormones. I was often pretty mercurial myself. If Lori was moody too, at the time it seemed normal. But was it? Or was it a sign of what was to come that I had missed?

All along, I now realized, I had never really worried about Lori. She so clearly had it all. It was always Mark who worried me. Mark, our middle child, had been shy and awkward. When we moved to Scarsdale, both Lori and little Steven were intrepid. Off they went into their new schools without a hint of self-consciousness. Mark, though, had trouble adjusting.

In high school, Lori was a good student, involved in all kinds of activities, surrounded by friends, and by and large cheerful. Mark, on the other hand, was always depressed, moping around, getting teary-eyed, listening to acid rock and writing poems about death and suicide. It was he, growing up, who kept me awake at night, not Lori. Now suddenly everything was reversed. Mark had blossomed in college, was talking about going on to business school, and was showing every sign of being happy and well adjusted. And Lori was in a mental institution. Where had things changed? What signs had I missed seeing?

And when I finally realized she was sick, was I too passive? Could I have done more to help? In particular, I berated myself for letting Lori be treated by that Dr. Kline. I never met the man, but I hated him. I thought he was awful. I didn't think he was helping these kids. All he seemed to do with Lori was give her more and more pills.

I could see the effects in her eyes. Just a few weeks after she began seeing him, her eyes became glassy and vacant, and she began to move like she was sleepwalking. She put on nearly twenty pounds. Her beautiful complexion began to break out, and her chestnut hair turned gray almost overnight.

Still, I didn't know how bad she was until one day in late spring. I came into the city to visit her often, and on that day I was on my way to meet her. I walked down a street in midtown, heading toward the corner where Lori and I had agreed to meet. As I walked, I passed a street person, a woman laden down with heavy shopping bags. Although it was late spring and very hot, she was wearing an overcoat, hat and boots.

Something about the woman made me look back. When I did, I was horrified. It was Lori.

Why hadn't I stepped in even then? Why hadn't I insisted she go to a hospital right away? I knew something was terribly wrong, but I had been unable to grasp it, helpless to act. Was there anything I could have done back then that could have saved her from the terrible fate she was suffering now?

So all through the summer, I walked that lonely route, up from the subway, past the ice cream store, past the flower cart, past the other sad-eyed parents who looked like me, into the bleak

colorlessness of Lori's room. As fall approached I b
pretzels from stands on the street, and pretty sw
Bloomingdale's. Her weight had ballooned up s
couldn't fit into her own clothes anymore.

Sometimes she was so sick she kept to her room, huddled up
and uncommunicative. Sometimes she was well enough to join the
other patients in some activities, like painting and crafts. Crafts! I
could scarcely believe it. My straight-A Lori, who had gone to
Tufts, nearly gotten into Harvard, and succeeded at everything
she did. And here we were feeling grateful that she was well
enough to paint designs on plates.

What was wrong with her? We still didn't know. No one was
telling us. Did they know? We didn't know that either. All we
knew was that they kept trying all the drugs they knew of, and
nothing seemed to help. The names of the drugs rang in our heads:
They tried lithium for her mood swings. They tried Thorazine
and Haldol for psychiatric symptoms. They kept boosting the
doses higher and higher. They gave her enough medicine to fell
a cow. But nothing was working.

The hospital seemed to be getting irritated with Lori. Why
wasn't she responding? And we were getting more and more
irritated with Payne Whitney. For one thing, it seemed they were
always changing doctors on us. Payne Whitney was a teaching
hospital, an offshoot of New York Hospital—Cornell Medical
Center, and we kept being seen by earnest young students doing
their rotation through a psychiatric clinic.

First there was a young man. Then a tiny young woman. Then
another man. Then another woman. Every time they changed,
we had to start all over from the beginning: Yes, Lori had seemed
normal through most of her childhood. Yes, sometimes she
seemed depressed. No, she had never had trouble functioning.
Look at her college record! Yes, her troubles seemed to have begun
in late college. If we were being put through this agony, we
thought, what about Lori? And what were they doing to help her?

Then one day in early July, we met with a young woman. Lori's
case was a difficult one to diagnose, she told us. Because of Lori's
cycles of racing energy followed by deep despair, the doctors were
considering that she had a bipolar disorder, which was another

ay of saying manic-depression. That made sense to me. I myself have pretty abrupt mood swings, from elation to gloom, although nothing that had ever been debilitating.

But then the doctor dropped a bombshell. Lori, she said, was hallucinating.

Hallucinating? I began to cry.

"I don't understand it," I said. "I don't understand what's going on with her, and I'm afraid."

Marvin was calmer. He didn't believe it. He didn't want to believe it. I think he felt Lori was letting her imagination run away with her, and that with a little encouragement, she could control it.

Still, we were both devastated by the news, and by the doctors' apparent inability to either figure out her symptoms or control them. So when the doctors proposed giving her electroshock treatments Marvin and I went along. We were willing to try anything. And electroshock, they assured us, was nothing like the horror that had been portrayed in the movies. It was a very mild current. Sometimes it provided enough stimulus to the brain to jolt it out of whatever was causing these wild swings. They brought us the papers. We signed them.

They wouldn't let us be there during the shock treatments themselves, so I never knew what happened or what they were actually like. But when I saw Lori in the evenings, she seemed much more subdued. Maybe she was just tired and out of it. But the evenings when she had been treated she always seemed so far away. After six treatments she seemed to be getting better, and she was allowed to do without the full-time nurse. One night we were even allowed a pass to take her out to dinner. But very quickly she relapsed. They shocked her six more times. Then six more after that. It went on and on, July, August and then into September. Altogether she had twenty treatments. Except for the lethargy on the days she had the treatment, we saw no lasting effects.

Payne Whitney, it seemed, was running out of tricks. It was a short-term facility. At first we had taken that as a hopeful sign. She was going to check in, get treated and get out. We never thought of the alternative: That she would not get better. That psychotherapy would not work. That drugs would not. That electroshock would not work. That she would not return home. That she would be moved someplace, to a longer-term facility, where the truly sick patients are sent.

Suddenly that alternative was thrust upon us. One day in early fall, we got a message that the doctors wanted to see us—together. Marvin and I met in an open area outside two offices. It wasn't in an office itself, but more like a waiting room, or rest area, a place where the physicians might relax between rounds. We were both tense. Marvin in particular seemed stiff, standoffish, defensive. There were two people facing us. One was a young woman, the doctor most recently responsible for treating Lori. The other was a young man. I had seen him around before, and he had from time to time been a part of our discussions about Lori's treatment. But there had been so many people, I wasn't clear what his real role was. Maybe he was a doctor. Maybe he was a social worker. Maybe he was a researcher. All I knew was that he was very young, and a stiff, scholarly type who seemed ill at ease.

The doctor began. "Lori has been here for over two months," she said. "We think we have some better idea of what her problems are now."

"What's wrong with her?" Marvin and I spoke almost together.

"Because of the combination of her severe mood swings and her hallucinations we think that Lori has something we call schizo-affective disorder."

"Schizo-affective disorder?" Marvin sounded incredulous. "What's that?"

"It's a combination of things. She's got some symptoms of manic-depression, and some symptoms of schizophrenia."

"So doesn't this diagnosis just mean you don't really know what's wrong with her?" Marvin sounded harsh. I think he was just shocked. It was the very first time we had ever heard the word "schizophrenia" applied to Lori. Even though they had told us before that she was hallucinating they had said that they themselves felt that could just be a symptom of her manic-ness.

The doctor shrugged her shoulders. "What we do know for sure is that Lori is a very sick girl. This hospital specializes in short-term treatments. Lori doesn't have a short-term problem. We'd like to recommend that she be transferred to another hospital in Westchester. It's also part of New York Hospital, but they do medium-and longer-term treatment there. It's also closer to your home."

Marvin was immovable. "I find this diagnosis very difficult to accept," he said in what sounded even to me like a very cool, professional voice. "All along we've been led to believe that she would be getting better very soon."

"I'm sure you know that her symptoms have continued to be very serious . . ." the young woman began.

"But just what are her symptoms? I'm not sure anymore what her symptoms are, and what was caused by the electroshock, and what by the medicine. Don't you think that we should take her off all the medications and see what she's like then?"

The doctor was dubious. Lori's problems have more to do with her condition than with her medication, she said. And in any case, since Lori had required so much supervision in the past, any experiments without medication would have to be done in some kind of hospital setting.

"But couldn't we take her home? You know that I am a psychologist. If she needs professional supervision, I could take time off and watch her myself . . ."

While Marvin and the doctor had been debating, the young man and I had sat silently. Just at that moment, though, he broke in.

"Schizophrenia is a very serious illness," he said. "It may be a very long time—if ever—before she will get better. She will probably never be able to live on her own again. It would be better for both of you if you faced facts."

I was in shock. This young man, a person I barely knew, had just told us there was no hope. No hope for Lori. The hospital was giving up on her, and we should too. My stomach was tied up in knots. I glanced over at Marvin, who sat there looking stiff and angry.

There were tears in his eyes. But I, who had spent the summer sobbing, couldn't squeeze out a drop.

Schizophrenia? What did that word mean? I didn't understand it. I didn't believe it. All along they had been talking about manic-depression. When they said schizophrenia I didn't know what they were talking about. What did they mean when they said she was hallucinating? And what did schizophrenia have to do with it?

Schizophrenia meant split personality, didn't it? I had heard about schizophrenia, and I had seen some movies about it. To me, schizophrenia was *The Three Faces of Eve*, the film starring Joanne Woodward about a woman who had three different personalities that came and went without warning.

How many personalities did they think Lori had? Was the girl who told us she could fly a different personality from the personality of the Lori we knew and loved? Where had this other person come from and how could we make her go away and get our Lori back?

I didn't think to ask those questions. And the doctors just seemed to assume we would understand what they were talking about, or at least accept it without understanding.

Who could I turn to? Marvin was still locked inside himself, and wouldn't talk to anyone. So he couldn't solve problems the way he usually did, by calling around to his friends and colleagues and seeking the best possible advice and information. He was a psychologist. Surely he understood what schizophrenia was. But he was too tormented to explain it to me clearly. Or perhaps he was shielding me from the truth. Once again I felt alone and confused.

I went to the Doubleday bookstore at lunchtime and bought three books on mental illness. To me, mental illness was tragic and upsetting, but the kinds of mental illness I was imagining for Lori had still been rather commonplace. Marvin and I had been devastated by Lori's breakdown, but that's all we had thought it was—a breakdown. People like Lori had nervous breakdowns. She had been under too much stress. She had been depressed. She had been unhappy. Even saying she could fly—it was awful, but if we thought about it as mental confusion caused by stress, we could still understand it. When the stress went away, and her symptoms were treated by drugs, the confusion would go away.

But schizophrenia? The word itself was horrifying.

I started skimming the books while I was standing in line, read as much as I could before I went back to the office, and the rest on the train on the way home.

All my ideas had been wrong. Schizophrenia wasn't a split

personality. It was a brain disease, a chemical imbalance. People with schizophrenia did hallucinate. They heard voices commanding them to do things. They heard voices talking about them. Sometimes they had delusions, like that they were the Prophet Elijah, or Moses. People with schizophrenia were very sick. Mostly the disease started in people who were very young, just starting their lives. Sometimes drugs helped get their hallucinations under control. Sometimes drugs didn't help at all. Very often people with schizophrenia didn't get better. Some of them spent their whole lives in institutions.

Suddenly I seemed to understand why they would want to transfer her out of Payne Whitney, to turn her over to some other hospital. All my suspicions were correct. They *were* telling us there was no hope.

9

New York Hospital, Westchester Division,
White Plains, New York,
September 1982–October 1982

HOSPITAL RECORDS

Schiller, Miss Lori
Admitted: September 24, 1982
Unit: 3 North

PSYCHIATRIC CASE HISTORY

IDENTIFYING DATA

Date of Birth: 4/26/59
Age: 23
Sex: Female
Race: White
Religion: Jewish
Marital Status: Single
Cultural Background: White, upper middle class, Jewish
Current Living Situation: Alone in apartment in Manhattan
Usual Employment: Insurance Salesperson

Patient, unreliable. Parents, reliable.

PRESENTING PROBLEMS

The patient was transferred from New York Hospital—Payne Whitney Clinic for long-term hospital treatment of depression, agitation, auditory hallucinations and confusion. Patient's complaint is that she is very confused, which she attributes to Electro-Convulsive Therapy that she received at the Payne Whitney Clinic and that she is hearing voices that tell her to hurt herself and criticize her.

DESCRIPTION OF PATIENT AND MENTAL STATUS

Upon admission, the patient's appearance seemed very normal. Her dress was appropriate. She seemed a little confused throughout the interview . . . She reported having hallucinations . . . She appeared to have no formal thought disorder, flight of ideas or circumstantiality. Cognition was difficult to evaluate because of her confusion . . . Her memory was poor, especially long-term memory. Her short-term memory was a little better.

RECOMMENDATIONS PROGNOSIS AND TREATMENT

Initially it would be important to clarify the patient's diagnosis. Historically she has been diagnosed as a bipolar disorder, but there are conflicting signs that would indicate a schizophrenic illness . . .

9/27/82 Nursing Note, 10:30 p.m.
Status: Constant Supervision

Lori is having frequent auditory hallucinations, including voices screaming at her, command hallucinations telling her to go out the window and "fly." She appears in much distress, often covering her ears. She walks near windows but can be easily encouraged to move away. She looks depressed and voices discouragement and anger over her lack of progress. She refused

9 p.m. medications for this reason, "they don't help take away the voices." Lori did look cheerful when parents visited.

10/1/82 Nursing Note, 11:45 p.m.
Status: Constant Supervision

While opening front door for another patient Lori tried to run out . . . Lori was caught before she got outside the door. Staff decided to take patient's shoes away and make her wear hospital pajamas.

10/3/82 Nursing Note, 3–11 p.m.
Status: Constant Supervision

. . . patient stated she hears two male voices, can't identify them. These two voices tell her to jump out the window, that she would be able to fly, and also that she should leave the hospital. Patient feels the voices in her head are coming from a "radio inside my head." Patient also stated she deserves to die because she is no good. Patient feels that dying would end her problem and would make things better for her.

10/15/82 Nursing Note, 3–11 p.m.
Status: Constant Observation

Patient had a visit from brother this evening. She appeared to be very pleased with the visit. She talked a little bit about still feeling suicidal and wanting to know why, since it was her life why couldn't she end it. She feels she has lived her life already and there isn't anything else to live for. Patient spacey at times. She also talked about her memory loss and [wondered] if it will ever return completely . . .

10/20/82 Nursing Note, 10 p.m.
Status: Constant Observation

Patient stated the voices are constant and tell her to hurt herself at times, other times she states she feels she should hurt herself as well without listening to the voices. Patient also mentioned that she feels she can fly because she feels she flew before. Patient stated she flew 2 years ago when she was in college. Patient stated she went sky-diving. The first time she used a parachute, then second time, the patient stated she went sky-diving without a parachute and landed on her feet. Patient feels that this is not anything magical . . .

10

Nancy Schiller
New York Hospital, White Plains,
New York, November 1982–April 1983

It's funny but I had never really noticed before that there was a hospital back there.

I had never given the long, elegant, tree-lined drive more than a passing glance—even though the big brick entrance gates into the hospital loomed over several big department stores I had visited for years. Saks, Bloomingdale's, Neiman-Marcus—forever, it seemed, I had been shopping, visiting, lunching and enjoying myself all in the shadow of a large, famous psychiatric hospital. It was New York Hospital—Cornell Medical Center, Westchester Division, on Bloomingdale Road in White Plains, and it was there that, on September 24, 1982, Lori was moved by ambulance.

Under other circumstances I suppose I would have been grateful that it was here my daughter had been moved. It was obvious that this was as good as it got. Payne Whitney in Manhattan and New York Hospital in White Plains were both part of the same overall medical center, but even in appearance the two hospitals were completely different.

Payne Whitney was a city hospital, dingy and grimy and overlooking the red-striped smokestacks of Queens, and the roar of twenty-four-hour traffic from the FDR Drive. New York Hospital, Westchester Division, on the other hand, was adjacent to some of New York's wealthiest suburbs, and surrounded by acres and acres of well-kept lawns, graceful old trees and formal gardens. Compared to New York Hospital in Westchester, Payne Whitney was gloomy and badly maintained, with scuffed walls and old motel-type furniture. The public areas of the Westchester hospital were filled with lovely old upholstered chairs, glass-front armoires and grandfather clocks. The patients' areas were furnished in a light, cheerful Scandinavian style.

The doctors at Payne Whitney wore white lab coats, which made the hospital feel remote and institutional. At New York Hospital, they wore street clothes. And while they were both teaching hospitals associated with Cornell University, here on Bloomingdale Road we somehow felt more in the hands of professionals who were trying to help us than as cases for students to practice on.

Still, we weren't grateful. We were angry. In the last weeks of her stay at Payne Whitney, our anguish at her harsh diagnosis and prognosis turned to rage at the messengers.

When I become angry, everyone knows it. I am mercurial, and my anger, like my happiness, is right out there for everyone to see: What had the hospital been thinking of, I raged, to put us in the hands of doctors as young and inexperienced as the ones we had been seeing? Maybe there were grown-ups working behind the scenes, making sure these youngsters didn't make mistakes— but why couldn't any of them have talked to us?

That young man, who turned out to be a resident in psychiatry, had told us to "face facts" in the same tone of voice he might have used to tell us he was breaking a dinner date with us. Did he know he was talking about our child, our child's future, our child's life, our child's fate? Did he know how parents felt when they heard news like that about their child?

They didn't care about Lori as a person, I concluded. They didn't care about us as a family. Payne Whitney was a hospital filled with a bunch of inexperienced students, and we were their guinea pigs.

Marvin, for his part, became even cooler, even more acerbic— and more demanding. The doctors told us to give up hope. We would not give up hope. They told us they couldn't get her well quickly. We wanted her well quickly. If Payne Whitney couldn't do it, then New York Hospital, Westchester Division, could.

Even though New York Hospital offered long-term care, we wanted her out of there as fast as possible.

We took our anger from Payne Whitney, and dropped it right on the staff at New York Hospital.

We had plenty of opportunity to do so.

We had, as much as possible, avoided dealing with the social workers on the staff of Payne Whitney. They always wanted us to talk about our feelings, and the last thing we wanted to do was share our feelings with strangers.

Still, much more even than at Payne Whitney, the staff at New York Hospital focused on Marvin and me. Right from the start, the social worker assigned to our case, a middle-aged woman named Jody Shachnow, began suggesting that we get more involved in Lori's treatment. She suggested family meetings. One-on-one meetings. Meetings together with Lori. Meetings with our sons. Telephone consultations.

I dreaded answering the phone. More often than not it was Jody Shachnow or another of the hospital's social workers on the other end of the line.

It was a new experience for us. We had never had to deal with social workers before. Why should we have? Social workers were nice, well-intentioned people who counseled people whose families were in trouble. They didn't have anything to do with families like ours. But with Lori's illness came a change in our family status. Now we too were a family in trouble, and in need of their help. I cringed when I answered the phone and heard the professionally concerned voice of Mrs. Shachnow on the other end.

The message "face facts" must have followed us from Payne Whitney. Or maybe Mrs. Shachnow had arrived at that conclusion on her own. In any case, we didn't want to hear her message to us: that we weren't "accepting" Lori's illness. By pressuring Lori to get better, she told us with professional kindness, we were denying the reality of her disease. Everyone would be better off, she said, when we came to "accept" that Lori was profoundly ill.

We knew Lori was very sick. But we—Marvin especially—couldn't accept that she was permanently sick, that she would not get better. I could see Marvin's back stiffen at the suggestion. And

then he would adopt a professional, detached air, and begin to
question the questioners: Had they tried this drug, or that treatment, or consulted this or that person? When he began to act like
a therapist himself, the room bristled with tension.

We both seethed at their hints that we stop putting pressure on
Lori. Lori worshipped us in a way that wasn't healthy, Mrs.
Shachnow said, ever so gently. But inside, she continued, there
was anger Lori was repressing, anger that was fueling her symptoms.

She wasn't telling us anything that we hadn't berated ourselves
for a million times over. But in a perverse way, the social workers
pushed our backs to the wall. As much as we tortured ourselves in
the darkness of our own room, we didn't want strangers shoving it
in our faces.

When it came right down to it, we just didn't want to talk about
it with them. When Marvin was home, we talked late into the
night. What had we done with Lori? What could we do about
Lori? We wanted information, and medical advice, and insight
into her problem. We didn't want to replay it over and over.

So we played little games with the social workers. When Mrs.
Shachnow tried to set appointments, we put her off.

"We'll be out of town then," I said, no matter when the appointment was scheduled for.

We made dates and didn't keep them. When we did show up,
we would get lectured about keeping appointments. Then we
would be even ruder. I tapped my feet, and Marvin pulled out
business correspondence. They asked questions and we gave
clipped answers. It was our little revenge. We don't want to be
here, we were saying. If you force us to be here, here's what you'll
get. We were like petulant children, sitting there with our arms
folded, refusing to speak.

"Are you feeling a little hostile, Mrs. Schiller?" Jody Shachnow
would say in her schoolteacher voice.

"Hostile?" I was sarcastic. "You might say that."

Inside, I was even more belligerent. Why shouldn't I be hostile?
I thought. You don't know Lori. You don't know what a beautiful, intelligent, charming girl she was. And now she is locked up
in your hospital. I don't know what's wrong with her. You don't

know what's wrong with her. And now you are treating me like a five-year-old. Wouldn't you be hostile?

Privately, Marvin and I mocked their professionally saccharine voices.

"And how are *you* tonight?" we would mimic in the car, and then collapse in peals of laughter. It was cruel. They were professionals, they meant well, and they were only doing their job. It was the only laughing we did those days. But at least it was better than crying.

For nowadays, there was no escaping it: Lori was getting worse.

Anyone could see she was hallucinating. Once the doctors at Payne Whitney had told us about it, I began to see it clearly. The staff at New York Hospital was doing what we wanted done. They were trying to take her off as much medicine as possible, to see what her symptoms were like underneath.

Off all medication, her symptoms raged. She was frightened, almost panicked, by what she was hearing inside her head. Sometimes when I would visit, she was able to carry on a conversation. She talked with me about her day, asked me to bring her cigarettes, or batteries for her Walkman. She would be very coherent, and aware of what was going on. Then all of a sudden—boom!— sometimes in the middle of a sentence even, she was gone. Suddenly the disease would take over. She was there, but not there. Her body was still with me, but her mind was far away and lost. She was looking at me, but not seeing or hearing me. She was listening to something else.

Sometimes when we were talking and she would begin to follow the voices in her head, I would grab her by the shoulders.

"Lori!" I would scream at her. "Lori! Pay attention to me. Stay here. Stay with me. Lori! Look me in the eye."

But when she looked at me, it was always with a secret in her eyes. "I know something you don't know," her eyes were telling me. It was a knowing, superior look, a look that had in it great distance, and great pity, and at the same time, an enormous amount of suffering. "I can hear something you can't hear," her eyes were saying.

And then one day, I recognized that look.

When the realization came, it was so sudden and so clear, I wondered why it had taken me so long to realize: I had seen the look in those eyes before. Not on Lori. No, my memories of those vacant eyes were much older than that. I had seen eyes like that—distant, remote, pitying, all-knowing, superior, preoccupied eyes—all the time when I was growing up. I had seen eyes like that on my mother.

My mother!

Suddenly it all made sense. My poor, scattered, bewildered, on-the-edge mother. Looking at my daughter, I saw my mother and suddenly I understood everything that had made no sense when I was a child. Suddenly I understood my mother's strange helplessness. I understood her odd behavior, the behavior no one ever spoke of at home. She was always talking to herself and eating her dinner in strange places. I remember seeing her take her plate into the bathroom to eat before the mirror, studying herself carefully as she took each bite. I saw in a new light the strange spells of false anger that seemed to come from nowhere and be caused by nothing. And her fainting spells that her brothers and sisters said she used to have even as a child—"to get attention" they said—suddenly even those made sense.

Everything fell into place. There were her regular disappearances. Every so often my mother would suddenly leave to visit her "cousin" in Florida—"to rest," people said. Only I knew what was never spoken about: There was no cousin in Florida. It was a Christian Science healer she was visiting.

Poor people are crazy, they say, and rich people are eccentric. My mother was rich, and so she was allowed to be eccentric. But now, looking at Lori, I realized that my mother hadn't been eccentric. She had been sick. And now I saw that sickness repeated in her granddaughter. For if Lori was schizophrenic, then so was my mother.

With a shock, I remembered the shame I had felt as a child. I remembered my mother meeting my friends, with an odd smile on her face.

"It's so lovely to meet you," she said in a girlish falsetto, prancing and swirling around like a marionette. Then the sudden fade-outs while she was talking, and the all-knowing, superior grin as she retreated into a world of her own. I watched my friends cover up their snickers, and I wanted to die from embarrassment.

Memories, long buried, came flooding back. Troubling, frightening memories that I had long ago tried to push aside. Memories that horrified me when they came bubbling to the surface. For my mother had not been the only one in our family who was sick, I now realized. Far from it.

I began to think back. Cousin Sylvia. How long had it been since I had thought of Sylvia? Sylvia had been a constant source of fear and embarrassment to me. Sylvia was "crazy as a loon" everyone said when I was growing up. She was fat and slovenly and always wore shoes with holes cut out around her bunions and calluses. She had flyaway gray hair and a triple chin. When she smiled you could see the spaces where teeth were missing.

As a child, I was frightened of this woman. She came every day and sat in the shoe department of my father's store, screaming and screaming.

"They're going to come and take your feet away," she screamed one day when I came in and put my feet in the X-ray machine to look at my feet in my shoes. I turned to my father, terrified.

"Don't pay any attention to her," he said. "She's a fat, old crazy cow."

My mind raced back to Lori. When I had seen Lori on the streets of New York, disheveled and out of control, what had I been thinking? Oh, please, I was thinking when I looked at Lori in the late spring heat wearing her long winter coat and snow boots, and carrying shopping bags, please don't let anyone see her like this. Please don't let them be repelled, point, fear. Don't let them laugh at my daughter. Don't let them laugh at me.

Looking back on that moment, I was aghast. With all my might I had been trying to keep from seeing what was right in front of my face. I had looked at Lori and seen my worst fears. I had seen a childhood full of embarrassment and humiliation. When I looked at Lori, I had seen Cousin Sylvia. I had seen my mother, and my friends laughing at her all over again. I had seen my past. It was something I couldn't bear to see again.

And then came an even more frightening thought. Suppose I was seeing not just my past, but my sons' futures? Schizophrenia,

I had read, ran in families. Clearly it ran in mine. Suppose Lori was not the only child of mine to be afflicted?

As much as I could, I tried to act normally. With Mark, it was easy. He was away at Tulane, and, it seemed, really happy for the first time in his life. He had shaken off the adolescent depression that had so troubled him and begun to blossom as a man. He was doing well in his studies. He had plenty of friends. He was dating a lot. It was apparent he was having a ball, and I was so happy to see that.

Steven was at home and in his senior year in high school. I knew he was devastated by Lori's illness. We all were. Nonetheless, Steven seemed happy to me. He was really funny, and could always make me laugh.

Things couldn't help but change. Up until I had gone to work, and Lori had gotten sick, Steven had been the child to whom I had been closest. The other two had left the house, and Steven and I had spent an inordinate amount of time together. He was my baby, and my life had revolved around him as a mother. Now with nearly every waking minute focused on Lori, there just wasn't as much time to spend with him as before.

Still, as best I could, I tried to keep up the things we had always enjoyed doing together. We went to museums together, played golf together, and talked about school and life.

I never mentioned my suspicions to my sons. I didn't want them to worry about themselves. They knew that my mother was strange. But I never told them my newly awakened suspicions about her. As for our other relatives, we had never had much contact with them, so the boys were barely aware they existed. In silence, I worried. Mark was twenty-one, and, I thought, more likely to be out of danger from an illness that seemed to strike in the late teens. But Steven had just turned seventeen. Was he going to be next?

We saw what we wanted to see, and believed what we wanted to believe. With enough time, and enough medication, Lori began to grow calmer, and we took it as a sign she was getting better. And we began to push for her release.

Actually, it was Marvin who pushed. My feelings were mixed. Her behavior was certainly improving. Her rages were beginning to diminish under the medicine, and her pacing was abating. She began to appear more relaxed and started to attend some of the hospital activities. By Christmas and New Year's she had calmed down enough to receive passes to walk with us on the grounds of the hospital. In February for the first time since she entered the hospital she dressed in street clothes, instead of the sweat suits she had been habitually wearing. After a time, she appeared well enough to go out to dinner with us, and to spend a weekend or two at home.

What she needed now, Marvin argued, was activity, a job, friends, a social life. She needed things to anchor her to reality, he argued, not to spend her days in a mental hospital surrounded by sick people. Being at home in a familiar setting with both of us there to help her would be the best thing for her, he argued.

Lori herself was begging to come home. Every time we visited she pleaded to be released. She often threatened to sign herself out against the doctors' orders, and once or twice she had actually tried to do so. She wasn't hallucinating anymore, she insisted. She wanted to get out of the hospital, and get on with her life. Marvin had promised her she could leave the hospital by her birthday in April. He felt she needed a goal to reach for. She grabbed on to that idea and wouldn't let go. She wanted to be home by her birthday. She would be home by her birthday.

My rational mind was screaming "No! No!" There was still something very wrong with this glazed, dazed stranger I saw before me. Thinking realistically, I could see that Lori was not better. She was drugged.

Still, who was I to argue? Marvin was the expert. If he said she would get better at home, I believed him. And while it was clear that Lori's doctors didn't approve, they were doing nothing to stop us. They did urge that she should be released, not to us at home, but to a halfway house. But when we rejected that option, they didn't press. What's more, it was hard to refuse Lori. She was so unhappy in the hospital, and so desperate to get out. She said she felt better, and who knew better than she?

Besides, all along the doctors had been telling us to face facts. Maybe the fact I had to face was that this remote sleepwalking stranger was my daughter. That this was what she would be like from now on. Maybe my expectations were too high. Maybe the doctors were right. Maybe I had to adjust, and learn to live with this strange new person who used to be my daughter.

So on April 22, 1983, Lori was discharged from New York Hospital, just four days before her twenty-fourth birthday.

Part III

There's Nothing Wrong with Me

11

Lori
Scarsdale, New York,
May 1983–August 1983

I was glad to be home.

Daddy had promised me I would be home in time for my birthday. And true to his words, he had brought me back to my old bedroom just in time for cake and ice cream. It wasn't that I cared so much about my birthday. I just couldn't stand the hospital.

Everything about the hospital infuriated me. I didn't know why I was there. I didn't know how I had gotten there. All I knew was that I was trapped. I felt like a prisoner doing my time. I looked out the window every single day and waited for my freedom. Outside was so inviting. I begged for a walk on the hospital grounds. Even with one hospital attendant—or two—at my side, I was so grateful to breathe outside air. I hated being locked up.

Most of all, though, I hated the hospital because everyone there thought I was sick. Well, naturally they thought I was sick! If you are in a mental hospital you must be sick. That was why I wanted to get out. I wanted to get out to be normal again.

There was nothing wrong with me. So why did they keep telling me there was? All these doctors and all these nurses kept saying all these things about me. The words swirled around my head. "There's some bipolar disorder. We should use some antidepressants." "I think she's definitely schizophrenic. A paranoid

˜he needs neuroleptics." "She seems to be very
Give her some sedatives to calm her down." "I
are borderline tendencies. She needs more work in
nerapy." When they finally settled on a diagnosis of
nzo-affective disorder—some schizophrenia, some manic-
depression—it felt like one of those everything-on-it bagels they
sell in the deli. Poppy seed, sesame seed, onion, garlic, salt, pep-
per . . . crazy, loony, insane, cracked, cuckoo. Daffy, demented,
lunatic, mad, maniac, nuts, screwy, wacky—use your imagination.

All the time I was in the hospital they told me I was sick. They
told me I was psychotic with hallucinations. I hated these two
words. I knew they were not true. Psychotic meant like the movie
Psycho and Norman Bates, and the Bates Motel. That was scary
and sick. That wasn't me. I wasn't a *Psycho*-tic woman with a
butcher knife.

And hallucinations? Another word that enraged me. Hallucinations meant that you were seeing something or hearing something
that didn't really exist. But when I heard the Voices screaming at
me, they were real. When the doctors and nurses challenged me,
told me that I was out of reality, and hallucinating, I hated them.
What made me the psychotic one? What about all those judgmental people? What made them the experts?

In fact, I knew they were trying to trick me, trying to torment
me into madness. I knew they could read my mind and hear all
that the Voices were saying about them. The doctors and nursing
staff told me repeatedly that the Voices weren't real. But if they
weren't real, then how did the staff know they were there? The
staff told me over and over again that they couldn't read my mind
either. But if they couldn't, then how did they know all about
what the Voices were saying?

My tormenters were real. I didn't want people telling me they
were false or unreal. I wanted help in making them go away.
That's what they should have been doing. But since they weren't,
I just wanted to get out of there, and fast. I was twenty-four years
old, and it was time I got on with my life.

But how could I?
I didn't even know what my life was. The one I had left behind

a thousand years ago didn't exist anymore. I didn't have a job. I didn't have an apartment. I didn't have friends. I didn't have a life.

It had been nearly a year since I had lived outside a hospital. I wasn't even sure how to do it anymore. I was used to having my life move with the rhythm of the hospital. Someone else had told me what to do and when to do it. Now that I was home, I didn't know exactly how to begin to make those decisions on my own. When I woke up in the morning, I just didn't know what to do with myself. Where was I supposed to go? What was I supposed to do? I found myself literally just standing around.

Because the medications made me at once lethargic and restless, I often just stood in one spot, moving my weight back and forth from one foot to another. I was taking so much medicine that I found it difficult even to smile. I walked around the house sluggishly, doing what I had to do like a robot.

Now that I was out, I wasn't sure how I was supposed to react to other people. In the hospital, I had had contact only with doctors and nurses, and with other patients. With the doctors and nurses, I was a patient. They would ask me questions, and I would answer them. The other patients were crazy. I had as little to do with them as possible. Outside the hospital were other normal people like me. But I couldn't figure out how to connect with them. I felt very awkward around people, even around Mom and Dad.

There was no one for me to hang out with. My old friends couldn't help me. I didn't really even want to see them. It hurt too much. When my old roommate Lori Winters came to visit me in the hospital, she looked like the Dove Soap girl, all slender and pretty with her clear peachy skin. I was so fat and ugly I could barely stand to be in the same room with her.

Everything had changed. Nothing was the same. Even my childhood plans with Gail Kobre. Ever since I could remember, we had planned to be each other's maids of honor when we married. We talked about it, laughed about it, planned what dresses we would wear, and who we would marry.

But on one of her visits to me in the hospital, Gail had some news for me. She and David were getting married in the spring. But I wasn't going to be her maid of honor. No one was sure if

I would be out of the hospital in time. And no one thought I could handle it.

Well, I was out of the hospital in time. She was married in May, just over a month after I came out. And I was there in the audience with everyone else, not up near the chuppah by Gail where I belonged. After the ceremony, the photographer took a picture with Gail and me together. He caught a big smile on my face, but he didn't catch the Voices that were shrieking in my ears, nor the sad feeling that everyone was moving on and leaving me behind.

Of course I did have my family. But even that had changed.

There we were again, 6:30 P.M. sharp around the dinner table, just as I remembered it from my childhood. But it was a pretty pale imitation of the old days. Like my friends, both my brothers were growing up and moving on with their lives. Mark wasn't there. He was in New Orleans, finishing up his senior year at Tulane, about to return to New York City to business school. Steven still lived at home. But he was at the end of his senior year in high school, had already been admitted to Johns Hopkins, and was hanging out with his own friends, doing his own thing.

So that left just me and Mom and Dad around the dinner table. And in place of the lively conversation I remembered from my childhood, there was now strained silence. What was I supposed to say to Mom and Dad? I felt a huge gulf between us. They had changed. They weren't proud of me. They hated me. I knew they loved me, of course, but they hated me too. They hated me, and they were afraid of me. The Voices told me so.

When my release from the hospital was first discussed, people in the hospital brought up the idea of a private-duty nurse. Shouldn't I have someone to stay with me while they were out of the house? Mom and Dad asked. I got angry with them. I would never consider such a thing. Never. Never. Never. I didn't need any more bodyguards. I had had enough of that in the hospital. I was out of the hospital, remember?

So at first, they took turns spending a lot of time with me. My dad took some time off from work, then my mom did. There was always someone around at first. What is Lori going to do? I was being watched like a prisoner, like a crazy person. When they began to leave me alone it was in frightened little jackrabbit bursts.

Mom dashed to the country club across the street to drop off her golf shoes, and was back in eight minutes. I was okay. The next day a kamikaze run to the supermarket. Back in twenty minutes flat. Still okay. Was Lori going to bug out and try to kill herself again? No, Mom and Dad. That's over. I won't do that anymore. I promise. I'm better now. Really. Pretty soon, I got them to believe me. So Dad went back to work in the city, and Mom followed soon after.

They tried so hard to please me. They knew that food was one of the few pleasures left in my life, so they took me to eat anything I liked. General Tsao's chicken and moo shu pork with pancakes and hoisin sauce; pizza with the works and spaghetti; soft-shell crabs, and burgers and fries—I'd wolf down anything.

They also did everything they could to help me put together the pieces of my life. My mom took me shopping for clothes, and tried to encourage me. "Go out and meet young people," my Dad said. "You won't have any kind of social life sitting around your room." He even encouraged me to hang out where young people hung out. "Go to a bar," he said. "You don't have to drink. Order a Diet Coke. Talk to people." He was always giving me some pep talk. And at the end, he always said the same thing: "It's better than being in the hospital."

But was it? I knew I hated the hospital. But the fact was, my memories of the past year were so foggy that I wasn't even completely clear what had happened in the hospital.

My last clear memory was of a morning in my apartment in the McAlpin. Lori Winters and I were leaning out the window, watching the Macy's Thanksgiving Day Parade roll by just beneath us. We were so close that the three-story-tall balloons were bobbing just about at eye level. Then the next clear memory I have is of lying strapped down in an ambulance, a pregnant nurse at my side, being transferred from the Payne Whitney Clinic in Manhattan to New York Hospital in Westchester. People told me that in between those two memories I had tried to commit suicide twice, and that I had already been in the hospital for several months. I didn't know whether to believe them or not.

These gaps in my memory were enormously frustrating. It was like everyone on earth was in on some secret about me. I knew that there were people around—doctors, nurses, my parents, my friends—who remembered things about me that I couldn't remember about myself. It made me paranoid and angry. What else did they know that they weren't telling me? What else were they hiding from me?

Again, I knew where the problem lay. It was with the doctors and the hospitals. While I was in Payne Whitney, I had been given shock treatment, lots of it. I knew that because the doctors at New York Hospital told me. That's what had destroyed my brain cells. They had fried my brain, fried me, fried away all my memories.

I was angry. I told the doctors what they had done to me. They always said the same thing. Shock treatment doesn't do anything to long-term memory, they said. They took me downstairs in New York Hospital, gave me tests, measured my responses and looked inside my brain. It's not the electroshock, they said. Bullshit, assholes! I knew better. They had electrocuted the memories right out of me.

It was awful. They had taken away big chunks of my life. Not only could I not remember being in Payne Whitney, there were all kinds of earlier memories I had lost too. Gail Kobre had visited me in the hospital, bringing with her a scrapbook filled with pictures of our time in London. Pictures of us together. In Trafalgar Square. Before the Queen's Guards. Skipping down the street, laughing. I must have been there. There was my picture. But where was the picture in my brain? Zapped. I felt like an outsider watching other people's memories in a movie that had nothing to do with me.

What did I remember from the hospital? I remembered the attendants assigned to be close to me at all times. I remembered the formal gardens, one of the few pleasures I was allowed while I was there. I remembered bingo and pizza nights in the hospital auditorium. But as for the rest, all I had was a mass of fuzzy impressions that bounced around in my head: Sound. Absence of sound. Jiggling keys. The dinner bell. Whispering. Yells. Tranquilizers. Visiting. Out of control. Showers. Walks. Sunshine. Reflections from outside off a freshly plowed snow bank. Mom. Dad. MEDICATION! MEDICATION! Cheek those pills. Tip the scale every Wednesday. Lithium vampires drawing my blood

Tuesdays. Faces watching from the nursing station. Two packs a day. The final chapter. Nothing to do. Carly Simon. Babies crying. Me crying. Tears of a clown. Forever and a day. Keys. Escape. Alcatraz. Nothing to do about nothing. A post office mug. Coffee in the morning? Spelled with two Fs, two Es. No thank you. And you're welcome. Blaring silence. Bomber planes. Sky blue. I love you. SHUT THE FUCK UP. Smiling faces. The sixties. Bouncing laughter. Can't breathe. This planet. Too terrified. Charles Manson. To die, they say. To die. Help me. Help me. Help me. Please. Tick. Tick. Tick. Goodbye.

Smash that window.

I can fly.

I desperately wanted to leave the hospital, so every time anyone asked me, I told them the Voices were gone. I would have been stupid to do otherwise. If I told them what the Voices were doing and saying, I would have been sent straight off to a state hospital for the rest of my life. That I was sure of. If, on the other hand, I was successful in convincing them that the Voices were gone, I could go home and live a normal life. What choice did I have?

By this time, I had become very skilled at concealing my Voices. I needed every ounce of skill I had. For days at a time, the Voices bombarded my brain with their nasty, raucous shouts. Concealing the Voices in college had been easy because the episodes were so few and far between. This time, however, it was much harder. The Voices were so much more frequent, so much louder, so much more forceful than they had been before. With practice, however, my concealment skills increased.

Many times they didn't work, of course. If someone addressed me while the Voices were actively assaulting me, there was nothing I could do. The Voices' power was too fierce for me. There was almost nothing from the outside that could pull me away. I had to listen to the Voices, had to engage in their world. For as long as these Voices chose to hold me, they were the most powerful thing in my world.

But in between these acute episodes, I usually could muster an adequate response to whomever was addressing me. When anyone—doctors, nurses, my parents, other patients—spoke to me, I learned to focus on the very end of their statements or questions, and respond to that. Usually I could manage quite an appropriate response. And then I would go back to the Voices.

Even though the Voices were far more intense in the hospital than before, in some ways they were less frightening. When I was in high school and college, they had sneaked up on me, blasting out of the airwaves almost without warning. By now, they had become almost familiar. I hated them. I suffered from them. But they seemed almost a normal part of living. I knew them. I understood them and they understood me.

When I got out of the hospital, the Voices were much softer, much less frequent than before. In the hospital, the doctors told me that it was because of the medicine I was taking, that the medicine was helping to fix whatever it was wrong in my brain. I knew better. I knew that this was just another sign that being in the hospital made me crazy. Wasn't it obvious? When I was in the insane asylum, I heard Voices that made me insane. When I got out, I felt better.

Still, I was so far from being the old Lori everyone knew and loved that I was constantly caught up in a storm of self-hatred. I was fat. I was ugly. Everyone hated me. My friends hated me. My parents hated me. They told me they loved me, but I knew they were lying. They hated me because I was a pathetic loser. I knew my brothers were afraid of me. I knew my mother was ashamed of me. I knew my father was disappointed in me. I was no longer the star my parents could show off to their friends. No more guitar. No more straight As. No more entertaining our friends with the Jerry Mahoney ventriloquist dummy. I wasn't sick. I was just a loser. Everyone wanted me to go away. Or die.

It was part of the deal everyone made with me on my discharge that I would continue to see a psychiatrist three times a week. Whoever I chose, they said, would help me work out the problems I was having, and would explain everything to me.

In the final weeks of my hospitalization, I chose the psychiatrist I would be seeing. My dad had always told me to go right to the top, try for the best, seek out the most professional help. So I chose Dr. Lawrence Rockland, the unit chief of 3 North, the unit where I had been hospitalized. While he and I hadn't been really directly involved when I was in the hospital, I used to see him walking through the unit, or coming to meetings. He was always friendly, saying hello when passing by, and taking extra time to touch base with me, and show interest in my condition and progress. I knew he was the boss, so he must be the best.

When I approached him with the idea of being my shrink, he was surprisingly enthusiastic. I didn't know the doc real well but I liked that he seemed to be the epitome of a descendant from the world of Freud, a cigar-smoking professional from the old, traditional days of psychiatry. He was bald, in his fifties, with a great sense of humor. He reminded me of my dad.

I wanted Dr. Rockland to help me but none of our sessions ever seemed to make much sense. What did I have to say to a psychiatrist? I was fat and felt kind of fuzzy, but otherwise I thought I was just like everyone else. The Voices were bothering me, of course, but I thought everyone knew that. I even thought most people heard them too. They were a normal, if troubling, part of existence.

I tried explaining that to him. The Voices had been around for quite a while, I told him. Even though I despised their presence, they had nothing to do with an illness. I was really quite sane.

He listened respectfully to my explanations without saying anything. When I had finished, he would rise from his chair, and go to his dusty textbooks filling up the shelves above his chair. Then, from the fat maroon books, he would begin a lesson in psychiatry, telling me how the brain worked, how thoughts worked, and what so-called normal people did and did not hear in their brains. I felt as if I were on an operating table. He was going to dissect my brain and insert logic into it. And that was just what I did not want him to do. I wanted help. I didn't want him messing with my brain.

So week after week, for a fifty-minute hour three days a week, I put all my energy into combating any help he might have to offer. He tried to get me to talk about my thoughts and feelings. I tried to keep away from just those topics. We shared jokes we had heard over the week, and laughed together as if this was therapy. We spoke about medication and the human body. We discussed the difference between the way tricyclic antidepressents and MAO inhibitor antidepressants worked. We discussed the dystonic reaction and the anticholinergic effect. He must have explained to me a hundred times how certain medications caused certain side effects, like a dry mouth. I always felt these were safe topics. When we talked about medicine, I didn't have to verbalize my feelings, my thoughts, my symptoms, or why the hell I was even seeing this man.

Sometimes we talked about my day-to-day life. Once when I admitted to him that I didn't know much about sex, and that I wasn't even sure exactly how it worked, he was very comforting. Once more he reached for his textbooks—only this time, they were anatomy and physiology textbooks. He sat down next to me on his couch adjacent to my chair, and explained everything to me in a low-key and comforting way. I found this session interesting, and was grateful for his help.

But mostly, I just stonewalled him.

"I don't know what to say, Doc," I would say over and over again.

"Just say whatever comes to your mind," he would encourage me.

"I have nothing on my mind."

"Is your head empty?"

"No, in fact, exactly the opposite."

"What do you mean?"

"You know. The stuff I always have on my mind."

"You mean the voices?"

Silence.

"What do they say?" He tried to coax it out of me.

Silence.

"You know, Lori, if you give me a chance, maybe I can help you. If you don't open up, though, I won't be able to help you."

"Leave me alone, Doc."

"Lori, just talk to me, work with me, and together we can at least try to overcome these horrible symptoms. They're obviously so painful to you."

Silence. A long, long silence. And then I tried, a little bit.

"The Voices are telling me not to trust you, and that you'll make me die."

"Do you believe that?"

What a jerk! "Of course I do, or I wouldn't ha
kind of games are you playing with my brain?"

"I know the voices seem real to you, but the
part of you deep down inside coming out in the for
tions. Do you understand that?"

How could someone like that help me? He was supposed to be a professional, the best. But my Voices knew more than he did. He didn't know anything.

He didn't even know enough to be concerned when there was danger. Once sitting in his office, I became aware that the room was filling up with floating paisley shapes that were out to murder both of us. They were sucking up all the oxygen in the room, and he and I were both going to suffocate. It was terrifying. I felt like a murderer. I had to warn him. But when I told him of the danger we both were in, he didn't seem concerned at all. He just sat there as if nothing was happening.

What could I learn from a guy like that?

So mostly I just sat there. Hour after fifty-minute hour, week after week, I sat there, silent. There he was, sitting in his chair, puffing on his cigar as if he were Freud himself. I sat adjacent to him in a big woolly chair, session after session, smoking cigarette after cigarette in silence. I wouldn't talk, and he wouldn't prompt me. So often we spent the entire session in silence. All I would do was pick the arm of my chair to shreds. It seemed like my project to destroy the chair before sitting in it somehow destroyed me. I stared at the clock ticking away in slow motion. I often fantasized about smashing that clock, or him.

My brothers didn't offer any help. Basically they kept their distance.

They had their own lives to live. Sometimes I would catch sight of Steven in the family room where his friends were drinking Coke and watching TV. He was all wrapped up in his job selling produce at Cherry Lawn Farm, and making his plans to go to college. I didn't resent him going on with his own life. I had been to college. I had had that experience. This time it was his turn.

I did resent Mark though. It was Mark who was living the life I wanted to live. He was graduating from college, going to graduate

...ool, moving to an apartment in the city, living the young, single life-style that was supposed to be mine. I wanted to live Mark's life. I even wanted to be him. It certainly would be better than being myself.

I had nothing to do and nowhere to go. I spent the rest of the summer lounging by the pool at my parents' country club. I was extremely self-conscious. I had gained so much weight since I had gone into the hospital. I felt like everyone was looking at me. I didn't fit in anymore.

It wasn't just in my head. People didn't know how to act around me. I could hear the chatter of my parents' friends as I strolled to the pool.

"Is she hearing voices now?"

"Does she remember who we are?"

"Can she still talk and carry on a conversation?"

"Is she going to change into another personality?"

"I think even though they let her out, she still may be crazy."

"Can you believe she's actually had shock treatment?"

"Poor Nancy and Marvin. What a tragedy . . ."

It almost made me long for the hospital. At least in the hospital I was just another patient, and not a freak.

12

Lori
Scarsdale, New York,
September 1983–May 1984

I was never without music. I'd wake up in the morning to music that had been playing all night. I drove my car flipping stations until I found one that I liked. When I came home, I made a beeline to my bedroom and immediately, like a reflex, turned on the stereo.

Sometimes I'd listen to music just to cover up the sound of the Voices. I'd turn up the music and focus on it instead of on the sounds in my head. Sometimes the Voices tried to shout over the music, and sometimes they succeeded. But often I could drown them out with tunes. Sometimes the music from the stereo was enough. But often, when the Voices were energetic, I'd have to do more. I'd plug a Walkman in my ears, turn the volume up to full strength and blast the suckers.

Music was a great mood bank. It was a kind of drug for me. It enhanced and tempered my moods. Just listening to the introduction of a favorite song was enough to make me feel some kind of exclamation-point emotion. Give me a dose of Al Jarreau and it picked up my spirits. Add a double dose of Neil Young to temper my feistiness. To get revved up, I popped a Pat Benatar cassette. Then I'd need a song to counter the wild state, so I'd play "Bridge over Troubled Water." And then I'd chill out in the early morning with the song "Easy" by the Commodores:

Everybody wants me to be
What they want me to be
I'm not happy
When I try to fake it.

Stevie Wonder's music was upbeat and exciting. I found myself playing "Golden Lady," swirling around and dancing with exhilaration and excitement alone in my room, feeling high as the Milky Way. Elton John, on the other hand, was in a category by himself. He was always the master of emotions, at both passionate ends of the musical spectrum. There were songs with powerful titles like "Funeral for a Friend." There were wild songs like "Saturday Night's Alright for Fighting." Elton John was my lithium. Elton Lithium John. We'll bottle him and keep him in the medicine cabinet, take as needed. Music is the doctor, as they say.

But if music was strong, my moods were stronger. More often than not I found that it wasn't the music that controlled my moods. It was my moods controlling the music. My moods would whirl around me, and seep out into the world, selecting the songs, filtering the tunes and lyrics not to alter my moods, but to harmonize with them and enhance them.

I never thought the songs or singers were speaking directly to me the way back in high school I thought Walter Cronkite was. Nonetheless, my moods sharpened the words and tunes like a knife, so they seemed to cut directly to my brain. The songs talked to my experience, shared my feelings. It was as if through music the world outside became a mirror image of my own inner world. The borders between the music and my mind would fade. As I became engrossed in the words and melodies, I often became captive to the mercy of the music.

One of Pink Floyd's songs seemed to be about my own obsession with time. I kept clock after clock in my room, and was always preoccupied with figuring out exactly what time it was. The song began with the clang of dozens of different alarm clocks, then the repeated sound of a heartbeat, then the din of drums and chimes. It felt just as I would feel when I would compulsively compare the analog dial on my watch with the digital clock and then, trusting neither, call 976-1616 to hear the comforting electronic voice intone the correct time, down to the right second.

I would hear Billy Joel's driving beat. Sometimes as he sang, he asked questions in his lyrics and then answered them himself. It seemed to me a lot like the conversations my Voices would have with each other when they were being relatively tranquil. Sometimes when Billy Joel sang about madness, depression or exhilaration he seemed to share my terrifying inner chaos. When he sang about loneliness, he seemed to understand the isolation I felt.

When the group Steely Dan sang "Any Major Dude," I could hear the song speaking to me, speaking of a woman, maybe me, hovering on the edge of a breakdown, trying to pull the pieces together again. Everyone seemed to live in a world of madness.

Crosby, Stills & Nash knew all about the terror I felt when a private reality consumed and became more real than the outside reality:

> *Now I'm standing on the grave of a soldier*
> *   that died in 1799,*
> *And the day he died it was a birthday,*
> *   and I noticed it was mine.*
> *And my head didn't know just who I was,*
> *   and I was spinning back in time . . .*

How wonderful it was in my depression to pop in a Jackson Browne tape, and roll around in his preoccupation with suicide. My own obsession became his obsession, and his became mine. I could internalize and heighten my feelings with his. I could feel someone else's suicide as if it were mine.

> *Though Adam was a friend of mine,*
> *I did not know him well.*
> *He was alone into his distance,*
> *He was deep into his well.*
> *I could guess what he was laughing at,*
> *But I couldn't really tell.*

Now the story's told that Adam jumped,
But I'm thinking that he fell . . .

Toward the end of that first summer at home, I began to look for a job. I realized I needed something to do. Much as I loved music, I couldn't sit at the other end of my headset forever. I couldn't lie around the pool for the rest of my life. So I began scouring the papers for something I could do. Late in the summer, I saw an advertisement in a local newspaper for a new restaurant opening in Scarsdale. They needed waitresses and bartenders. I decided to apply. My parents were very encouraging. "It's a great way to meet people," my father said.

I was determined to land the job and I did. With all my waitressing experience with Tara and Lori at Mug 'N Muffin in Harvard Square, I thought I'd be perfect in the job.

So much had changed since then. For one thing, this was a much more complicated restaurant than Mug 'N Muffin, which was little more than a two-coffees-one-black-with-Sweet-'n-Low-one-extra-light-with-sugar-and-two-blueberry-muffins little breakfast bar. This restaurant was one of those darkly lit trendy places where working people stopped by for lunch, yuppies dropped in in droves to hang out with their friends after work, and older people—people in their thirties—went out for prime rib in the evening. Sometimes—usually on Friday or Saturday night—it was so crowded that it seemed all I did was say "excuse me" all evening, and the only way I made it through the night was by ignoring about half my customers.

I had also overestimated my abilities. Whatever waitressing skills I had back in college had been lost in the chaos of the intervening years. Here I was a lousy waitress. I couldn't keep up with the work. I found the pace terrifying, and the world of the restaurant chaotic. Everything about the job was strange and difficult, everything seemed to slip out of my grasp. I wasn't fast enough dishing out cole slaw and pickles during setup. I was too fat to fit into my uniform. When the dinner hour began, I could handle couples, and the occasional single who came by for a solitary supper. But when four friends came in for an evening out, I panicked. My thoughts were so scattered that I couldn't remember orders. Who ordered the steak teriyaki, and was it a baked potato or French fries to go along? Not only could I not remember orders, I couldn't even read my own writing when I wrote them down. My hands shook, so I couldn't carry all those plates at one time, which meant I had to make extra trips. When it came time to total up, I was constantly making mistakes. The cash registers were computers, and I never could master them.

To make matters worse, the Voices in my head kept up a steady roar of commentary about everything I did. Between their shrieking, the pace of the work, the thundering din of the crowd talking all at once about the Mets, their Saturday night date, that jerk Rodgers in marketing, the last movie they saw and the next movie they were going to see, the last guy they dated and the next guy they wanted to ask them out, sometimes I would want to scream.

After a while, I switched to working downstairs in the cocktail lounge on Friday and Saturday nights. The pace was just as fast, but the job was a lot easier. There were fewer things to remember. With ice. Straight up. Frozen margarita, with salt, without salt. Nothing to it.

Still, there were a lot of creeps down there, and sometimes it was hard to keep my temper. Sometimes I came close to losing it. Once I actually did when a particularly rowdy group began to tease me and laugh at me and make fun of me. There were both men and women in the group, and they were all getting off on the wisecracks of one particularly obnoxious guy who was the ringleader.

As I tried to ignore the taunts, the Voices were taking over. They were yelling orders at me. They were telling me all kinds of vile and violent things to do to that jerk. I served the customers as quickly as possible, and tried to keep away. I was afraid of what I might do. But the restaurant was crowded, the tables nearby kept ordering, and those people themselves kept calling me over. There was no way I could escape their ridicule.

I took it as long as I could, long enough to get their orders, go away and fill them. But when I came back to pass out the orders, and this guy started in on me again, I decided it was time to strike back. I gave all his friends their drinks, saving his for last.

"Did you say that you wanted that on the rocks, sir?" I asked him demurely. Then I poured the whole thing into his lap.

I couldn't blame that one on the Voices. That was all me, and I loved doing it.

Still, despite the hassles, I stayed on. They apparently needed me. I needed the money. I liked the company. Before too long, there was another big attraction: It was here that I got turned on to coke.

I had dabbled in drugs in high school, smoking pot with some friends, sorting out the seeds from the leaves on the fold of an opened-out record album cover. In college, I had tried cocaine with friends at parties. And when I found myself really strung out I tried Quaaludes. I couldn't drink. Something about alcohol just didn't agree with me. Even when I just tried some beer at a fraternity keg party I'd always throw up. Those little pills or a quick snort on the other hand could make me feel incredibly relaxed when the Voices were making me tense. But drugs had never been a big part of my life until I got out of the hospital.

By the time I left the hospital, though, cocaine seemed to be everywhere. In fact, I rarely had to seek it out. It came looking for me. I found that plenty of people coming to the restaurant were into cocaine. In fact, every so often I found that some regular customers would offer to tip me, not in cash, but in cocaine. At the end of the meal, the happy customers would simply ask me to share some lines with them.

At first I was cautious. It was a pretty public place, after all, just down the road from my parents' home. But gradually, as time went by and no one tried to stop us, I became more and more relaxed. Just as I had begun to recognize the good cash tippers, so too I began to know who did coke and who didn't. There seemed to be so many who did! First it was an occasional line just for fun. Then it became a daily event. Then gradually cocaine became a regular part of my life.

Soon I began to get friendly with the people I knew who did the drug. Often I would see a big-time drug dealer, a man I knew had been in and out of jail for dealing drugs, sitting at the bar. Often he'd call me over from across the bar and invite me to do some lines in the bathroom. I liked it when people shared. It was cheaper and easier than getting cash. When a customer tipped in cash, I just mentally calculated it for my cocaine fund. When one passed me a quarter gram, however, it was much more valuable. I got to do more of the stuff, and I got to do it right away.

All I was trying to do was to feel better. Those medications they gave me in the hospital were useless. I took them because people told me they would make me better. But lots of times I didn't know why I bothered. The only thing those fistfuls of stupid pills did was make me feel fuzzy and disoriented, as if I were at the bottom of a swimming pool. And the Voices still raged away at me, mocking the drugs, the doctors and me.

Cocaine, on the other hand, helped me ignore the Voices. For as long as it lasted, cocaine made me feel alive. It made my senses feel sharp and clear again. When I did a line, I felt good, I felt real, I felt vital in a way I hadn't since long before the Voices entered my life. Cocaine directed my attention outside of myself. As long as I was high, I had enough strength to ignore those Voices calling me back into their world.

So for a while I found the relief I wanted. When the crash came as it always did, I went back for more. When the crashes came closer together, the search for relief began to consume more of my time and my life. Before too long, the search for cocaine— and of ways of getting it—began to be the single-minded focus of my existence.

Eventually, it was cocaine that brought me to Raymond. Then Raymond brought me cocaine. Then Raymond and cocaine became so intertwined with each other that I could barely tell them apart, and I couldn't do without either one of them.

I met Raymond through one of my fellow waitresses who lived in his building. Nicole and I had become friendly, and liked to hang out with each other. Raymond was her friend. At first I would go over to see Nicole. We would talk, listen to music, and I would watch her put on her globs of makeup. And then we would both go down to see Raymond. Raymond always had cocaine. If he didn't, he knew where to get it.

For a long time, we had a friendly threesome. Nicole and Raymond and I would all get high together. But as time went by, I slowly found myself bypassing Nicole and going straight to visit Raymond.

Like drugs and music, Raymond took me away, for a little

while, from all the pain. For before too long, he fell in love with
me. And I guess I fell in love with him. He wasn't exactly the
kind of guy my parents would have picked out for me. But I liked
him. He was cute, a black man with light brown skin the color
of chocolate milk. He was over six feet tall and had a smile that
would melt a brick. He had a great in-shape body, not rippled
and bulging like a bodybuilder, but just nice and toned all over.
Even without the cocaine, he turned me on.

He was an emergency medical service technician. He had a
girlfriend he lived with. Or maybe she was a wife. He wasn't
clear. But that kind of made it more exciting and romantic.

For a while, Raymond gave me something fun to look forward
to. He was a bright spot in my life that was otherwise nothing
other than miserable. My head was full of pain. I was confused
and lonely. There was something wrong with me, and I didn't
know what. I worked so hard at dating, but the guys who were
interested in me were geeks and creeps. The ones I liked never
called back. Most of them thought I was too porky. Raymond
thought I was perfect, cuddly and beautiful. He told me so all the
time. How could I resist?

Mom and Dad were trying hard to help me. But being around
them wasn't fun either. Dad wanted so much for me to be well.
He was always lecturing me, questioning me, pushing me, encouraging me. I wanted so much to be well for his sake that being
with him was a constant effort. I had to hold myself in, watch
myself, control my actions and impulses. It was hard work.

And I was so consumed with self-hatred that it was hard for
me to do anything with my mom. How could I go shopping with
her when looking in the mirror made me sick? How could I go
to the country club with her when I knew I was so fat and ugly. I
couldn't stand to be around my beautiful, trim, outgoing mother.

Raymond never wanted to hear about my illness. Whenever I
started trying to talk about my symptoms, he would cut me off
or change the subject. To Raymond, I was as normal as the next
person, and that was that. So we talked about him. I liked that.
To me, he was someone outside the system, and especially outside
my system. We talked about his work, about his mother, his
house, his little son, Ray Jr., his girlfriend.

But mostly we did cocaine, or talked about it. Where were we going to score? Whose car were we going to take? Who was going to drive? Do you have any? No, do you? Was there any stashed? Who's got money?

Together, we got high on coke every single day and night. When I got off from work, we would go off together in search of a place to get high. We couldn't go to his place; we certainly couldn't go to my parents' house. So our relationship was filled with cocaine and endless hours in cheap motel rooms. We took the four-hour special and spent the time watching the Playboy channel and sniffing coke. I was so desperate for the drug that I let him do anything he wanted with me, just short of having sex. But when the coke was gone, so was I. No coke, no Ray and Lori.

As I became more and more consumed with the drug, just getting enough for the day became a major focus of my life. Raymond was doing some buying and selling, and often shared some of his with me. But that wasn't enough. I was working long hours at the restaurant, and still getting some tips in lines. Nearly all my wages were going to purchase cocaine, too. Some days, when I didn't have enough money for that day's hit, I would even steal small amounts from the restaurant.

Staying high became my entire goal. I did coke everywhere. In an elevator. In Grand Central Station. Walking down the street. I even did coke in Dr. Rockland's waiting room. I was continually high, continually fighting the Voices, continually feeling rotten. I hid cocaine in my pockets, in my socks, in my sneakers, in my room and in my car, for emergencies. The one thing I was afraid of was of being without coke when I needed it.

Cocaine was definitely a form of self-medication. My mind began to obsess over getting as much as I could, more than my body actually craved. I was literally consumed with everything and anything having to do with the drug.

I even began to hear my own cocaine-filled life reflected in the music I listened to. Eric Clapton sang about cocaine. Neil Young sang about Raymond and me:

> *I love you baby,*
> *can I have some more?*

I always needed more. For when the fall came, it was horrendous. It was a tremendous crash. Coming down from an artificial high was like riding down a roller coaster dramatically spiking down, and then derailing off the track. I couldn't sleep because I was so coked up. And without any more to bring me back up, I just got into bed and lay there with my mind racing, trying to fight off the bad thoughts entering my brain, the bad thoughts telling me to kill myself and end all this misery.

Once when I crashed and I was out of cocaine—including everything I had hidden away in all my secret stashes—I panicked. I had to have something. So I decided to snort a lithium capsule. I broke it open and sniffed the white powder inside as if it were coke. It was horrible. My entire face burned. I felt like my nasal passages were on fire. I tried shoving water up my nose, but nothing worked, and it was hours before the pain subsided. I thought the walls of my nose were going to cave in.

Need for the drug began taking me deeper and deeper into a world that I never knew existed before. To get coke, I went with Raymond to places I would have been afraid to go otherwise.

One of our favorite cocaine stops was in the South Bronx, at a store about as big as a table. Upstairs was one of the most disgustingly filthy bathrooms I have ever seen. There was also a little room with a TV and a bed—and lots and lots of coke. It was piled up on a mirror. We would go there. I would wait. Raymond would do his deal. We would do a line, and then leave with enough to keep us satisfied for a while.

It was a frightening, dangerous, awful place. Once when Raymond took me there, there was a rifle in the upstairs room. When he left me there, and went off with the dealer, I became wild. I was so wired that I didn't even go for the pile of the stuff sitting right there in the open on the mirror. Instead, I went for the rifle. I would end this fucking horrible existence right then, I thought. I would blow my brains out, splatter them on the wall. I tried to put the gun to my head. But I couldn't manage it. I couldn't maneuver the rifle to my head with one hand, and reach the trigger with the other hand. Besides, I was shaking so hard I could barely keep the rifle still. I could hear Raymond and the dealer coming back up the stairs. I put the rifle down, and waited for them, trembling all over with fright.

The more drugs I did, the more suspicious people around me got. Dr. Rockland was beginning to question me more. Early in my therapy sessions I had told Dr. Rockland I was doing coke but I made light of it. I never told him how much I was really doing, or how important it had become to me. I told him it was just an occasional thing, a line now and then with friends simply for recreation. I could tell he was beginning to realize that wasn't true. By now, I was sometimes consuming nearly $1,000 a week worth of cocaine.

Gail Kobre—now Gail Kobre Lazarus—was growing concerned. Even with her new husband and her new house, she still tried to keep in touch with me. It wasn't the same as before, but still she would occasionally drop by. I had told her I was doing drugs. I even tried to get her to share a line with me. She indignantly refused. One afternoon she and I were together in the backyard of my parents' house. I was lying on the hammock, and Gail was sitting on the rocks by the roses.

"I'll always be your friend, Lori," she told me. "But I can't stand by and watch you ruining your life like this."

As for my parents, I had tried hard to conceal it from them, but they weren't stupid. They were hoping they weren't seeing what they were seeing, but they were beginning to catch on. Raymond and I called each other as many times a day as we could. I called him at his work. He called me at home at midnight, and teed my parents off. I'd have to lie to my folks, that it was a wrong number, or else that it was my friend Nicole calling. I knew the lies weren't working.

13

Marvin Schiller
Scarsdale, New York,
June 1984–August 1984

At first, Nancy and I were delighted when Lori got herself a job. We didn't have any problem with our daughter working as a waitress. It was honest work, and we knew she would be good at it. She seemed to like it too. After a very short time, it seemed that she was spending most of her time there. Just about every evening she worked a shift, and most weekends too. Many weekends the only way Nancy and I saw Lori was to go over to the restaurant for dinner.

That was all right with us. We would head over about dinnertime and wait for a table in her section. I would order a burger or spare ribs and Nancy would get a salad from the salad bar. To my eyes, Lori was doing pretty well for someone who had just been locked up for almost a year in a psychiatric hospital. I would sit waiting for my food and watch her moving briskly through the crowds. She was lively and efficient, and she knew she was in the service business. I would watch her laughing and chatting with the customers, keeping up a cheerful repartee as she took orders and made change.

Sometime the previous fall she joined a video dating service. That seemed like another good sign. Even though Lori was living at home, Nancy and I thought she ought to be making a bigger effort to make friends with people her own age. She paid $500 for a subscription to the dating service, and I told her I thought it was a good investment.

Very seriously, she explained to me how the service worked.

"There was a lady off camera asking me all kinds of questions about what kinds of guys I like, what kinds of things I like to do, how I feel about different things."

It seemed that she was given the chance to see similar videotapes done of men, and select the ones she felt she'd like to date.

"So if I pick Andrew and Scott, then the service calls them in and tells them someone's interested. They come in, see my video, and decide if they're interested in meeting me too."

Lori was, like me, old-fashioned. She liked the idea that if the attraction was mutual, the woman's phone number was given to the man to call. The attraction must have been mutual a good bit that fall, for men were always showing up at the door. One man showed up with a big bouquet of roses. On another evening she returned home laughing: She had just had dinner with a magician who had performed his tricks over the meal.

All through the winter I loved to hear the phone ring. It meant to me that our Lori was back.

I was so grateful she was back, so grateful she was out of that hospital.

Now that she was out, I felt my job was to encourage her, to shepherd her along, to make sure that she didn't get stuck in the hospital system. I embarked on a program to encourage her. Marshal your forces, Lori, I told her. "You are in charge of the way you present yourself to others." She was a fighter, a winner. She could pull it together and hasten her own recovery.

Although she was up off the bottom, I knew she wasn't altogether well. I had only to look at her to know that. I could see it in her eyes. From the time Lori was a baby, I used to say that Lori had devilish eyes. There was mischief in them, and intelligence and sparkle and fun. These eyes were dead, their stare vacant. Her walk was different too. Her arms hung lifelessly from their sockets. She looked like a zombie, moving as if walking in her sleep.

It wasn't the Lori we knew. But it was better than the Lori we had seen over the last several months. I figured that she was in the early stage of recovery. When she picked Dr. Rockland as her psychiatrist, we all agreed that what she needed was to be eased back into her own life. With work and friends, meaning and purpose, she would merge herself back into the life she had left behind.

Lori herself seemed to feel that way too. In May of the year before, just after Lori left the hospital, Nancy threw a wonderful party for my fiftieth birthday. It was at a restaurant in SoHo in Manhattan, and about two dozen of our family friends were there. Mark and Steven were with us, so it was the first time the whole family had been together in one spot in a very long time. The boys were getting punchy, acting silly, calling for a toast and then passing chunks of browned bread around the table. Everyone was in a good mood.

Lori, with a new, short and bouncy haircut, looked lovely that evening. And then, when the real toasts began, she did something that brought tears to my eyes. She stood up before our guests and thanked me for all the help I had given her while she was in the hospital.

"I'm sorry for all the trouble I caused you then, Daddy," she said. "Thank you for helping pull me through a rough time."

When you make a jump from a 1 to a 3 it's not like the 10 you had, but it's still progress.

I tried to keep our relations simple and on an even keel. On Sunday afternoons, we walked on the golf course together. On Saturday afternoons, we did errands. We drove up to Central Avenue in Yonkers to pick things up for the house or the car or the garden. Sometimes we stopped at Caldor's and I would buy her a Diet Coke and a soft hot pretzel, which she seemed to like, and I loved. We tried to make some fun out of simple things. We had a little competition to see who could find the cheapest 93 octane gas in Westchester County. I found a station in New Rochelle; she found one in Eastchester. We'd compare notes and then go out of our way to fill up at the winning station. We probably spent dollars saving pennies, but I didn't care. It seemed to amuse her, and gave us something to talk about.

Nancy was always troubled by my psychologizing. "Why don't you leave that to the doctors?" she kept saying. "Don't get in-

volved in her therapy." But when Lori returned home I felt I
owed it to her to give her my best. I had good training. I would
use it to try to help her.

I tried to talk to her about her voices, what they were saying,
who they were, what they meant to her. I encouraged her to write
down her dreams, and for a while she kept a paper and pencil by
her bed. She was having such a difficult time communicating,
talking to us—or to anyone—about how she felt, that I encouraged her to write down as much as possible. If she felt free to
bring those feelings to me, then I would try to interpret them for
her. Over and over I would say to her that it was important to
remember how she was now, so we could all look back and
appreciate how far she had come.

One thing I insisted she talk to me about was suicide. She had
already tried to kill herself twice, and many times in the hospital
it was obvious that she would have tried again if she had been
able. I tried to talk with her about how final death was. That if
she attempted suicide she might actually succeed. That even if she
weren't completely serious about the attempt, there was always
the possibility that she'd make a fatal error.

"It's not like so many other things, Lori, where if it goes wrong
you can try again and do it over," I told her. "If you make a
mistake, you don't get another chance."

As the weeks went by, I kept asking her: "Are you planning
on killing yourself, Lori? You have to tell us if you are." I would
try to drag it out of her. More often than not she would become
belligerent.

"Stop hounding me," she would snap. "You're just trying to
provoke me. You don't understand."

But strangely enough over time our relationship began to grow
closer. She had always been my little girl. But these days it was
clearer to me than ever before just how much she needed me. She
needed my support and my reassurance and my encouragement,
and she was actively seeking them out.

She would walk up to me and say, out of the blue:

"You're mad at me."

"No I'm not, Lori."

"Well, you're looking at me like you're mad at me."

Over and over I had to reassure her.

"You hate me," she would say.

"Lori, I don't hate you. I love you." Finally it began to dawn on me. When she challenged me like that, she wasn't making a statement. She was asking a question. And she needed to hear the answer. She needed to hear that I still accepted her. She needed to hear that I still cared for her. Over and over again she needed to hear me tell her that I loved her.

During this period, my life was difficult on all fronts. My clique of partners had won the power struggle and had become the new management of my company. That meant much more responsibility and power. It also meant more work and travel. I was now responsible for fifteen offices all over the country, and I had to visit them often. It also meant more worries. Now that I was in charge, helping the company thrive was my responsibility, and I took it very seriously.

Nancy and I continued to support each other emotionally, but our lives these days were far from the carefree frolic that I had expected when our three little ones had left the nest. Life for me these days largely boiled down to work, Lori and sleep.

Earlier in the spring, I had told my firm about Lori's problems. I had been forced by necessity to confront the issue with them much sooner than I had been ready to. Because Lori had already graduated from college, she was considered an independent adult, and no longer covered on my medical insurance. Her coverage had lapsed by only a few months when she was hospitalized. She had no insurance of her own, and her bills were mounting by the tens of thousands of dollars. The costs were more than I could comfortably handle on my own. So in March I wrote a memo to my firm, asking them to help me out.

The memo went to the board. I was a member of the board. That should have made things easier for me, but—emotionally at least—it made things harder.

I had spent years cultivating my hard-nosed, cost-conscious, demanding image. I was the guy who operated by the book, played by the rules, and didn't believe in special deals. I built my career on that philosophy. I helped build our firm on it. And here I was, Marvin Schiller, the macho manager, coming to my colleagues with hat in hand, saying, "Please guys, can you help me out?"

They asked me to leave the room while they deliberated. I stood outside the large room where our board meetings were usually held around the half dozen rectangular tables pushed together to make one huge square. I was usually inside making decisions. Now I was outside, waiting for a decision to be made about me.

After the better part of an hour they called me back in the room. They had dictated into the minutes of the meeting a series of stern little warnings, including one to other employees to plan more carefully for the health insurance needs of their children who no longer qualify for coverage. The firm can't be responsible for the coverage of dependents who no longer qualify, they said. But then, after a reminder that this was a one-time-only exception, they agreed to extend my coverage for long enough to cover half of Lori's bills.

Still, I continued to keep disclosure to a minimum. About a year earlier, just as Lori had left the hospital, my new secretary, Anne Schiff, had joined our firm. She must have quickly guessed the situation, for she always put Lori's calls through to me right away. But I never mentioned Lori's past, and Anne didn't ask. During the ordinary chitchat that precedes business, I would talk about my one son heading for college, and my other son heading for graduate school . . . and then I would talk about my daughter who "worked" in a hospital. I figured it was a play on words. After all, she was working hard at getting well and was in a hospital. I didn't see any point in being more explicit than that. It would just make people uncomfortable in situations where we were aiming at being relaxed.

With our friends, though, we dropped the charade. Once she had transferred from Payne Whitney to New York Hospital's branch in Westchester, we knew that this was no short-term thing that could be brushed into the background. With doctors at Payne Whitney telling us to give up hope, I realized that this was not something that she was going to shake in a few weeks, that this was a very serious, and probably a long-term illness. I never believed she wouldn't get better, but I was beginning to realize that the hills we had to climb on the way back were steeper and higher than we had hoped for.

So Nancy and I talked it over and agreed that we would be open with our closest friends. We tried to be as matter-of-fact as possible in breaking the news to them.

"Do you remember that we told you that Lori was working in Boston?" we said to our friends. "Well, she wasn't. She was actually in New York Hospital. She's attempted suicide a number of times, and she's really very ill." We explained as best as we could what we understood was wrong with her, and we tried to explain that we had concealed it for Lori's sake, hoping to shield her from stigma.

People were polite and seemed concerned.

"When did this happen?" they would ask. "What is happening with her now?" "I didn't realize." Their expressions were sympathetic, but we could see they were shocked. Some seemed confused about what to think about her illness, about how to react to us, or to her.

We were surprised too. People didn't behave the way we had expected them to. Some of our closest friends had the hardest time dealing with the news. One couple in particular had been very close to us and to our children. But they seemed to be particularly uncomfortable. They never asked about Lori and never visited her in the hospital. In fact, very few people asked about her, and fewer still actually visited her. They didn't know what to do.

As time went on, I began to wish that our friends could understand better, or be more empathetic with our situation. But in a way, how could I blame them? We had such a hard time understanding and accepting the situation ourselves. How could we expect more from them? And after all, what did they know about mental illness? A few bizarre stories about serial killers or cannibals, or young men who went up in towers and shot at passersby. Deep down, our friends were probably afraid of Lori, afraid of what she might do. In the end, Nancy and I realized that this was our struggle, not theirs, and that we couldn't look to anyone else to ease the pain or make things better.

As Lori settled into her job, we began to let ourselves believe that things were getting better. But then, in the spring of 1984,

Nancy and I started detecting a strange pattern to Lori's life. Phone calls came at odd hours, and seemed to be from odd people. Sometimes when Lori answered the phone, she spoke in hushed tones. Sometimes, Nancy said, Lori would leave the house suddenly after one of the calls.

Nancy began noticing that a lot of the calls were coming from one man. I had met this guy before when he occasionally came to call for her at the house. His name was Raymond and he was black. That in itself didn't bother me. What bothered me was that his background seemed odd. Something about him made me uncomfortable too, a furtiveness and unease he seemed to exhibit around us.

"Marvin, I think that guy is selling drugs to Lori," Nancy said one day.

Parents were always being admonished in those days to be alert for signs of drug abuse. Be on the lookout for unusual behavior, the public service announcements said. Watch for unexpected mood swings, running nose, tremors, bloodshot eyes. We watched, but what could we tell? We couldn't separate out her illness from anything else that might be affecting her. Lori's moods were so unstable that she had initially been diagnosed as manic-depressive. She slept so little that her eyes were often bloodshot. And she was taking so much prescription medicine that there was hardly a time when her hands didn't tremble.

At first if there were any signs we took them as positive. She had been so fat coming out of the hospital, and she had begun to lose some weight. Her moods seemed to get brighter.

For a long time my concerns about Raymond were of a different sort. I thought she was having a sexual relationship with him. That bothered me. I thought she could do better than that. I told her so.

"Are you having a relationship with this guy?"

"No, Daddy. He's just a friend. I need friends. You know you are always on my case to meet people. Well I met someone."

The other boyfriends came and went. Lori let her membership in the dating service lapse. But still the phone calls continued. Nancy was getting more uneasy. She told me how worried she was, so the next weekend I confronted Lori again. I was in the family room watching TV when she came in. I turned to face her.

"Lori, why is this guy Raymond calling you all the time?"

She shifted around uneasily. "Dad, I told you. He's a friend."

"Lori, do you think I'm stupid?" I kept my voice low, but she could tell I was serious. "There's something more going on, and I know it. Your mother is worried. I'm worried. Is that guy selling you drugs?"

"No, Daddy," she said. Her denial was vehement, but I felt she was lying. "He doesn't have anything to do with drugs. He's just a friend I met from the restaurant. We just hang out together."

"I don't want you meeting that kind of people. I don't want him around here, and I don't want him around you. I think he's a drug dealer."

"No, Daddy. He's just a friend. He's got nothing to do with drugs."

There was a long pause. I looked her straight in the eye. "He'd better not," I said.

But soon it became apparent that she was indeed lying. Even to us it became clear that something was affecting her, something more than her illness. Her mood swings were becoming much more pronounced, and much more rapid. ("Maybe she isn't taking her medicine," I thought.) The tremor in her hands had increased so that she had trouble performing ordinary tasks like pouring herself a soda. ("Maybe she is taking too much medicine.") And she was increasingly agitated. ("Is she taking enough medicine?") In fact, it seemed like she hardly slept. ("Does she need sleeping pills?") I was away during the day, so perhaps she slept then when I didn't notice. But at night, I could hear her coming in at one or two o'clock in the morning, and then pacing about until dawn.

Finally, Nancy and I decided it was time for a showdown. Lori was involved in something dangerous, and we couldn't stand by any longer. This time I was going to find out what was really going on. Once again I confronted her.

When she finally confessed, I blew up.

She wasn't going to do one thing more until she got herself off the drug, I told her. If she couldn't do it herself, then she was going to have to get help. So with a recommendation from Dr.

Rockland, Nancy and I arranged to have Lori visit a drug treatment program in Stamford, Connecticut. Three times a week, she drove up there for counseling, group therapy and surprise urine tests.

I knew she could do it, and she did. By August, she was clean.

14

Lori
Scarsdale, New York,
September 1984–March 1985

By early fall, I was ready to try again with another job, this time one in the mental health field. I knew a lot about it, obviously. Maybe I could help somebody. Dr. Rockland and I talked about it, and he gave me a list of the hospitals in the area. I prepared a résumé—which didn't include my stays at Payne Whitney and New York Hospital—and sent it off.

I didn't actually believe it would work, but it did. I had a number of interviews, and several job offers. I chose to work at Rye Psychiatric Hospital Center because it reminded me least of New York Hospital.

Where New York Hospital was big, with over three hundred beds, Rye Psychiatric was small, a thirty-bed hospital. The road in was short, but it was lined with greenery. It had well-kept lawns and a soothing atmosphere about it. There was a main building and a small side building called "The Cottage" that really did remind me a bit of a country cottage.

But the most important thing was that, unlike New York Hospital, Rye Psychiatric Hospital was not a closed-door facility. As long as they stayed on the hospital grounds, patients were free to come and go as they liked. There were no bars or safety screens on the windows. There were no passkeys or security people in jeeps riding the grounds.

Suddenly, from being a psychiatric patient, I was in charge of
other psychiatric patients. After a brief orientation, I began han-
dling the same kinds of jobs that all the other mental health workers did. I helped patients in an assertiveness training group. During
recreation, there was arts and crafts, where I helped the patients
make wallets and moccasins. During art therapy time, they drew
pictures and I helped analyze them.

When I worked on the evening shift, which went from 3:00
P.M. to 11:30 P.M. the workload was lighter and I could be sponta-
neous. I went out in the garden with the patients or played horse-
shoes or croquet or took people out for walks.

The day shift was the busy one though. That's when all the
patients had to be woken up, helped with getting washed and
dressed, and assisted through breakfast and lunch. Daytime was
when we got most of the admissions too. During my orientation,
I had been trained to take admissions reports, and do all the other
required paperwork.

I wound up doing a lot of paperwork because, unlike the other
staffers, I enjoyed it. I liked to write, and I liked to interview the
incoming patients and their families. I asked them questions about
their problems and complaints and wrote them down in great
detail. And I helped with the record keeping about the daily events
of the hospital. I also learned how to do EKGs, which were
required for all admissions, hooking people up to the electrodes
and taking the totally painless reading of their brain waves.

I never mentioned my past to anyone, and at first no one asked.
But a few weeks after I began working at Rye Psychiatric, Eddie
Mae Barnes called me into her office. She was director of nursing,
and a stout, no-nonsense person. She had noticed a tremor in my
hands, she said, and wondered if I had "seen anyone about it."

"Yes," I said, holding my breath.

"Do you take any medication?" she asked.

"Yes."

"Have you ever been under a doctor's care for it?"

"Yes."

"Are you under a doctor's care now?"

"Yes." By now I was really shaking.

"A psychiatrist?"

"Yes."

"And have you ever been in a psychiatric hospital yourself?"

"Yes," I said. And waited.

But miraculously, she didn't fire me. She didn't even cut back on my duties. After that, I did notice that she was watching me more closely. But aside from that, nothing else happened. I was amazed, and grateful. It wasn't common in those days to use former mental patients as mental health workers. She was being creative—and taking a chance.

Within a very short time, I began working marathon shifts at Rye Psych. I was usually scheduled for day shifts, beginning at 7:00 in the morning and ending at 3:30. But often when another worker didn't show up or was sick, I found myself taking the next shift too, which ended at 11:30 P.M. Or sometimes I would do the evening shift, and then stay overnight to cover until morning. Sometimes I would do the morning shift, go home at 3:00 in the afternoon, catch some sleep and come back at 11:00 at night. Sometimes I'd be home asleep when Eddie Mae called at 5:00 A.M. to ask if I could be there by 7:00. I almost always accepted.

Once, during a raging blizzard, I worked all three shifts in a row, staying there, and awake, for twenty-four hours straight. It was snowing too hard for anyone else to report to work, or for me to get home.

I liked doing all the overtime. Partly, I liked the money. Very soon, I was making more from my extra shifts than I was from my regular salary. But partly, I discovered I was good at the work. I was a hard worker, a good writer, and conscientious. When the state came to recertify the hospital once, the examiners pulled reports I had written to explain to the others that this was how a report should be written.

I was trying so hard to be normal.

My mom and I went on errands together. We bought groceries, stopped at the pharmacy, the dry cleaners. We went to buy flowers for the house. Doing errands was safe. We didn't have to talk. When my Voices yelled at me to jump out of the car, I could focus on the radio and keep myself under control. Down to the Golden Horseshoe shopping center we went. My mother gave me assign-

ments, I carried them out. But when I went into the pharmacy to
fill a prescription, the owner and his assistant, who had been there
for years, didn't recognize me.

All right. All right. I know. I'm a big fat tub of lard. I couldn't
stand my weight. I hated the way I looked in the mirror. I especially hated buying bras and bathing suits. I'd ask people what I
looked like, but nobody dared tell me for fear of hurting my
feelings. All they'd say was that I was a "little overweight."
"Don't worry. You'll lose it," they said. "It's probably from the
medicine." And then the worst of all: "You have such a pretty
face." I knew what that meant. It meant I was blubber. Only Dr.
Rockland and my parents dared to tell me the truth.

Dr. Rockland encouraged me to exercise. That would be a way
to lose the pounds, he said. He also said it was a proven medical
fact that vigorous exercise was a good antidepressant.

So I tried to do what he said. I walked four miles on the golf
course with my parents on Sunday. I found that too boring. I
walked with my mother to Gail's mother's house, two miles each
way. That was too hard. I tried long bicycle rides. Sometimes I'd
ride my bike the seven miles from my parents' house to New
York Hospital. The hill up Gedney Way was a killer, but I stood
up from the seat and pumped up. I made the five-mile trip from
home to the village of Mamaroneck. Once when I was making
that run Dr. Rockland, who lived nearby, happened to be driving
by, and he beeped with pleasure at catching me in the act of
actually listening to his coaching. I felt I should be wearing a
bumper sticker: Honk if your mental patient is exerting herself.

Dad said go off, be with young people, make friends, enjoy
life. So I went on a group vacation, a Club Med–like thing, to
Jamaica. I liked swimming at Negril Beach. I liked parasailing,
because it reminded me of skydiving. I liked pigging out on the
all-day buffets. We played bingo and cards, watched crab races
and went snorkeling. But most people were there to drink and
sleep around. Because of the medication I was taking, I would get
sick when I drank alcohol, so I felt queasy all day. And I had no
intention of getting involved with any of those big-time losers on
this trip.

I even tried to go to nursing school. I thought that would be cool. It would prove I was okay. Along with a B.A., I'd have an R.N. after my name. I couldn't be sick if I was a nurse.

I needed to take preliminary courses, so I signed up at Westchester Community College to take nutrition and chemistry. We analyzed the nutritional content of food. The teacher brought in the milk carton, and we studied the information on the side. I wanted to impress the teacher with my knowledge so I sat in the front row munching Snickers bars: The TV commercials said that Snickers were nutritious and gave people energy. When we saw a movie about the famous nutritionist Jean Mayer, I got all excited. I went up after class and told the teacher I knew Dr. Mayer personally. I didn't. He had been the president of Tufts while I was there, but I had never met him.

In chemistry class, I found myself leaving the room two or three times in each ninety-minute lecture out of sheer antsiness. Sometimes when there was a break, I just left and went home. I missed tests and pop quizzes but it didn't matter. On the first day of class I had seen the periodic table of the elements. My eyes had zoomed in on the "Li"—lithium. I knew all about this element in a very intimate way. I even ingested it. From then on, what I did in class never really mattered. The very fact that I knew what lithium was made me feel superior to everyone else.

I couldn't concentrate. I couldn't sit still. Too many things were distorted in my brain. I wanted to be a nurse, but I didn't want to study. After a while, I just stopped going to class.

Even so, I was trying so hard that I almost never did anything inappropriate at Rye Psychiatric. Once, though, I passed my hand, palm side out, before the eyes of a catatonic patient, trying gently to bring him out of his inner world. Eddie Mae saw me and called me into her office.

"Don't ever do that again," she scolded. "He could come to and be frightened, and get out of control."

Sometimes patients sensed my wildly fluctuating moods. One patient went to Eddie Mae, confused and flustered.

"What did I do wrong?" she asked. "Lori seems so depressed I think she must be mad at me."

Again Eddie Mae called me in. Had I done anything off-limits, like confiding my personal history of mental illness to this patient? I told her I hadn't. And I lied about my moods.

"It's nothing," I said. "I'm just tired."

But mostly I did fine. So well, in fact, that after I had been working there for about a year, I decided to apply for a job at New York Hospital. That would be the ultimate, I decided, the real proof that I was okay. After all, if I were a mental health worker in the same hospital where I had once been a patient, I must be all better, right?

Meanwhile, Rye Psychiatric, which had been sending patients out for electroshock treatments, had just begun doing them themselves, and I volunteered to assist. It was something new to learn, of course. I had another motivation too. I knew, because people had told me, that I had had twenty electroshock treatments at Payne Whitney. But I couldn't remember any of it. And of course I blamed the electroshock for my loss of memory. I wanted to see the treatment used on other patients to see what had happened to me.

I found it very upsetting.

First we had to make sure the patient ate and drank nothing after midnight. Then, around the time of the scheduled treatment, I would help connect the electrodes to their temples, and watch while the doctor gave anesthesia. The patient lay, covered, on a bed. Then the doctor would administer the current by flipping a switch. The whole thing reminded me of the scene in *The Wizard of Oz* where Dorothy and her three friends find the little man behind the curtain flipping switches to make thunder and lightning go off.

My job was to help hold the patient down. For when the jolt of electricity went off, the patient would have a seizure, and arch up from the bed. Then, as the seizure subsided, their toes would curl. That was a sign that everything had gone well.

I couldn't stand watching it happen. I couldn't stand thinking this had happened to me, not once, but many times. It made me feel so helpless and out of control.

So pretty quickly I moved to the recovery room, where I found the job less scary. As the patients revived from the anesthesia, their faces were flushed and they were disoriented. It was my job to reorient them.

"You are in Rye Psychiatric Hospital," I told them softly. "You've just had ECT. You're fine. Today is Tuesday." I would keep talking to them in a low voice as they gradually came to. Then, because they had already gone so long without eating, I would feed them snacks, first juice, then half a sandwich. As they gradually began to feel better, I would help them with their shoes and escort them back to the main building.

I enjoyed helping the patients, but I hated mentally putting myself in their shoes. Every time I thought about it, I got upset.

Still, in many ways, my own experience had made me empathetic with patients in a way that many other people weren't able to be. I knew I wasn't a trained therapist. But I was a good listener, and I gave good feedback.

I found myself growing close to some special patients. Carla was a sixteen-year-old Puerto Rican girl, very sweet and likable. She seemed like the kind of girl who should have been excited about just starting out on her life. But instead, she seemed kind of lost, as if she didn't know where her place in the world was. For some reason she clung to me, following me around, seeking me out, wanting to talk to me whenever she was able. And I in turn got swooped up by her. She seemed so innocent, so sad. I could see myself in her in some ways.

When she talked about trying to kill herself—she had tried many times—I could understand how she felt. She needed help, and I could offer the same kind of support that had been offered to me over the years.

"It would be a tragedy if you killed yourself," I told her. People had said that to me all the time, and so those were the exact words I used with her.

"There are people who love and care for you," I told her. "Your mother, and your brother, and your sister—how would they feel if you killed yourself?"

"They'd be happy," she said. I remembered feeling exactly that way in the past.

"No, they wouldn't," I told her firmly. "They would never get over it."

And on and on I talked to her, telling her about hope, and the future, and living. I told her how valuable she was, about the good times she had ahead. I was using all the words that had been

used with me, all the messages that people had tried to ram into
my own depressed brain.

It seemed to comfort her. At any rate, she didn't kill herself,
and after a while she was discharged. She must have believed some
of the things I had told her. The problem was, I didn't quite
believe them myself.

15

Lori
Scarsdale, New York,
April 1985–October 1985

Suicide was on my mind again.

One of my favorite movies was Frank Capra's *It's a Wonderful Life*. I watched it all the time. My parents were so happy to see me engrossed in such an upbeat, wholesome movie that they bought me my own copy. I guess most people find it makes them feel good to watch Jimmy Stewart playing George Bailey, who is rescued from despair by a sweet guardian angel. That's not the way I felt. The part I fixated on was the scene in which Jimmy Stewart/George Bailey decides he'd be worth more dead than alive. That's just what I felt. I had put a tremendous burden on everyone. I would be better off dead.

My head swarmed with suicidal fantasies.

The Voices in my head were using megaphones. They called me waste, rubbish, junk, bile. "You're nothing but a piece of shit," they screamed at me. I told Dr. Rockland what they were saying. To try to tease me out of believing in them, he made up an acronym for their message: I was LOWPOS, he said: A Lazy, Obese, Worthless Piece of Shit. I think he meant to make fun of the Voices, but it seemed he was making fun of me, and I felt worse and worse.

I felt hopeless. I was never going to get better. All I was doing was spending time that was really wasted since I was ultimately

going to get done what had to be done. Put your finger in a bucket
of water and pull it out. The hole left is how much I'd be missed.

Killing myself was my job, my responsibility. I mentally punished myself each day for not having done it yet. The notion that
suicide is against the law always preyed on my mind. What were
the authorities going to do? Put my corpse behind bars? Handcuff
my wrists with no pulse? Me-Murder, I called it. Would they take
my lifeless body, peel it off the pavement and make it stand trial
for that Me-Murder? Hah! Let's see them try to stop me.

Several times I tried to get a pistol to blow my brains out. But
for someone who had been as sheltered from violence as I had
been, it wasn't easy. You can't just go to Bloomingdale's and
charge a revolver to your account.

I didn't want to just take an overdose or slit my wrists. I wanted
something powerful that would reflect the despair that haunted
me every day of my life. As the pressure of these thoughts built,
my imagination went wild seeking ways of accomplishing my
aims. I thought about jumping in front of a car, or better yet, a
truck; or even better yet, a train. I thought about jumping out of
a moving car onto the highway. I thought about standing on a
bridge, pouring a can of gasoline over my head, lighting a match,
and jumping in flames to my death. Splat. Rocks in a bathing suit,
then into the ocean? How about jumping into a vicious animal's
cage in the Bronx Zoo?

I tried desperately to dodge these fantasies. Planning on jumping
off the top of the Galleria Mall? Then keep away from it. Don't
even drive by it. Thinking about dumping all my capsules into a
McDonald's shake? Never go to McDonald's again. Not even for
French fries.

As frightening as the scenarios were, however, they gave me a
chance at eternal peace. The Voices would alternately chant, "To
die! To die! To die!" and then, "Peace! Peace! They are waiting
to give you peace!" There was only one route to peace. The
pressure was building. Finally, it became unbearable. I had to act.

It was the middle of the night when the bubbling kettle of my
suicidal fantasies finally boiled over. I was in my bedroom, and
the Voices were chattering away like Fourth of July firecrackers.
They were condemning me to die, making me feel like shit. They

were suffocating me and there was no way out. My urge
them for good was so impulsive and powerful that I d
time to act out any elaborate fantasy. I used what I had at hand

I had a huge mirror on my bedroom wall, and it watched me
as I prepared to murder myself. I made my own precise death-
calculation. I had a bottle of Mellaril, a major tranquilizer I took
every day for my psychotic symptoms. I knew what the highest
safe dose was. I decided to take three times that amount, plus a
little bit more. If I took more, it might make me sick enough to
throw up. If I took less, it might not be lethal. So one by one I
swallowed most, but not all, of the bottle of pills. I was going to
die deliberately, as an expert.

Then, about thirty-five minutes into the overdose, I decided on
some insurance. I went into the kitchen, and selected a knife. The
paring knives were too small. The butcher knives were too big. I
chose a medium-sized serrated one. As I gently drew the blade
across first one wrist and then the other, I marveled that not only
did it not hurt, it actually tickled. It felt good! I watched the red
stains spreading across my arms.

I went back to my bedroom to watch my blood—and my life—
seep out. I felt exhilarated. I did it! I finally did it! I felt like a hero
on my way to finish a crusade.

A second later, I panicked. I was going to die. Really going to
die. The thought terrified me. I bolted to my parents' bedroom.

It was a little after 4:00 A.M. when, blood dripping from my
wrists, I shook my dad awake. He knew immediately what I had
done. He sprang out of bed. He jumped into his clothes and,
dragging me spraying drops of blood behind us, pulled me into
the car.

All the way to New Rochelle Hospital he screamed at me.

"Make yourself throw up, Lori. Make yourself throw up. Stick
your finger down your throat."

I couldn't do it. So it wasn't until we got to the hospital when
they helped me throw up, then pumped my stomach and band-
aged my wrists, that I was out of danger. For all the rest of the
night, my dad waited by my side for the crisis team to arrive.

Because of the amount of tranquilizer that had made it into my
system, I slept most of the time. While I was awake I begged my

out of the hospital. He put the responsibility in
134 I felt I wasn't going to harm myself again, I could
home.

mised. I was only looking for relief, I told him. Relief
what? From those chattering, nattering, vicious, unforgiving
ices. And somehow with that suicide attempt they had been
satisfied. The wild frenzy that reached its crescendo a few hours
earlier had peaked and was now receding. I felt tired. I was distressed at upsetting my dad. But, as the Voices had promised, I
did feel peace.

For the next several months, I felt better. It was as if in trying
to kill myself, I had made an acceptable offering to the Voices.
The volcano of their rage had erupted, and then subsided. I was
more tranquil, more in control. So by spring, I decided to try to
take another vacation.

I booked a trip with the Tufts alumni association. There would
be people my own age there, from my school, my parents reasoned. I would meet people, make friends and have a good time.
I picked a trip to Morocco. It was music that governed my choice.
The Crosby, Stills & Nash song about riding on the Marrakesh
Express had always fascinated me. Morocco seemed like an exciting, adventuresome place. I wanted to go someplace exotic where
no one I knew had been.

But the trip was a disaster from the start. There were no Tufts
alumni in the group, and no single young people. Everyone was
old, or in pairs, or had young children. I felt alone and frightened
the moment I stepped on the plane.

I hated Morocco. The people in the streets seemed so pitifully
poor that I ended up giving away my meals to the little bug-eyed
kids who looked so hungry. Mopeds were the vehicle of choice,
and their buzzing about confused me.

But the worst thing was the sun. It was incredibly hot, beating
down on the white buildings. It was so hot and so fiery that even
in normal circumstances it was uncomfortable and dangerous for
people who weren't used to it to walk about. For me, it was even
worse. After the suicide attempt with Mellaril, Dr. Rockland had
switched me back to Thorazine. I was taking huge doses of it, and
one side effect was to make me hypersensitive to the sun. I had a

tough time dealing with ordinary daylight. The fierce Moroccan desert sun was murder.

I used lotion on my skin, and wore long-sleeved shirts. But I couldn't do anything about the part in my hair. I lathered the part up with sun-tanning lotion. I couldn't find a hat anywhere, so I put a towel over my head. Even that didn't work. The sun fried my scalp through everything. I came home from my first day walking and sightseeing in tears from the scalp burn.

So I decided to stop the Thorazine.

I arrived in Morocco on Sunday. By Wednesday, I was actively psychotic. People were wailing around me. My room was filled with candles, burning all day and all night, on the bed, on the floor, on the walls. When I showered, I heard my father's voice screaming at me out of the shower head. He was using words I didn't understand, speaking in a language I couldn't comprehend. Then his voice became many voices and I couldn't understand them either. I tried to figure it out. I was in a foreign country. Maybe the voices were speaking in some other language. I doubted it though. I was going crazy. That was it. My Voices were being taken over by other voices. It was petrifying. I longed for the relief that street drugs could bring me. I tried to get some the first opportunity I could.

And opportunity presented itself almost immediately. As Raymond had before, Mohammed brought that opportunity to me. That afternoon in Morocco, I met Mohammed when I was looking for a leather jacket. I had heard leather was a good buy in Morocco, but everything I had seen was too expensive. I met Mohammed in front of my hotel. He said he was a guide. His fee seemed reasonable. He showed me his driver's license to show me he was legitimate. We took a trip just outside the main part of the city to a leather store he knew. They showed me a red leather jacket that I loved. I haggled a bit. They served me mint tea. And I left with a jacket that I thought was a good deal.

After that we shopped for some little things, did some sightseeing and he returned me to my hotel. He seemed respectable. So when, on parting, he asked me if I wanted to go out that evening to ride on his moped and smoke some real Moroccan hashish, I readily agreed.

That night, he showed up in a cab, not a moped. We drove

around and before long I found myself lost. We were in a strange residential neighborhood. The buildings didn't look real. There were no lights on in any of them, nor was there any sign of life anywhere. Mohammed explained that he had to go home for a moment first, and courteously invited me up. I began to feel tense. I decided to stay in the car. He flung some instructions at the driver in a language I didn't understand, and then left.

Then I began to get scared. I tried to talk to the driver, to ask him to take me back to the hotel, but he spoke no English. I sat there telling myself that everything was going to be okay, when finally Mohammed returned. More instructions to the driver, and off we went. We hadn't driven far, when he said something else to the driver and the cab pulled over.

"We'll walk back to your hotel from here," he said. The cab rattled off.

Everything was completely dark. We were by a huge field surrounded by big trees. Mohammed pulled me by the arm under some of the trees. He wrestled me to the ground, and pulled out a knife.

"If you make any noise, I'll kill you."

I felt sick, and psychotic. I hadn't taken my medicine in many days. The Voices were screaming that I was going to die, and not by my own hand this time. I tried to struggle some, but I was too afraid of his knife.

He made me take off all my clothes and lie on the ground. Then he climbed on top of me. I was crying and trying to explain to him that I was a virgin, and afraid. But he either didn't understand, or didn't care. He tried to penetrate me anywhere he could.

Miraculously, he couldn't do it, no matter how hard he tried. Finally he got up from on top of me and helped me get dressed to walk back to the hotel. As we crossed the field, he kept telling me to say that I loved him and hold his hand. I was repulsed and frightened and angry. He wanted to kiss me, but I felt like throwing up.

As soon as I spotted the hotel, I began to run. "See you tomorrow!" he shouted at me as I bolted.

Back in my hotel room, I took off every single item of clothing and threw them in the trash. Over and over I bathed myself, taking shower after shower and bath after bath in the hopes of cleansing myself. I felt gross and dirty and filthy.

I was in one piece physically, but scattered into a zillion pieces psychologically. My head reeled with the punishments my Voices and my wild imagination wanted to inflict on Mohammed. I would pin him to a tree and castrate him. Or force him to cross a field full of land mines.

Terrified, I decided I needed to talk to Dr. Rockland. I sneaked down to the reception desk. The people could barely speak English. It took what seemed like hours to place the international call. Then I heard the phone ring. One ring. Two rings. Three rings. Four . . . and then his answering machine picked up. I was so nervous all I did was say my name, and that I was in trouble.

I returned to my room to hide. I was still hearing crazy Voices, and I was afraid Mohammed would return. My flight home wasn't scheduled till Saturday. I spent the next three days in my room in tears, afraid to leave. When the phone rang, I wouldn't answer it. When someone banged on the door, I wouldn't open it.

That was the beginning of the end for me.

I went back on the Thorazine while I was still in Morocco, but I stopped being diligent about taking it. I hated taking it. It literally made me sick. It made me feel dopey and heavy and on the verge of being comatose. And the Thorazine had so many side effects that I wound up taking more and more medicine to counter them, and all the drugs whirled around and around in my brain like a hurricane.

After I got home, I began to feel reckless. In addition to the Thorazine, Dr. Rockland had prescribed Nardil, an antidepressant. It was a kind that belonged to a family called MAO inhibitors—Dr. Rockland explained it to me in one of our endless safe conversations about medicine—that required a special diet. No cheese, no chocolate, no caffeine, or else the blood pressure gets out of control. I began showing up at Dr. Rockland's office after a big meal of double-cheese pizza, Diet Coke and M&Ms, which I would proudly disclose to him.

I began to feel bolder. I careened up the winding Old Mamaroneck Road at top speed. Sometimes I drove off the road, but who cared? Life was awful. Life on the edge was no worse. I hated being sick, hated being myself, hated every hour of every day. What difference did it make?

When Dr. Rockland suggested the hospital again I was furious. I told him I would definitely kill myself before I went back in that place. He told me he thought I already was trying to kill myself.

It would just be for a short time, he promised me. Just for a week or so, just to "adjust my medication." I would feel better, he said. He tried to be soothing. Mom and Dad chimed in. Just a short stay, they all said. Nothing like the last one. You aren't sick like you were the last time. You just need a little help.

So finally I agreed. I signed myself back in to New York Hospital. Within a week of my admission, Mom and Dad brought me a letter—from New York Hospital. They were offering me the job I had applied for before as a mental health worker. Sure I'll take it, I thought. Why not? After all, I'm already here. And I laughed and laughed and laughed.

Part IV

The Quiet Room

16

Lori
New York Hospital, White Plains, New York, November 1985–February 1986

So here I was back again and everything seemed so familiar.

The first unit had been an intermediate-stay unit; this one was for acute care. Both units had a long and a short hallway that joined to make a kind of a T-shape with a glassed-in nursing station at the junction of the T. Each unit had its own dining room. Each had a music listening area with smoking allowed in the back. Each had a day room with a television set and a card table for games and puzzles.

Both men and women were housed on the same unit in separate rooms. Each person had his or her own bed, dresser, an armoire for storing clothing, and a bed table with a reading light. I jumped the waiting list and was given a single room of my own. No roommate could put up with me because my status was always close to the lowest possible one on the unit.

Status! Ha! I knew for sure that I wasn't a rookie anymore. When I was first hospitalized, I thought status meant married or single, or how much money you made. Now I knew all the lingo. Status meant the level of privileges you had earned by your behavior. The highest level—O.U.—was Open Unit, which meant you could come and go as you pleased after checking in. At the other end of the spectrum—the one I knew a lot about—

was C.O., or Constant Observation. That meant some jailer always had to be within arm's length.

I knew lots of other new words too. Nice, romantic-sounding words like "elopement." Here it meant to run away. "Danger! Elopement Risk!" read the signs on the doors to the unit, warning everyone to be careful to lock up behind themselves.

Yes, I was a savvy veteran, all right. But it wasn't a good feeling. I saw patients around me I recognized from my last stay. I didn't want to be like them, living a lifetime of bouncing in and out of the hospital.

I had boldly convinced everyone around me that Lori Schiller was never going back into the hospital. That it was a one-shot deal for me. I believed that myself. So the second time around wasn't going to be any fun. All those admitting people would be sorry. I would make them sorry.

This time I wouldn't listen to these doctors and nurses who had gotten me into this fix. This time I would listen to the Voices. They would be my allies. They would protect me and keep me safe. They would guide my behavior and help me to understand my mission.

From the first, my days in the hospital were long and dreary and painfully empty.

For much of the time, I was considered too much of a danger to myself and to others to be allowed to wander freely. So every day I watched as my fellow patients left for music group. Or to go to the library. Or on a group walk to the formal gardens on the grounds. Or on a pass to White Plains to shop or go to the movies.

Fall turned to winter. The days outside grew shorter. I watched the leaves fall from the trees, saw people go from sweaters and caps to full-blown winter clothing, all without breathing a mouthful of outside air or looking straight up at the blue sky.

Every day I awoke early. Sometimes I was first in line for breakfast. Sometimes I burrowed deep under my covers contemplating my long day ahead. Either way, I wished the day away. After breakfast, we all lined up to receive the little cups that held the pills that were supposed to make us better. Next was a community meeting at 8:30 A.M., where everyone—doctors, social workers, nurses, mental health workers and patients—talked about such mundane things as how much money the unit had earned at a bake sale last week, when a certain nurse was going to be leaving the hospital, or the announcement of a weekend trip to Nyack for a street fair.

After the community meeting my long, disturbed days really began. I had no attention span for TV. No one particularly wanted to talk to me, and I certainly didn't want to talk to them. So I paced. I'd begin by walking up the short hall, then down the long hall. Around and then back. Up and down, up and down. Everyone else was leaving the unit for activities. My activity was pacing.

When I got tired, I headed for the day room and my cigarettes. After puffing for an hour, I'd get bored again and resume my walking. I'd walk to the bulletin board and study the notices for five minutes as if they were the most fascinating things on earth. Then I'd walk away, pace some more, and return to the bulletin board for another five minutes as if I were mesmerized by the notices. Then back to the day room for more cigarettes.

Just as I put my tenth butt out, it was time for noon medications, followed by lunch. I swallowed my pills, snarfed down my foot-long hot dog and was back in the day room smoking my after-meal cigarette all in twelve minutes flat.

The afternoons dragged on as if they would never end. Three afternoons a week, I met with my psychiatrist. Because of a hospital rule that doctors couldn't see private patients in the hospital, I couldn't see Dr. Rockland anymore. I didn't like the doctor I was assigned instead. He didn't understand me. I didn't care if I understood him or not. So our sessions were a dreary waste of time.

At 5:00 P.M there were more medications, and my day brightened a bit. For after the late-afternoon medications was dinner, and then by 6:00 I could go to the window, and begin anticipating my parents' arrival.

When they came, which they did nearly every day, they brought me packs and packs of bubble gum. They brought me chocolate. They brought me sweatshirts and sweatpants in a variety of colors. They brought me little windup toys that I had a passion for. And they brought me themselves, and love and reassurance.

Just after visiting hours, the staff put out snacks. It always seemed a particularly touching gesture. So many of us were aching from our visitors—or absence of them. It seemed like a way of consoling us. "Your visitors have left and gone home," the snack table seemed to say. "One day, you too will go home." The snacks served their purpose for a lot of us. It changed the focus from intense to casual. I started in on the cherry Italian ice, moved on to a bowl of Cap'n Crunch, and then packages of Sugar Wafers and Oreos.

At 9:00 P.M., it was time for the last medication of the day. After that, most patients fell almost immediately asleep. Not me. I stayed up until 11:00 so I could pig out on "midnight" snacks. What a pathetic existence, I thought to myself.

The next day was exactly like the one before, including all the same feelings, Voices and overpowering fears. The only difference was that at lunch they served spinach quiche.

The only thing that punctuated the bleakness of my hospital day was my rage. I became really furious after Christmas in 1985 when I was transferred to an intermediate-care unit, where the sicker patients were housed.

I had been conned. Dr. Rockland had tricked me into going back into the hospital to have my medication adjusted. It all sounded so simple. Take away one pill, add another, home again just like that. But one week had become two weeks, two weeks had become two months, and now they were settling me down for an even longer stay. I was a captive.

I fantasized about beating the crap out of Dr. Rockland. He lied to me. Psychiatrists weren't supposed to do that. My Voices became extra-vindictive, fueling the fire of my already sizzling rage.

To make matters worse the staff of the new unit was unsympathetic.

Some of the nurses and mental health workers, of course, truly seemed to care for me. At night, Jean, a nurse, and J.J., Gladys and Danny, who were mental health workers, always seemed to be like a team on my side. J.J. was an enormous black man, truly huge. He was kind to me even when I ripped his favorite sweater right down the middle in one of my struggles.

He and the others were always sympathetic. One night I escaped and was found shoeless in a snowdrift. When they found me, the four uttered not one word of reproach. Jean made sure I was warm. Danny tried to figure out why I had bolted. J.J. was reassuring: "You know you won't be in the hospital forever," he said. And Gladys slipped me a Scooter Pie that she had swiped from the kitchen.

But most of the others seemed cold, indifferent and hateful. Everyone, it seemed, had simply decided I was a problem that had to be solved. So everyone was extra tough with me. One of the nurses sitting supervision at my door almost seemed to hate me.

"Stop feeling sorry for yourself," she barked in my door when I was sitting on my bed one day crying. "You're acting like a chronic mental patient."

Another woman, a social worker, seemed to delight in lording it over me. I tried explaining to her how badly I wanted out of the hospital.

"Well, if you're hearing voices, you belong in a hospital," she said coldly, in a snippy, social worker voice.

For his part, my psychiatrist had decided that I could control my behavior but had chosen not to.

"You're not cooperating with your treatment," he said.

I fought them every way I could. Underneath, far from where even I could become aware of it, the Voices and I were collaborating on a secret mission: to act up so badly that I would be kicked out of the hospital. For just as the last time, I firmly believed I was not sick, and did not belong in a hospital.

The problem was, as I let the Voices gain power over me, I lost all power of my own. I started out not wanting to control myself, and ended up not being able to.

Impulse became action.

At first, I was simply provocative and rude.

At community meetings, I would spray the room with my hostile comments.

"Who's going to miss that big cow anyway?" I'd say when a nurse's departure was announced. "Big deal. A load of stupid cookies and brownies for $37.50. Who cares?" I'd respond to the bake sale announcements.

After a while, my behavior escalated to violence. I threw a backgammon set that other patients were playing with across the room. I banged on the walls and windows. I overturned furniture. I was constantly trying to escape.

Once I ran away to Dr. Rockland's office. It was early evening but the sky was already dark and there were no stars. Someone going in or out of the unit was careless; the door was open a fraction of a second too long, and off I went, down the stairs, down the halls, and then outside the hospital. The ground was cold under my feet. I had no shoes on. The staff had taken away my shoes as a precaution against just this kind of escape. Luckily, I didn't have far to run outdoors. Dr. Rockland's office was just in the old 2 North Annex.

When I arrived, I thought I was in luck. For there, still working, was Dr. Rockland's secretary, Elaine. She was a friend of mine and I was glad to see her. My whole body was trembling. She gave me a cigarette.

I thought we would keep on sitting and talking until Dr. Rockland arrived. After all, it was what we had done so many times in the past. When Dr. Rockland was late for sessions, many was the afternoon I sat chatting with Elaine while she offered me coffee and candies to make up for his tardiness. I could trust Elaine, I thought.

How wrong I was. She was just like the rest of them. She called the unit. Almost immediately, they came from the unit to carry me back like an animal. Why did Elaine turn me in? I was only trying to get help. If I could only get to Dr. Rockland, he would tell them I was fine and didn't need to be in the hospital anymore. He had put me in here, and he could get me out. I felt like Elaine was a traitor. My Voices were harsher.

"Witch! Bitch! Sorceress!" they shouted at Elaine as the burly staffers lugged me up the stairs and back to the unit.

My Voices egged me on, but they never seemed satisfied. I was never good enough for the rude chanting demons in my head. The only thing that really seemed to placate them was when I hurt myself. At their orders I twisted the cord of my lamp against my neck to try to strangle myself. I unscrewed a light bulb during the night hours when no one could see and hid it in my room, trying to break it and cut myself with it. I tried to stab myself with the point of a tiny charm that my father had brought me from one of his trips to Hong Kong.

Finally the Voices commanded me to stop taking my medicine. It was poison they told me. So dutifully I lined up for my daily dose, popped the pills in my mouth in front of the nurse, and then walked away. Around the corner, I spit them into my hand. "Cheeking," it was called. My idea was to save enough pills to do myself in later.

Without my medicine the Voices went wild. After five days I was nearly out of control with madness. The staff found my stash, realized what I had been doing, and immediately switched me to liquid medication.

Liquid Thorazine, the medicine they used against my Voices, burned deep grooves in my tongue. I hated it and so did the Voices. But the Voices knew what to do. The very next occasion, I dutifully poured the cups of medication into my mouth—and then spit the whole mess into the nurse's face.

The Voices howled with laughter. And I wound up in the Quiet Room again.

The Quiet Room.

I first made the acquaintance of this place back when I was in the hospital the last time. The other patients made grim jokes about it. They called it "Hotel California"—the hotel you could never check out from.

The thought frightened me. Where was this place? What did someone have to do to get there? Then one day I saw someone, one of the staff, sitting on a bar stool looking through the window of a closed door. He didn't seem to be having a particularly exciting time, or to be even particularly interested in what he was looking at. The next time I walked the hall, there was no bar stool, no person, and the door was ajar. I peeked my head in. All I saw was a room, empty except for a green vinyl mattress on the floor. The window to the outdoors was covered with a heavy, industrial-quality mesh. Between this mesh and the window was a fan. In the corner of the ceiling there was a mirror tilted so that the person on the outside looking through the window had a complete view of the inside of the room. So this was the Quiet Room.

The Quiet Room was supposed to be a safe and tranquil place, a place where patients could be alone, free to relax and calm themselves down during or after a crisis, or hopefully before one occurred. Some people liked it. It made them feel safe from whatever was tormenting them. Some people walked in there voluntarily, and stayed until they felt in enough control to come out.

Me, I was usually carried there. I hated it. It was almost a routine. I'd hear the Voices, would feel the need to do something, would immediately carry out some destructive act, and be sentenced to the Quiet Room. One or two staff members escorted me there, down the long hall past the other patients, who looked on at my humiliation. I was agitated and jumpy, on the verge of losing control. I struggled with the staffers, trying to keep from having to go back in.

At the door, a two-step routine: A dose of sodium amytal, a big-time tranquilizer, to calm my agitation. Then staffers took everything away from me—jewelry, shoes, anything in my pockets. Thus stripped, no matter how desperate I was to hurt myself, there was very little I could do about it.

Once inside there was nothing to do at all. When I was really agitated, I paced. Eight paces forward. Eight paces back. Sometimes when I was calmer, I lay on the mattress and thought. Sometimes I lay on the mattress and slept.

The worst part of the Quiet Room was how lonely it was. Two patients were not allowed in the Quiet Room at the same time, and staffers usually only entered to bring medication or to check vital signs. If the Quiet Room was successful in stripping me, for the time being, of my Voices, then the silence itself became overpowering. If not, then there I was, all alone with my tormentors.

The idea was to lower my stimulation, to calm me down when I became too hyper. I'd stay there for a while and when I was finally deescalated and back in control, I'd be allowed to return to my room.

But I thought of the Quiet Room as the Punishment Room. And so did my Voices. They taunted me, and teased me, and threw my confinement in my face. No sooner had I quieted down enough to leave, they would begin to torture me again. I wanted to put an end to their torment, so I lashed out again. And back I'd go to the Quiet Room again.

It was as if I was stuck and unable to break myself from the chain of commands of the Voices. Within several hours, the pattern repeated. Sometimes even on my way from the Quiet Room back to my own room I would fall apart and have to turn right around and go back. Over and over the cycle repeated.

I began getting more and more sodium amytal, sometimes several doses a day. Soon, the oral doses were no longer working fast enough and I had to receive the drug by injection.

My Quiet Room visits stretched longer and longer. After a while I lost track of time. I could see through the screened window if it was night or day outside, but sometimes even those distinctions blurred. The Quiet Room had to be kept lit even at night, so the staffer on the stool could see inside. I could count the meals brought to me on plastic trays, but usually I was too agitated to keep track. It seemed as if I were captive in there for weeks at a time, left alone to face the Voices that were rising up to consume me like water in a sponge.

It seemed so strange that my fellow patients could enjoy the Voices they heard in their own heads. On my unit one young man had Voices who told him he was the Messiah. Another young woman always sat by herself, laughing happily. Once I asked her what she was laughing about.

"Hubert is telling me jokes," she said. She called him her playmate, and often talked about how much she liked him.

I was jealous. There was nothing about my Voices that was friendly. I had tried to make them my allies against the hateful staff. But in reality the Voices terrified me. Sometimes I told the staff they were gone, but I was lying. The Voices were with me when I awoke. They were with me when I got dressed. They were with me when I ate. They were with me when I sat around the day room, trying to think of something to do. I could not even find relief in sleep. The Voices yelled so loud they woke me up, leaving me shaking and frightened.

The closest I ever got to a friendly Voice was that of the Narrator. He described my actions instant by instant, not leaving out even the tiniest, most insignificant thing. A hundred times a day, he commented on my movements.

"She is now walking through the door," the Narrator said. "She's wiping her feet, little ass. Wiping her feet on the rug in the entryway. She's going into the kitchen. Ha! Ha! You fat piece of lard, of lard. Go to hell. Ha! Ha! You look sad. You look like shit. You are shit. She's now walking into the day room. She's going to turn down the TV set. To die, asshole. Ha! Ha! Ha! . . ."

The Narrator taunted me, made fun of me, sometimes even threatened me a little. But mostly he just talked about what I was doing. And his manner was less intrusive, his Voice level less loud, and his overall demeanor less scary than the others. I didn't fear him as much as I feared the others. I just wanted his annoying banter to go away.

Sometimes I heard one Voice laughing, a single witchlike Voice that screeched and cackled in derision. Sometimes that Voice would be joined by a second, and then a third. Sometimes they chanted the same thing over and over again, like Voices rehearsing for a play.

"To die!" they chanted. "To die!" I must have heard that a thousand times a day.

Sometimes more and more Voices chimed in, until all the Voices joined into a horrendous crowd, an appalling cheering section that had suddenly turned into a riot. These crowds of Voices were loud, painfully loud. When I heard them coming, I would run for my Walkman. But often it was no use. They would scream and shout over even a rock tape turned up to 10.

But even more than the Narrator and the crowds, the Voices I feared the most were the men who talked to me of hell.

I don't remember thinking much about hell when I was growing up. Jews don't really have a hell, and in any case, my family wasn't religious. My brothers were bar mitzvahed, and I was confirmed. But other than that, my family was what was jokingly known as "twice-a year Jews." That meant we appeared in temple only on Rosh Hashanah, the Jewish New Year, and on Yom Kippur, the Day of Atonement. No one ever taught me to fear punishment or eternal damnation.

No one before the Voices that is. The Voices taught me about a hell that was beyond all religious beliefs. It was worse than the worst horror movie I had ever seen, worse than my worst nightmare. It was beyond all imagining, beyond all human hope.

And it was completely and totally real. The Voices told me so. And the Voices told me they would take me there.

As I sat in the Quiet Room, the Voice that spoke to me was as clear and real as any other voice around me. In fact, he was more real, because he was both inside me and outside me. He spoke directly to me, in low, gravely tones, hoarse and husky, a true demon from hell.

"Come to me," he crooned. "Come to hell with me."

I didn't want to listen. I didn't want to hear. But I had no choice. Where could I go? How could I escape? He seemed to know that. He began to sneer.

"Come to hell, cunt. You whore. You bitch. You asshole. To hell! To hell!"

Beyond him I could feel the hell of his imagining yawning up to swallow me. There were red and orange devils and smoke and fire everywhere. There were only two kinds of people in his hell, the tortured and the torturers. Everywhere, almost as if on an assembly line, men were having their balls cut off and hung onto wooden poles. Women were being raped by piles of disgusting men at a time. The sounds of that inferno filled my ears, filled my head, began to consume my whole body. There were shrieking, shrilling, squealing sounds of victims in pain, and the hysterical laughter from their tormentors. This was to be my fate. This was my destiny. The infinite pit of hell was reaching out to claim me.

And then it got worse.

This Voice was joined by another, and the two began to argue. They shouted angrily at each other, struggling over my fate. I was at the mercy of these Voices. Whatever they commanded would happen. I was totally helpless before their wrath. Their quarreling surrounded me:

VOICE NO.1: She must go to hell.
VOICE NO.2: She will be punished.
VOICE NO.1: She must be punished.
VOICE NO.2: She will be punished, that fucking whore.
VOICE NO.1: She must be punished in hell.

VOICE No.2: Ha! Ha! Ha! To hell! To hell! To hell, that bitch.
No!

VOICE No.1: Don't cry, little bitch. Hell will come.

VOICE No.2: Hell will not come.

VOICE No.1: Hell will come.

VOICE No.2: There's worse than hell. There's hell's hell, and
she will take us there.

VOICE No.1: She must DIE and we will take that pussy to
hell with us. That trash!

VOICE No.2: Why so soon? Needs to suffer more. Needs to
swallow our presence.

VOICE No.1: Needs to die! Ha! Ha! Ha!

VOICE No.2: To hell!

VOICE No.1: To hell now! Come to me. Come, you fucking
bitch.

VOICE No.2: Ha! Ha! Ha! You whore. You will be punished
and you will go to hell . . .

I tried to escape. Tried to flee. Tried to punch them, wrestle
with them, strangle them. Too late I tried to leave their world,
tried to return to the other world, the world of patients, the world
of the hospital, and nurses and dinner. I shouted for the Voices to
leave me.

"Stop it! Stop it!" I screamed at them. "Shut up! Shut up!"

"Ha! Ha! Ha!" they taunted me. "Take the pussy to hell!" one
said.

"Not now. No, later. No, later. No, later," said the other.

"To hell! To hell! To hell!"

I screamed and writhed and fought with them. I covered my
hands with my ears to block out their taunting. It didn't help.

"Come to me . . . come to me . . ." shouted No. 1.

"To hell! To hell!" screamed the other.

"No! No! No!" I screamed. I tried to run. Nowhere to run. Tried
to hide. Nowhere to go. Nowhere safe. They're everywhere. A
chair. A window. Must break away. Must break. Must punch. And
I punched, and I kicked, and I flailed. The shrieking, the tormented,
the buzzer sounding, running feet. Cries and shouts. They're coming! They're coming! I can't stop them! I can't stop them!

I must break something. I must hurt something. I must hurt someone. I must hurt myself.

Stop! Stop! Stop!

Far from calming me down, the very emptiness of the Quiet Room became the screen on which this terrible fantasy projected itself. The Voices spoke to me through cracks and vents in the walls. The overhead light transmitted messages to me. I couldn't breathe. My skull was coming undone and the Voices became megaphoned until I was sure they would deafen me. I panicked. I had to make them stop. I had superhuman energy, superhuman strength. I literally punched a hole in the wall. I pounded my hands across the safety screen on the windows, opening my knuckles and fingers till the bones showed, and blood ran down my arms.

I was beyond even the Quiet Room.

From far away I could hear the buzzer's blast echoing all through the other units, as the alarm pressed at our nursing station set off lights and alarms all over the hospital. Our staff had called for reinforcements. The big men were coming running. I could hear their footfalls pounding the stairs and halls. I could hear the thumping and grunting as equipment was being dragged into place. I could hear ice cubes rattling in a cooler.

It was going to happen again. I was going to be cold-wet-packed.

Cold-wet-packing was a form of restraint that was only used to calm the most violent and out-of-control patients. Most people quieted down under the influence of other methods. If the Quiet Room wasn't enough to keep patients from hurting themselves, patients were sometimes given tranquilizing shots, and then temporarily put in two-point restraints with their wrists tied. There was also four-point restraints, where wrists and ankles were bound to the bed. Sometimes patients were strapped into Geri—for geriatric—chairs, which were little wheeled contraptions usually used for propping up old people. I broke three Geri chairs by struggling. From experience, the staff knew that only cold-wet-packing would do for me now.

The idea behind cold wet packs was to chill the patient thoroughly. As the body struggled to warm itself, it would use energy.

And as the person tired from the effort to get warm, he or she would calm down, ultimately relax, and, it was hoped, fall asleep.

In order for a patient to be cold-wet-packed, a doctor's order had to be signed. As the buzzer was sounding, the staff was paging an M.D. to come to the unit to write the order as quickly as possible. I was so violent that the packing was usually well underway by the time the panting psychiatrist arrived.

When the big men got there, they restrained me while I was being packed. The shot of sodium amytal hadn't taken effect yet. The big burly attendants looked to me just like the horrid rapists of my Voices' hell. My terror flared. My adrenaline shot up. My strength and power intensified. I could fight off a whole Quiet Room–ful of men. They weren't going to touch me. That I knew for sure. I kicked. I flailed. I bit. Even against a roomful of big men, for a moment it seemed I was winning.

And then they were back in control. It was just as the Voices had shown me. It was just like the rapes in hell. Big strong men held me down while unseen hands stripped off my clothing. Off came my high-tops. Off came my favorite blue sweatshirt with the green frog on it. Off came my only pair of jeans that fit. Off came my socks one after the other. How was I going to cause any problems by keeping my little socks on my little feet? And then finally off came my bra. My undies were all that stood between me and the rape that my imagination had fabricated. I was truly terrified.

And then came the real horror. They hoisted me onto the elevated bed that had been set up for me in the kitchen, or in a special room off the short hallway, or in the hall itself, or wherever they could get set up fast before I totaled the place or hurt someone or myself. With strong hands holding me flat, others began wrapping me securely in sheets that had been soaking in ice water.

They wrapped me tight as a mummy, arms and hands at my side. All that was left uncovered were my feet and my neck and head. And there they left me, with a single attendant by my now helpless side.

I was laughing hysterically. But there was nothing funny about it. It was cold, freezing cold. My teeth began chattering frantically as if they were the Voices speaking. I was going to die a shivery

Arctic death and the Voices were going to have the last cold icy laugh. My whole body was frozen.

Cold-pack protocol mandated a full two hours as this freezing mummy. The attending person sitting by my side regularly checked my vital signs on my feet or on my neck. I tried to refuse to let anyone take my temperature. It was my final effort.

As the sodium amytal began to take effect, and the shivering to wear me out, I did begin to calm down enough to complain. I had been bound with my elbow digging tightly into my side. Too bad. No one was going to unbind me before my two hours were up. I found myself thirsty. All I could have was sips of water or juice from a straw the attendant would hold to my lips. What if I had to go to the bathroom? That's tough. If I needed to go badly enough, I just had to go right where I was, and feel the warmth spreading out underneath me against the icy cold sheets.

When two hours were up, a decision had to be made. Was I calm enough to be unpacked? If not, an order had to be signed for an additional two hours. If I was deemed calm, then female staffers had to be called. The men were there for their strength during emergencies, but it was women who had to be there when I was un-cocooned. It was one thing I was glad of. After the two hours were up, I had usually recovered enough of myself to be self-conscious about what had transpired, and modest about my nakedness.

So two female staffers would have the honors of demummifying me. I'd be freezing, wet and cramped, and feeling embarrassed, degraded and demeaned by the whole process.

But the most amazing thing was how truly calm I felt. Never again, I'd say.

17

Steven Schiller
Baltimore, Maryland,
January 1986–March 1986

Visiting Lori in the hospital this time around had been so much easier than it had been the first time. It wasn't that she was better. If anything, she was much sicker than before. It's just that I had changed so much.

When she was hospitalized the first time, I was not quite seventeen, an awkward, lonely teenager just growing out of my baby fat. Three and a half years later some people had a hard time recognizing me: I had spurted up so that at twenty I was six foot three and lanky. The first time she was hospitalized I was in high school. This latest time I was in college.

When I set out for college in September of 1983, Lori had already been out of the hospital for six months. She and Dad drove me down to Baltimore. Dad and I sat in the front. She sat in the back, quiet and pensive, smoking heavily.

We hadn't exactly been hanging out while she was living at home. But as I was leaving for college she gave me a piece of advice.

"Enjoy yourself at college," she said. "It's the best time you'll ever have. It gets a lot worse after that."

It made me sad to think how true that must be for her.

When we got to Baltimore, I bounded out of the car, and leaped off to my dorm room without even much of a goodbye to my father or Lori. I wasn't really worried about what people would think of her. I was more focused on my new life and what people would think of me.

I spent my freshman year trying to adjust, trying to make friends. It was tough. Johns Hopkins is a very serious school, very scientifically oriented. And here I was, a political economics major, thinking I would prepare myself for a law career. I began thinking I'd made a terrible mistake. I've come to the wrong school. I'm not going to be a doctor or an engineer like everyone else here. This is all wrong.

But at the beginning of my sophomore year, everything changed. I was given a psychology professor as my adviser, and that gave me an idea: I would major in psychology. I would become a psychologist like my dad. I would learn enough to discover a cure for Lori.

I threw myself into the psychology classes. I took organizational and industrial psychology. I took cognitive psychology, and dutifully copied into my notebooks all the maps of the brain and neural pathways. Even though I never did very well in any of the classes—and really badly in the more statistically oriented ones—I loved the work. It appealed to my sense of order. My dad always used to say that everything had a reason, that nothing ever just happened. In my psychology classes I began learning just how much we know and don't know about why things happen in people's brains. I began to learn why people do what they do. I became involved in research, studying and investigating conditions like Alzheimer's and Huntington's disease with professors and fellow students.

In addition to studying, I also became involved in people's lives. I was trained as one of a group of peer counselors, who were taught to help identify people who were having crises. We learned to ask open-ended questions, and to find out if people were suicidal.

I never mentioned Lori to anyone, not even to the professor with whom I was working. Still, people began to associate me with psychology, and psychological issues. Friends started to think of me as someone who could help people with their problems. When a friend's girlfriend started seeming depressed, I was asked to talk to her. I made sure that she didn't have an active suicide plan, by asking her about her plans for the future.

With everything I learned, I thought, I was just one step closer to finding a cure for my sister. And in the meantime, I hoped, I would find out more about myself. For the thought that someday I too might be in Lori's place had never quite gone away.

The winter after I came back from my junior year abroad, I visited Lori several times.

Overall, she seemed far more agitated than when I had left. She had big scabs on her hands from where she had cut herself banging on the window screens. She showed me a big hole she had pounded out of the wall. She talked about losing it, and how many guys it had taken to hold her down. At times, she seemed almost in awe of the impressive numbers. Sometimes we sat on the bed and she would suddenly drift off, seeming to retreat into a world of her own. At those times, I now realized, she was hallucinating, and I waited uncomfortably for those moments to pass.

Sometimes she was very drawn, dragging herself around like a zombie. But on other days, she would seem much better. Sometimes we played pool, or listened to music or just talked. On those days, she often focused on her status.

"I have to get my status up," she said. It was clear that in the hospital everything that related to your quality of life came from your status.

We seemed much closer than ever before. I had spent my junior semester abroad at the same place she had been six years earlier, so we had that in common. While I was in England, I had taken up smoking, because I thought it was European and cool. I brought her Silk Cut cigarettes that I had bought in London. She liked them, and going to the smoking room gave us something to do together, and something to talk about.

She told me her troubles. Sometimes she pleaded with me to get her out of here.

"I can't do that, Lori," I said. "You know I can't do that." I tried to get her to focus instead on what I could do to make her life easier. Could I come visit her more often? Call her from school? Bring her anything from the outside?

My psychology studies gave us something else to talk about. I tried to talk to her about the different symptoms she had, the medications she was using, and the side effects she was experiencing. I looked up every drug she was taking, and talked with her about what they did and how. By observing her shaking hands and the involuntary movements she was making with her tongue, I diagnosed that she had some tardive dyskinesia, one of the side effects of the antipsychotic medication she was taking. I wrote a paper on lithium and, as part of my research, talked with her about what effects it was having on her.

I was convinced we were going to find a cure for her. But then one visit something happened that changed my mind about becoming a psychologist at all.

Lori and I were sitting and talking when, all of a sudden, I heard loud voices down the hall. One of the patients was having an argument with one of the orderlies. The patient was an older dark-haired woman, maybe in her late fifties, very drawn, wearing a man's dress shirt that hung almost to her knees. She was wearing socks, but not shoes. I knew what that meant. Lori had told me that her own shoes used to be removed as a precaution against running away.

The woman patient was screaming and shouting profanities. The orderly was speaking calmly and firmly. He was telling her that if she didn't control herself, she was going to have to be put in the Quiet Room. I looked at Lori. She was turning white.

Then, down the hall, the patient lost control. She lunged at the orderly, flailing and hitting. Other workers saw it, and rushed to his aid. Someone hit the emergency button, and it was pandemonium. The other patients were getting agitated, standing up and pacing jerkily around, or wringing their hands. I could tell by her face that Lori herself was getting more and more upset. I was upset myself. There was running and screaming, and bells ringing all over the place.

Everything seemed in turmoil. Lori began pushing at me.

"Go! Go! Go!" she yelled frantically. "Get out of here! Get out!" And suddenly hands were behind me, I don't know whose, pushing and tugging me toward the door. Then just as suddenly I was no longer on the unit, but outside it, standing on the landing in a stairwell, facing a locked door. From outside, I could still hear the emergency alarm ringing, and the sounds of running and shouting, but now it sounded far away.

I was shaking. Lori had told me about this kind of thing before, but I hadn't realized what she had meant until I had seen it myself. Sometimes that kind of thing happened to her too, I realized. All the old fears resurfaced. That commotion I had just seen could have been my sister.

It could have been me.

I didn't stop shaking until I got home. And somewhere along the way I realized that if this was the reality, I still couldn't face it. If someone was going to find a cure for Lori, it wasn't going to be me.

18

Lori
Futura House, White Plains, New York, April 1986–October 1986

The more wild and out of control I became, the more the doctors and nurses and social workers reached for their trump card: the state hospital.

Time and again my doctor sat me down. "We can't keep you here forever, you know," the psychiatrist warned. "You don't want to have to go to a state hospital, do you?"

I was terrified of state hospitals. I had never seen one, but I had heard all about them. They were grim and depressing. They were where people went forever. Every time they threatened me, I made an effort to control myself. But sooner or later the pressure built, the anger of the Voices rose, and off I would go again.

For another two months the cycle continued. Crises. Quiet Room. Threats. Calm. Then another explosion, more time in the Quiet Room, more wet-packing, more talks with the psychiatrist, more threats of the state hospital.

Finally, their patience wore thin when, just after one state hospital threat, I punched out a window during a fire drill. That was it, they said. They could do no more for me. I was going to be discharged immediately.

For months and months, all through my hospital stay, I had been agitating for this. Now, suddenly, with their ultimatum, I panicked. Leave the hospital? What was I going to do? How was

I going to exist? Suddenly I realized that, while I hated being in the hospital, at least I was safe there from hurting other people or hurting myself.

Give me a little more time, I begged them. Just a little more time to get used to going outside, to make some plans, to find somewhere to go. I was resentful, fearful, almost panicked at the thought of being pushed out of the hospital. But somewhere, deep inside me there was born the tiny, flickering germ of some insight. Perhaps I was sick after all. Perhaps I did need some help.

I tried to clean up my act as quickly and as completely as possible. I tried to obey all the rules, to attend every community meeting, to take my medication without protest. And I tried to endure silently the fear that accompanied the raging Voices. It was my will against theirs: I held firm and refused to heed their commands, refused to become lost in their screaming, refused the relief of screaming myself.

Slowly, I began earning off-unit privileges. I walked one day, alone, to the dental clinic to have my wisdom teeth extracted. Back again, without incident. I began attending therapeutic activities with the other patients, and participating in a cooking group. I started going for walks with other patients and a mental health worker and then on my own. Then came passes off the grounds. I went with another patient into White Plains to see a movie. The very next day I went shopping. Then a weekend home with my parents.

Meanwhile, we were all discussing where I should go. All along I had refused halfway houses, or day hospital programs. Now, however, I went along with their ideas. My dim new self-awareness told me that I couldn't survive otherwise. I couldn't go back home and take care of myself. I couldn't face a day without structure. For the first time since the Voices leaped into my life so long ago, I was beginning to realize vaguely that I needed help.

A day hospital program would give me somewhere to go during the day, as well as therapy and guidance. My hospital treatment team, Dr. Rockland and I all agreed that the day program at St. Vincent's Hospital in Harrison was best for me. The halfway house I chose, Futura House, laid down ground rules: I had to be out of the hospital for two months, and on my best behavior for that time, before they would permit me to enter. My reputation had preceded me, and they didn't want any troublemakers. When I was discharged on March 21, 1986, I set myself a challenge: to get into Futura House early. With that goal in mind, I was a model of good behavior. So five weeks later, in late April, I moved into Futura House.

My doctor on the unit and the social worker congratulated themselves. Their plan had worked. My bad behavior had turned out to be just that—bad behavior. Their threats and entreaties had pushed me into getting "better."

Only I knew the cost of my newfound appearance of health. I felt caught in a crazy bind. On the one hand, after many long years of therapy I was beginning to understand the importance of expressing my feelings and thoughts. On the other, expressing the way I really felt to a psychiatric team meant being locked up in a loony bin forever. I couldn't act on anything that was really in my brain. If I dared to, I'd be threatened with a state hospital. Either way, I would lose.

Everything they did to me in the hospital was a form of control. Medicine helped contain me, but not my thoughts. Sodium amytal helped mellow my behavior, but did not tame my brain. Cold wet packs restrained my impulsive and explosive behaviors, but did not muffle all the clamor and upheaval going on inside.

And as for my newfound "cure," that was all a matter of control too. Everyone needs to breathe, but people can still hold their breath underwater. If you practice, you can hold your breath for much longer than you ever believed possible. That's what holding my Voices inside was like. Sure, I could hold it for a few seconds longer. But the explosive rage was building inside all the more for not being allowed to be expressed.

If you go underwater, and take a big breath and hold it in longer than you think you should, when you come up for air you will be gasping for breath, and more desperate for air than if you had come up sooner.

Futura House was actually two apartments in a building in White Plains. One apartment was for men, the other for women. There were nine of us women in our house, three in a triple room, and six divided up into doubles.

Despite our formal cleanup schedule—we each had our own

tasks to perform, from vacuuming to scrubbing bathrooms—the place definitely looked lived in. It was kind of tattered and messy all the time.

We shared cooking duties too, and all ate together at one long table, family style. I didn't really like helping to make dinner, so when it was my turn, I'd pop a couple of packages of frozen fish sticks in the oven and serve it with a side order of warmed-up Tater Tots.

My biggest problem was learning how to fill my days. My hospital days had been filled with aimless pacing. My real-world days had to be more structured than that.

Every day I made a fifteen-minute drive over to North Street in Harrison to the day hospital. I left the halfway house every morning at 8:45 to be there by 9:00. The morning was filled with nonsense. We had art therapy, assertiveness training, group therapy, and classes in leather, wood and jewelry working as well as grocery shopping and cooking. I felt they treated us like morons. I'd sit for forty-five minutes sanding a piece of wood. Then a staff member would give me the okay to sand another piece of wood.

I had lunch there every day—every day an ice cream sandwich—and by 1:45 it was over. Then my problems began. How could I spend the rest of the day? Because Futura House wanted us to find meaningful things to do with our days, the house was closed and locked between 9:00 A.M. and 4:00 P.M. So what was I to do with my time?

While I was in the hospital, I had insisted I would return to work at Rye Psychiatric. After I was released, though, I decided not to even try. There were too many staffers from New York Hospital who moonlighted there. I didn't want to keep bumping into people from my patient days. What's more, after I had been hospitalized for a while, Eddie Mae Barnes had, with my permission, announced to the staff where I was. They sent me flowers, which I appreciated. But now I felt uneasy going back knowing that they knew. So that left me with nowhere to go, and nothing to do.

I tried to do something fun, like getting my hair done. My mom promised to pay for my appointment if I wanted to improve my appearance. But I couldn't get my hair done every day. And besides, somehow the hairdresser managed to let me know, sub-tly, but nonetheless clearly, that in my porked-out state I was never going to look like a movie star no matter how many perms he gave me.

Mostly, though, I just went home. I'd get in my car at the day program, drive to Scarsdale, climb right into my old bed in my old room, and stay there until Futura House opened up again in the late afternoon. My dad and mom were both working. My dad never came home early enough to find me. And on the few occasions my mother did pop in, I tried to charm her. I complained about the rules that had locked me out until late afternoon, and the fact that I had nowhere to go.

"I didn't think you'd mind if I came here."

Surprisingly, she didn't seem to.

But before too long Deanna, my social worker, got wind of what I was doing, and she did mind, a lot. After that I was forbidden to go home, except on weekends.

A couple of times I tried using my key to sneak into my room at Futura House, popping out after 4:00 P.M. when it was safe. But mostly I just wandered about aimlessly. Usually I wound up in the park across from Futura's apartment building, sitting on the benches talking to the bums, the crazy people, the bag ladies and druggies. We talked mostly nonsense. But still they fascinated me, especially Isaiah, a tall man who wore white robes.

When in a burst of candor I described my new friends to De-anna, she hit the roof again. The park was off-limits too, she said. Together she and I worked out a new plan. I was to remain at St. Vincent's Hospital until 3:00 P.M., and then spend one hour in the library before coming home.

My new day just underscored the meaninglessness of my whole life. At St. Vincent's I watched the end of a soap opera, knowing nothing about the plot or the characters, and caring even less. Then I watched a half hour of Tom and Jerry cartoons. Then to the White Plains library, where I took out books on anatomy and physiology and hid them in the shelves, pulling them out when I arrived, and poring intently over them a page at a time until my hour was up.

And then sometimes I would stop at a bakery in White Plains. There I would sit, eating a bagel with cream cheese and lox. I looked out the window, and wondered why I got sick. I felt so alone. Life just didn't seem worth it. All by myself in a world of billions of people.

The more I began to realize I was really sick, the more I became aware of the vast gulf separating me from everyone else, and the lonelier I became.

My old college friends Lori Winters and Tara were still off doing their own thing. Gail was caught up in her home and her husband. My brother Mark was in Chicago for his new job, and Steven was at college. I was even feeling distant from Mom and Dad. They didn't come very often to visit me at Futura House. I felt they were ashamed of me, their freak daughter. I went to visit them at home, often hanging out all weekend with no particular purpose. But I wouldn't go to the country club with them to be scrutinized by all their cronies the way I was the last time I came out of the hospital.

I resumed seeing Dr. Rockland. But nothing in our sessions did anything to overcome my loneliness. Despite meeting three times a week, I didn't feel that we were getting anywhere. I felt he cared about me. I felt he wanted me to get well. But somehow we just weren't clicking together. We continued to have long silences punctuated by discussions about medication.

As for my fellow residents at Futura House, I just couldn't relate to them. My roommate was as involved in music as I was, but her tastes were unbelievably old-fashioned and nerdy. She was mostly hooked on Broadway musicals, which she played over and over and over again. I felt she was torturing me.

I mean, how many times can you listen to "The Impossible Dream"? "Oklahoma"? "If I Were a Rich Man"? *The King and I? West Side Story?* And *Annie.* By the end of the day, I wanted to smack that twerp Annie.

When I got my turn, I put on the most intense songs I could think of, like Pink Floyd's "The Wall," fierce music about rebellion, pain, suicide and death. I played them loud, until she finally left the room with her Pollyanna music and gave me more quality time with my own wild strange brand of tunes.

Many of the other women were quite talented. One was a

superb artist, her work hanging in local galleries. One woman played the piano. One knew how to cook. One had been out of the hospital and holding down the same job for years. They all seemed more adept at relating to other people than I did. I envied the free and easy way they had of talking with the staff people.

I didn't seem to be able to relate normally to anyone. Instead, I engaged them in a continual game of "Can you top this?" What else did I have to offer or make intelligent conversation about? I saw my psychiatrist three times a week, more than any of them did. So I offered that as conversation. We swapped stories of the times we were sickest. I talked about cold-wet-packing. Someone else talked about eloping to Boston. I talked about liquid Thorazine burning holes in my tongue, someone else would talk about cheeking her medicine for a week.

In the end, I just couldn't deal with them. I plopped myself down on the couch in front of the TV. The Voices were shouting at me so that all I could do to try to muffle them was turn the TV volume up loud and giggle uncontrollably. I sat on the sofa and laughed and laughed and laughed to myself until my fellow residents rebelled. They didn't understand my pain at all. They just wanted some peace and quiet. So I felt all alone, with no friends, no one to talk to, no one to help distract me.

No one, that is, but Deanna and Robin. The two women couldn't have been more different. They were like my good angel and my bad angel. And yet somehow I came to rely on them both.

Deanna, my assigned social worker at Futura House, seemed like a goddess to me. She was older than I—maybe in her late thirties, with long blonde poodle-like hair. She had a lively, free-and-easy attitude toward life. She took courses, vacationed in interesting places. She had a neat husband, a man who owned an art gallery. She swam all the time, and was fit and relaxed. I wanted her to like me. I wanted to be like her.

Somehow we clicked in a way that Dr. Rockland and I never did. Every Monday at 4:00 P.M. Deanna and I had our weekly session. We met at the Futura House office and talked for as long as I could last.

I felt safe with her. She wasn't going to judge me, or reprimand me, or laugh at me. She wasn't going to send me to the state hospital if I said the wrong thing.

And I didn't feel bad if I didn't come up with heavy stuff to talk about. I didn't have to bring into sessions stuff about my childhood, or sexual experiences, or what I felt about my parents. We talked about day hospital, about my friends, about my lack of friends. I was still so restless from my inner turmoil that I needed to talk about it. Deanna opened doors of emotions for me to explore.

I guess I understood that I could have done this with Dr. Rockland, but somehow sitting in his office with him smoking his phallic, Freudian cigar, I felt that if I didn't talk about sex, or my father, then I was being a bad patient. With Deanna I could just talk about whatever was on my mind at the moment.

She was supportive, always encouraging me to keep fighting. And I believed somewhere in my heart that she really did like me. That notion kept me going.

Robin, on the other hand, was clearly a bad influence on me. A resident like me, she was tall and blonde with hair down to the middle of her back, and an acne-scarred complexion. The only thing we really had in common was our diagnoses, both schizo-affective disorder. Still, we were pretty much inseparable. We spent a lot of time together smoking cigarettes and shooting the breeze.

Our pasts were completely different. Her parents hated each other; she couldn't believe mine were so close. She barely spoke to her mother; even when I was angriest at mine, we were still friends. I talked to Robin about my relationships with men. She talked to me about hers with women, for Robin was gay. I found speaking with Robin easy and comfortable. I hadn't had a buddy like her in a long time. Like Deanna, she was easy to talk to.

Unlike Deanna, she liked to egg me on into getting in trouble. Robin was into shoplifting in a big way. It scared me, but it was kind of exciting too. She always went for the challenge. We went into a college bookstore and she spirited off the biggest, fattest textbook she could find. Once we were in a Hallmark store and she spotted a coffee-table book on unicorns that she wanted. I didn't want us to end up in jail, so I dug into my own pockets for the money to pay for it. But before I could say anything, she had lifted it right out of the store. She was fast!

She urged me to try it. I didn't really want to. I was scared. But she was daring me, so I made an attempt. My heart was pounding and I was moving fast. But when Robin and I reconnoitered, she was completely unmoved by my efforts.

"Is that all?" she said when I pulled from my pocket a little green fluorescent marker, the first and last thing I was ever able to bring myself to swipe.

Robin and I worked out another little scheme we found mutually beneficial. I was prescribed a tranquilizer called Xanax, a kind of high-tech Valium, to take four times a day. I got into the habit of skipping a dose here and there to build up a reserve fund for emergencies. Then I got the bright idea that they could be a kind of currency.

From then on, I paid Robin in Xanax to do my household chores. We worked out an elaborate system. Different doses of Xanax were different colors. One color would be worth cleaning out the refrigerator. Another color was to do the bathroom, and a smaller dose for vacuuming and dusting. I'd sit in front of the TV with my feet up while Robin, high on tranquilizers, mopped the kitchen floor.

It became a kind of a game. Quietly, just as in the hospital, I was trying to push the edge, just skirting the danger zone.

Then that summer I tipped over the line. Once again I decided to stop taking my medicine. Despite my growing new awareness of my illness, deep down I still equated taking medicine with being sick. If I stopped, I thought, I'd get well.

Of course I didn't get well at all. I got much sicker. At first I just began to feel a little weird. Then the voices started dancing about, popping in and out more and more. They got louder. I started to panic. The staff at the day hospital began to sense my agitation and question me. I told them I was fine. I wasn't.

Then one day the Voices became too strong to resist. Inside the day hospital were pots of blooming roses. The Voices ordered me toward them. "Take that fucking rose plant and kill yourself with those thorns. Now!" I didn't feel like I had a choice. I followed those directions, and tore up my arms with the rose thorns.

n the day hospital staff found me, bloody among the blooming roses, they summoned the doctor in charge. He felt I needed to be rehospitalized. He tried to convince me to sign myself in—to move from being a day patient downstairs, to an inpatient upstairs.

"It will only be for a short while, just long enough to adjust your medication," he said.

Ha! I had heard that one before. No way. I wouldn't do it. I had the doctor in a bind. I had tried to hurt myself. I was clearly in a mood to do it again. He couldn't let me go. But I wouldn't check in.

He sat me down outside his office, under the watchful eye of some mental health workers. From the doorway, I could hear him trying to solve the problem. He tried Dr. Rockland. No luck. Dr. Rockland was on vacation and couldn't be reached. He tried my parents' home, but there was no answer. My dad was on business in Chicago. Finally, many phone calls later, he did track my father down.

He put my dad on the phone with me. Daddy pleaded with me to admit myself voluntarily.

"Lori, it's for your own good," he said. "You need help." I didn't believe him. Hadn't he and Dr. Rockland convinced me before to go back to New York Hospital for a "short" stay that stretched on for months? I left him with no choice, Dad told me. He gave the approval to commit me involuntarily.

And involuntarily it certainly turned out to be. I put up a hell of a fight. Immediately, as soon as the decision was made, mental health workers appeared to carry me from the day hospital, and the freedom of the outside world, to the locked inpatient hospital upstairs. I struggled, and yelled, and writhed, but nothing worked. They stripped me down, gave me an anti-crazy shot and put me in seclusion.

Another hospital. Another Quiet Room. And not even surroundings I recognized. St. Vincent's was so different from New York Hospital. It was grungier. The rooms were different. I didn't know any of the staff. The protocols were all different too. We weren't allowed to receive phone calls directly, for example. All calls had to come through the nursing station. And patients weren't even allowed to handle matches. Staff walked around with lighters hung from their necks to light patients' cigarettes when they asked.

As soon as I had quieted down, I began telling everyone around me that I was leaving soon. The patients all laughed at that. They had heard that before. But I meant it. And this time I knew how to do it. With medication newly running through my blood and my brain I calmed down enough to carry out my plan. I followed every rule, obeyed every order. And every time anyone asked, I said the Voices were gone, I felt better, and had no intention whatsoever of killing myself.

It worked. I was in and out of St. Vincent's Hospital in nine days flat. Back I went to the day program as if nothing had happened. Still, I stayed furious at my parents for a long time afterward. I was mad at my father for committing me. I was mad at my mother for a different reason: She was so upset and angry at me for this latest hospitalization that she had refused to visit me even once.

Once again a suicide attempt had blown the lid off the seething bubbling kettle that was my brain. And once again, the Voices placated, I was visited by a strange calm. It was in this calm that I decided to make another go at nursing school.

Suddenly and without any warning, I quit going to the day program at the end of August, and enrolled instead in Pace University's School of Nursing. I didn't want to go back to the school where I had failed before. I thought of this as a new start. Besides, Pace had a terrific reputation. I even decided I'd go directly into a special master's program they offered, but my entrance scores were too low. What a joke! I could hardly believe I was the same person who had graduated with honors from Tufts just five years ago. Tufts University? A real grind school? Impossible. These days I could barely put together two consecutive thoughts.

Still, my scores were good enough that Pace undergrad accepted me, and I began work with a vengeance. I used every bit of guts I had. I forced myself to concentrate. I pored over the lecture material, over and over again. I must have done something right. I passed the first semester with a C plus average. It wasn't my old A self, but at least I wasn't failing.

Still, the attempt was taking its toll. The effort of fighting back my symptoms was weakening me. The temporary calm was ebbing. I was holding back the Voices by dint of superhuman control. But they wouldn't be contained for much longer.

You can only hold your breath for so long.

19

Mark Schiller
Chicago, November 1986

Every time I came close to bringing Sally home to meet my family, we broke up. Sometime near the scheduled visit, I would start to back off.

"You know, maybe we should start dating other people, just to make certain . . ." I would begin. Sally would react in horror. What had she done? What was wrong? Then we'd have a big fight and storm apart. We'd stay apart until the danger of the visit passed, and then make up. Because my father traveled to Chicago often on business, Sally had met him. But we had been dating for almost a year, had pretty much decided to get married, and she still hadn't met my mother and I still hadn't brought her back home to Scarsdale.

I wasn't deliberately sabotaging things. It's just that I had been running away from home for so long, it was hard to run back. I finally had this nice life, a nice job and a nice girlfriend safely far away in Chicago. I didn't want anything to mess it up.

My mother finally did manage to meet Sally—but only when my parents took matters into their own hands. My mother flew out to Chicago with my father. When I showed up alone at the restaurant—announcing that we had broken up yet again—my father demanded Sally's number, phoned her himself and ordered her to get dressed and get downtown, and then yelled at us both for being so silly. The rest of the meal was uneventful, and the ordeal I had been dreading was finally over.

Now Thanksgiving was coming, and another ordeal was about to begin. Sally and I were about to announce our engagement. This time she really was coming home with me for the holiday. And I was scared.

For this time, Sally was about to meet Lori. And I realized that for a long time one of the things I had been running away from was Lori.

Growing up, I never felt I was good enough. I was a typical middle kid, I guess, always feeling like I never got enough attention.

Steven was the baby, and Lori was perfect. She was a straight A student. She was popular. She was a great dancer in the discos, a great writer. She had a great sense of humor. My parents just reveled in her accomplishments. My parents were always telling me what a great kid I was, and how bright and how accomplished. But it was Lori who was always getting all the kinds of attention that I wanted.

I was unhappy in high school. I very much wanted to be part of the in crowd—the jocks and the cheerleaders—but I wasn't cool enough. I wanted to play sports, but I wasn't good enough for the varsity team. I wanted to be recognized for my brains, but although I graduated with a 3.7 average, I wasn't even in the first fifth of my class.

By late high school, I had worked myself into a pretty gloomy state. I hung around in my room writing poems about death. I thought about suicide a lot and got my parents all riled up. They tried to say all the right things.

"This is all part of growing up," they said. "We went through it when we were your age." But I didn't believe them. I thought I was a real loser, a real failure.

When I chose Tulane as my college it was my first assertive step away from my family and toward independence. Tulane, in New Orleans, wasn't exactly the kind of place kids from Scarsdale went to college. In Scarsdale, if you didn't get into Harvard or Princeton or Yale, then you went to Brandeis or Colgate or Tufts. Very few people ventured even to Chicago to go to Northwestern, or to the University of Chicago. And it was almost unheard of to go south as I did.

That was fine with me. I wanted something completely different. I liked the warm weather. I liked that fact that Tulane was a big school. I liked the fact that it was a major party school, and that accomplishment seemed a secondary consideration. I liked the fact that I could be at the top of the class here, and would be one of the smartest people. I wanted to start over. I wanted to have fun.

It worked.

I enjoyed Tulane. Out of the pressure cooker of Scarsdale High School, I achieved as never before. I got lots of As. I was elected to an honor society. I was a member of a fraternity. I was popular. People liked me. I liked being somewhere where I was only known as myself, and not just as Marvin's son—or Lori's brother.

After college Chicago became another place for me to start over, just as New Orleans had been. I did well at my work. I was clearly going to be promoted. And then in a small neighborhood bar in November of 1985, I met Sally, a girl I had known vaguely at Tulane. I had been in Chicago since August. I had had a few dates since I had arrived, but Sally was different.

She was attractive, she was funny, and she was smart and easy to talk to. Since we had gone to the same college we had something to talk about on our first dates. We went to blues clubs and to bars. We went dancing. She fixed her friends up with my friends and we all double-dated. We went out on our first date in early December. By January we were seeing each other four or five times a week.

Early on in our relationship I told her about Lori. I was worried. I didn't know how she was going to react. But Sally was great. She was sympathetic, but not too sympathetic. Interested, but not too curious. Willing to listen, but not too eager to pry. I was relieved.

Nonetheless, as Thanksgiving and the trip home rolled around, I got more and more nervous. Sally had only met my mother once, and she had never met Steven. I was worried that my family was going to come on too strong. I was worried that Lori was going to do something strange. I was worried that Sally would think Lori was weird, or be frightened of her or hate her. I was just plain worried.

As it turned out, I needn't have worried for Sally's sake. The Thanksgiving table was loaded with wonderful things to eat—turkey and stuffing, my mom's homemade ambrosia and homemade pies. There were fresh rolls filling the house with the smell of baking and pitchers of cider. Little turkey and Pilgrim and Indian figurines were scattered about the beautifully set table. What's more, there were guests there, and that relieved a lot of the tension. Our friends the Mossbergs had come with their two daughters, who were close to the ages of me and Lori and Sally. Having other young people around helped a lot.

Lori herself was more quiet than anything else. She seemed to be on a lot of medication. She slipped off fairly often to take quick naps. She and Sally chatted briefly about her halfway house and about nursing school. The whole thing was no big deal.

And on the way home Sally surprised me.

"Don't you think Lori should be a bridesmaid at our wedding?" she asked.

Sally's reaction surprised me. It wasn't that it was kind—I knew that Sally was a good-hearted person. No, it was that it was so matter-of-fact. Sally had simply seen Lori and taken her for what she was. I, on the other hand, had been devastated by what I had seen. For it was at that Thanksgiving dinner I really realized for the first time that Lori was terribly sick. And that realization was jolting.

My own experience with depression had made me less, not more, understanding of Lori's illness. When I learned Lori was seeing a psychiatrist my reaction was: Is that all? So? That wasn't anything to worry about.

My parents didn't know it, but when I was in high school I had been so unhappy that I had gone to see a psychiatrist myself once. I poured out to him all my woes, my fears about being unpopular, my thoughts of death, my need for attention. Nothing had come of it. Psychiatry had seemed like such a scam. I talked. He listened. And I paid to have him listen. Big deal. Anyway, now that I was older I wasn't so unhappy anymore.

When Lori tried to commit suicide and was hospitalized, I just thought it was a transparent plea for attention. And I felt the beginnings of a little tug of annoyance. Here she was, the main attraction once again.

Even when my parents told me Lori was hearing voices, I was skeptical. Hearing voices? Sure, I thought. Sure you're hearing voices. It just seemed too weird to be true, and just weird enough to be made up. It was something no one could see, no one could prove, and that would scare everyone. A perfect ploy for attention, I thought once again. I was actually angry that she was so smart that she could make up an illness that no one could disprove.

Lori was perfect. Lori was everything. Nothing could ever happen to Lori. I had had Lori on a pedestal for so long, it was nearly impossible to topple it and accept that something was seriously wrong with her.

When I had first seen her in the hospital several years ago, she had seemed sick, but she had still seemed more or less herself.

This time at Thanksgiving, however, she seemed like a different person. She was lethargic, and goal-less and aimless. Her weight was up, her skin was broken out, and her lips were all shriveled up. Her attitude toward me had changed too. Before, she had seemed depressed, but still accessible. I may not have liked what she was saying, but at least I could talk with her. Now she was refusing to talk, withdrawing completely, acting hostile.

But it was the realization that while she was in the hospital she had been mutilating herself that really got to me. Finally I understood. What she was going through and what I had gone through were not the same thing at all.

I had done a zillion things growing up to call attention to myself. Once I had even gone to school with Band-Aids all over me, hoping to be asked what was the matter. But underneath, nothing was the matter. Hurting myself had never been an option. For all my cavalier feelings about suicide the first time I heard she had tried, I always thought about it in the abstract. I couldn't really imagine people hurting themselves on purpose.

And then I got it: Lori was different, really different. There was something really wrong with her. In some ways the realization made everything much easier. I could take her illness seriously now. She wasn't just a kid like me going through some rough times. I could feel the sympathy and shock that my own disbelief had shielded me from before.

But in some ways it made everything much harder. It turned my world upside-down. The perfect Lori I had worshipped since I was a child was gone. In her place was someone I didn't know and didn't understand.

At that Thanksgiving dinner, my father did his usual thing, going around the table, asking each one of us what we had to be thankful for. When his own turn came he grew very emotional. We were family, he said, and family was all there was. We were lucky we had each other, he said, and we all had to stick together through good times and bad.

Lori had been a terrific big sister to me. She was always there when I was having problems. She helped me with my school-work, and listened to my woes. When I felt out of it in high school, and Mom and Dad were reassuring me with platitudes, it was Lori who consoled me. I couldn't face this new, odd, ill person.

When my turn came I mumbled the right thing, about how glad I was to have my sister home, and that she was feeling better. It wasn't what I wanted to say. It was what I was expected to say. What I wanted to say was: I can't take this. Get me out of here.

20

Lori
Futura House, White Plains, New York, December 1986–April 1987

Things began to fall apart. My lungs were screaming for air. The Voices were screaming to be released. My control was becoming harder and harder to maintain.

Soon I began hearing the call of cocaine again. One of the first things I did was try to find Raymond. I found him, but something had changed while I was in the hospital. Raymond had never wanted to have anything to do with my illness. While I was in the hospital he never visited me, never even tried to contact me. Now that I was out and living in a halfway house, he couldn't deal with that either. I spoke with him sporadically, but he definitely did not want to make himself the man he was to me before I was rehospitalized.

I could still get cocaine. I had a lot of other sources around town. All you had to do is step into a bar, preferably one with a druggie reputation, and get friendly with the bartender. In that kind of bar they liked people like me scouting for coke. It meant good tips. Cash-and-carry was the name of the game.

And if I didn't have Raymond, at least I had Robin. She had her sources and I had mine. Together, we could always manage to stay high. When we weren't doing lines, we smoked marijuana in the stairwell at the halfway house, spraying deodorant around after us to mask the smell. It was good to have a buddy like Robin.

Still, I wanted Raymond. I was especially lonesome around the holidays. My mom and dad were traveling and I wound up alone in Futura House with two other residents and a counselor. I whipped us up a fancy lobster dinner for Christmas—years ago my daddy had taught me how to prepare it—so we had some festivity. But as New Year's rolled around, I began to pine for the comfort of a man.

Against all evidence, I had it in my head that Raymond and I would spend New Year's Eve together. So as the clock ticked in the new year, I sat in the pay phone in the halfway house, waiting for the good news that Raymond had some blow, and that we were going to see each other again.

The hours dragged on. No calls. So I began to call him. Once he answered, made some vague, uncomfortable excuses and hung up. The rest of my calls went unanswered. Over and over I dropped my quarter into the resident pay phone trying to reach him. The phone rang and rang and rang. Midnight came and went. I saw in the new year alone, sitting in a phone booth. By 2:30 A.M. I finally realized. I was alone.

Very shortly afterward came another disaster. Robin and I got caught. We had usually been careful about using drugs at Futura House. It was strictly prohibited, so we knew that if we did it there, we had to be careful, indulging only late at night when no one was around. But after so long without getting caught, we grew careless. We laid some lines right out on the dining room table. Of course someone saw us, and ratted.

Deanna called me into her office. There was no warmth in her voice.

"Have you been doing cocaine?"

I was cocky. "What if I say yes?" I asked her.

No answer.

"Well, what if I say no?"

Back and forth we went. Finally I confessed. Deanna was angry. As I left the office the first thing I did was make a beeline to Robin. I had to warn her what was in store. But Deanna was quicker than I. By the time I reached Robin, Deanna had already gotten to her and delivered the news: We were both suspended for a week.

Mom and Dad were livid. They let me come home for that week, but they weren't happy. Dad roared at me.

"So this is what you do with the money I've been giving yo

Mom just shook her head that I would be so stupid as to ad
drug addiction to my other problems. The week I spent at home
was pretty tense.

Futura House accepted me back on one condition: no more
drugs. I accepted the condition, but things got worse anyway. I
was beginning to understand how sick I was. But I was far too
overwhelmed by my secret symptoms. I kept encouraging myself
to hang on a little longer but I didn't know how long I would
last, and I didn't know how to communicate my suffering to
anyone else. My anger was returning. I was screaming for help,
but the language I was speaking no one seemed to understand.

I played sick games with myself. Late at night when it got
warmer, I went outside Futura House in shorts and a T-shirt, but
no shoes. I walked to the curb, put my Walkman on my head and
turned it up full-blast. Then I closed my eyes and crossed the
street, one foot in front of the other. Cars zoomed by honking. I
imagined hearing the drivers yelling and cursing. Smiling slyly, I
finished my crossing and opened my eyes on the other side. My
record was six round trips. Then I got bored with the game.

My violence was escalating. I smashed a window. I punched in
my closet door. At the Thursday weekly meeting, the staff made
things very clear to me: one more incident and I was out.

At nursing school my performance grew more and more erratic.
I wanted desperately to succeed. But no matter how hard I tried
to stay in control, I found myself doing wildly inappropriate and
even dangerous things.

I couldn't even handle bed making properly. My first patient
was a woman who had had surgery just the day before. I went
into her room, introduced myself cordially as a nursing student
and asked her to please get out of bed, as I had to change her
sheets. She didn't want to climb out of bed so soon after surgery.
She resisted. I persisted.

I knew she had had the surgery. I knew she was in great pain.
I also knew that I had to make her fucking bed if I was going to
pass this part of my nursing rotation. I finally helped her out of
bed and seated her in a chair nearby. I tried to make her bed as

le, but in my haste I caught my finger in the
d oozed out everywhere. I never did get repri-
the poor lady move. Instead, I wound up in
room for bandaging and a tetanus shot.

all kinds of crazy things. Instead of washing my hands for
twenty seconds as instructed, I scrubbed for two minutes by the
clock. I went into a geriatric's room, and tried to cheer an old lady
up by borrowing her cane and tap dancing like a fool around her
room. I walked out of an anatomy and physiology exam because
I didn't know where the parts of a dissected cat belonged. I faked
patients' blood pressure because the Voices were screaming so
loud in my ears that I couldn't hear anything when it was my turn
to take a reading. I was clever, though: I always wrote something
close to the last reading on the chart. If the last true reading was
110/80, then I'd write 110/70.

In the first semester, I had just managed to pass my exams. This
semester, I couldn't pass my exams, because I wasn't really taking
them. I gave that job over to my Voices.

While I was sitting before my examination paper, I would hear
the Voices whispering. "Pick B! Pick B!" they'd say. I believed
everything the Voices told me, and knew that under their command I could do no wrong. I raced down the sheet answering
question after question according to their instruction. I would
finish a fifty-minute, fifty-question test in five minutes, hand in
the paper and waltz out of the room confident I had aced the
exam. Later when I got back a paper with a failing score, I was
crushed. The Voices were fakes! They had deceived me and let
me down.

Still, I couldn't study well enough to prepare for tests on my
own. Was this really my brain? Was this really the same brain that
had achieved for me a 3.9 average at one of the most competitive
high schools in the country, and a 3.3 average at one of the most
competitive colleges? Was this the same brain that learned to speak
Spanish? That wrote papers the professors praised?

My thoughts ran all together, veered and careened and strung
themselves together in ways I could not control. I couldn't concentrate. I couldn't corral them.

I sat in class watching the instructor show us how to give shots.

"You do it firmly," she said, grasping the syringe. "Don't hesitate. Pretend you are throwing a dart."

"A dart. A dart," my mind chanted. "Do it like a dart." And then, as the lecture droned on, my mind was off in flight. "Do it like a dart." The ultimate injection. A shot in the ass. Syringe. Cringe. To die in room 404. Dead. Gray plastic features. Cinema I and II. Last row. Row, row, row your boat. Don't be a cutthroat. Cut your throat. Get your goat. Go out and vote. And so I wrote. Topic: nonsense. Sense of none? The flying nun. Flying high on coke. Diet Coke. Ninety-nine cents. Two-liter bottles. Bottle it up. Seethe. Fester. Bubble. Explode. Ha! Ha! Ha! They're at it again . . .

To be sick. To be well. To wish in a well. Please let me be courageous. Another quarter in the fountain. Please let me be like everybody else. The outcast. Loser. Pitiful. Hate that word. Fighter. Winner. Delusional. False beliefs. Who am I kidding? Daffy Duck? Loony Toons. Deranged. Demented. Unbalanced. They're manic. I'm crazy. I'm crazy. That's insanity. It's cracked to be like Humpty Dumpty. Zcdera = crazed! Is a cuckoo clock wacky or just screwy (as in needing a Phillips screwdriver to be cured). What do I need to be healed. Will a wrench work? Maybe I can wrench my neck? Suicidal ideation seeping out? Too tense and nervous. SNAP! (and not as in "crackle, pop"). I'm suffocating as if a Ziploc bag has zipped my head off. That's witless; incredibly bugged out. It's like an overdose of Chinese mustard burning your brain beyond the Outer Limits of your nostrils. "You can pick your friends. You can pick your nose, but you can't pick your friend's nose." I have no friends anyway. How about just a buddy? How about a Budweiser? How about a budding flower? How about a beer and a rose? How about a wedding? To love and to cherish forever and always. Isn't "always" a panty shield or a pregnancy test or tampon or something? Now I'm getting grosser by the minute. My second-hand first-hand Swatch watch's second hand is busted. Around and around the time goes, and where it stops, you may win a prize on *The Price Is Right*. Let's go to a club and eat cold cut sandwiches on club rolls, and bring clubs with us like we were in *The Flintstones*. Dr. Rockland is Fred's and Wilma's and the Rubble family's psychiatrist too. He

back to Stone Age times to give family therapy. Do you
_____ime? Does anybody know what time it is? Do you care?
Sealed with a kiss. No valentines except from my daddy. Why
can't I find a boyfriend? Why can't I find any friends? Maybe I'm
a blockhead or a huge blackhead. No, I have a good complexion.
I scrub my skin off. I will come to your aid with a Band-Aid. Fix
me up. I want to be cured. No more schizo-affective disorder.
Get it out of me. Not interested. Go to fucking hell. They always
find their way into my mind. I'll show you assholes. All I want
is a man and a family that makes it in this world. Please, dear
God, I pray and pray for an advantageous kind of life. I promise
to be a worthwhile contributor to this life and perhaps beyond.
Crazy or just a bit touched? Either way, as they say, I'm my best
buddy. High five, self!

Robin realized I was in trouble before anyone else did. Maybe
she knew the signs because she had been there before. I started
giving away things. I gave Deanna a photograph I had taken of a
red bird that I loved. I gave away all my record albums, every last
one, to the residents in Futura. I tried giving my stereo to the
house. My dad would take care of my car. For several days I
talked to Robin about wanting to kill myself. I was sick of the
Voices. Sick of feeling depressed. Sick of feeling worthless. Sick
of feeling hopeless.

She threatened me: "If you do anything, I'll kill you," she said.

Ha! If I had my way she'd be too late. I had made the final
decision. There was no other way out. This was to be my last
night to plan, to think, to feel, to say goodbye to the Voices and
to pray that I—and my parents and friends—would finally find
some relief.

I had a plan. A real plan. This wasn't going to be another
botched suicide attempt. This was it. After hearing about hell for
so many years, I hoped that heaven would welcome me.

My plan was simple. During the day I would drive home. Mom
and Dad would be gone for the day in Manhattan. I would put
my car in the garage filling the empty space where Dad's car
belonged. I would close the door to the garage. I had already
noted that the garage door hit the driveway all the way down,
and I wouldn't need blankets or sheets to fill the space. I would

turn on the keys to my car, and also to my mom's car for good measure. I knew where the keys were always kept, hanging in the kitchen.

No one would be home for hours. The car fumes would fill the garage. I decided to play "Comfortably Numb" by Pink Floyd in the cassette deck of my car, and I decided to play it loud. I imagined putting the seat back listening to this mood music and going to sleep painlessly and forever. I felt confident that I could carry out my blueprint this time for sure. This was really it.

I was anxious to fall asleep. Tomorrow was the big day. I lay in bed, tossing and turning under my covers. I popped my head out. I buried it in my blanket. I turned on some Cat Stevens music. I got out of bed and paced around. My heart was pounding big-time. I tried taking a hot bath. I went back to my room and started staring at the ceiling. And then the tossing and turning started all over.

I needed to sleep. I needed to dream. I needed to prepare for tomorrow. I went to my supply of tranquilizers. I took one. I took two. Then four. I had to sleep. Five. I'm going to die in the morning. Six. Seven. I can't fall asleep. Eight. Maybe if I walked around enough I'd get tired. Nine. Ten. It was getting late. I couldn't keep track.

I thought about watching TV. I had to get out of bed, but I was feeling fuzzy. I tried to make it to the living room, but the walls knocked into me. I felt uncomfortably wasted. I could barely walk. How was I going to make it till tomorrow?

Robin intercepted me in the hall. She had been worried about me for a week, she told me. She had been keeping an eye on me. She helped me back into my room, where she saw the near-empty tranquilizer bottle. She begged me to turn myself in.

As clearly as I could, I explained to her that that was impossible. I needed to die. But that was okay, I told her calmly. This time it was going to work.

Robin was crying. She was frightened. "Lori, I love you," she sobbed. She didn't want to rat on me. But she didn't want me to die either. She knew she had to act quickly. Finally she turned me in.

The counselor on duty took one look at me, called Deanna and then a taxi to take me to the White Plains Hospital emergency room. I don't know how much time went by, but very quickly, it seemed, both Dr. Rockland and Daddy were there to meet me.

I was still very groggy. I tried with my slurred speech to beg them to let me die. I had to die. I dozed on and off. I seemed to fade in and out of consciousness as I recounted my lovely plan, my strategy to end my life tomorrow.

All of a sudden, I woke up. It was tomorrow. I didn't like being awake. I wanted to go back to sleep. Wait a second. Where the hell was I? It wasn't hell. I was in a bed. It wasn't heaven. Too many colors. Some obscure, undefined being was sitting in my doorway eyeballing me as if she had nothing better to do with her time.

And then I realized: I was back in the fucking hospital.

Part V

The 9925 Key

21

<hr>

Lori
New York Hospital, White Plains,
New York, May 1987–June 1988

On Tuesday, December 15, 1987, I arrived on 3 South—one of New York Hospital's long-term units—in time for lunch.

But even though I was starving, I refused to eat. Instead, I went straight to my room. I didn't want to see anyone. I didn't want to talk to anyone. I was tense and upset and on the edge of tears. As I walked through the halls on my way here, I had seen the other patients staring. I knew that they were laughing at me and relishing my discomfort.

In my room, I unpacked my belongings. I covered my single bed with the pink comforter my mother had brought me. I put the boxes with my three hundred cassette tapes on the floor. Into the closet went the tons of clothes—in three sizes—that had been bought to accommodate my increasingly porky figure. I lined my windup toys on my desk. My parents were always on the lookout for new ones. They knew that I could fill hours of my empty day fiddling with these little children's playthings. I had a lizard with a wagging tail, a set of teeth that chattered, a walking pig that wiggled its tail and ears and snorted, a walking hamburger, a cackling witch and a psychedelic slinky.

But even the sight of my familiar possessions didn't reassure me. Everything about this place frightened me. This wasn't just a new hospital unit. I had seen plenty of those. No, this was the

end of the road. This was the place I was going to learn to live—
or die.

Months earlier, when I had awakened from my suicidal slumber
on that first night in the hospital, I had begged to be allowed to
go back to sleep. I wanted to sleep forever, I told everyone. Let
me sleep or let me out, I ranted. I wanted to finish the job. I
wanted to die.

Once the intensity of my suicidal urges had passed, however,
the staff offered me a different choice. I could be discharged immediately as I wished. Or I could sign myself into an extended care
unit. There I could plan on a stay of at least a year, maybe longer.
There, the doctors would make every possible attempt to find a
medication that would help me. At the same time, though, I
would have to learn to help myself. I would have to undergo
intensive therapy. I would have to begin to acknowledge that I
had an illness. I would have to begin to learn to control my illness
on my own. No more in-and-out. No more revolving door. Go
or stay, the choice was mine.

Everyone waited expectantly. I was well known at the hospital.
Many of the staff had been around me during my first and second
stays. They knew how vigorously I had fought each time to leave.
No one could believe it when this time I chose to stay.

What no one realized—not even me—was that the hospital's
ultimatum had spoken to a tiny gleam of insight that had begun
glimmering in me. Even while I had been fighting my hardest,
little cracks had begun appearing in the steely armor of my denial.
Toward the end of my last stay at New York Hospital, their
threats to discharge me had panicked me into realizing that I might
need help. Those months living in the halfway house, spending
lonely afternoons in a pastry shop watching the rest of the world
live their lives, had convinced me that I was different from other
people. The three-times-a-week lessons Dr. Rockland had given
me for years were at last having an effect. Perhaps he was right,
I admitted grudgingly. Perhaps I did have an illness. And if I did
have an illness, perhaps they were right. Perhaps I did belong in
a hospital.

I considered the first option. Down the road, I saw a discharge
to a halfway house, another few months of misery and despair,
another suicide attempt, another hospitalization—in other words

the wretched half life of a chronic mental patient. I knew I couldn't take that. I realized what really lay down that road: death. Not the amorphous welcoming, relieving death of my sick fantasies, but real death. I had failed again this time but sooner or later I was going to succeed. This last attempt had come too close.

So when the doctors handed me the choice to go or to stay, something snapped inside me. This time, instead of trying to die, why not try to live? The last time I had been in the hospital I had fought their programs. This time why not go along with them? The last time, I had allied myself with the Voices. This time, why not fight them?

My decision seemed like a good idea at the time I made it. In fact, having made a decision gave me hope. If I had an illness, maybe it could be cured. If I was sick, maybe I could be made well. Maybe they could pull these Voices right out of my skull. Maybe I could have a real life. I agreed to transfer to the long-term unit.

Yes, back at that time it had all made sense. Now that I was here however everything seemed different.

It was clear that this wasn't going to be easy. This was going to be war, a war against the Voices. And the Voices weren't going to give up without a fight. They were going to struggle against me—and anyone else who tried to conquer them.

The Voices were yelling so loud I could barely hear over them when, later on that afternoon, I had my first meeting with Dr. Doller.

Dr. Jane Doller. Jane Doller, M.D. I had first met her on my old unit, during the months I was waiting to be transferred here to 3 South. She often came through to visit another patient on the unit where I was staying. Once I found out her name, I instantly became part of her fan club. For some reason, I got such a kick out of the pun in her name that I looked forward to her visits just so I could greet her.

"Hello, Dr. Doller!" I called out. "Hi, Dr. Doller!" I just loved saying that name. Dr. Doller. Dr. Doller. Each time, she returned the acknowledgment with a nod of her head, or a quiet hello.

I knew she was a psychiatrist. But she didn't look like a psychiatrist. She didn't look like any kind of doctor I had ever seen before. She wasn't angular and crisp like so many of the young professionals I had met. Instead, she looked like the Pillsbury Dough Girl, all pudgy and squeezable. She was always rushing and busy whenever I saw her, but somehow her manner was different from that of the other doctors. She wasn't brisk and businesslike like so many of the others. She was soft. Her face was soft. Her hair was a soft brown. Her manner was soft, and almost retiring. Her voice was soft. Her words were soft. Everything about her seemed soft. I liked her immediately, without knowing why.

Still, except for the several-times-a-week hello, Dr. Doller and I had nothing else to do with each other until I transferred over to 3 South. So when she came to my room, and gently steered me to a bank of chairs in the hall of the unit, I was nervous and apprehensive. I had just found out that she was not just any psychiatrist. She was one of this unit's bosses. She was staff psychiatrist of 3 South, and she was going to be the administrator of my case. I was impressed immediately.

The Voices chattered and wailed and screamed as Dr. Doller asked me questions about my experiences. It amazed me that she was not writing everything else down as psychiatrists usually did. She was just listening, her head tipped slightly to the side, a quizzical look on her face.

I knew that as my administrator she would be the person in charge of my overall treatment, from prescribing my medications to assigning my privileges and my status. What she wanted to know, though, was who should be my therapist. The therapist would be the person who would work with me closely, one on one as Dr. Rockland had, to try to find out what was going on in my head. The choice of therapist was hers; she was trying to find out what I wanted before she made her decision.

I tried to concentrate over the din of the Voices. I would like a woman this time, I said. Over all my years in and out of the hospital, I had mostly worked with men. There had been a few women, but only for very brief periods. In Futura House, I had felt so comfortable with Deanna. It made me realize I related better to women, and wanted to give it a try. It amazed me how well I was able to verbalize my wants and my needs.

Dr. Doller listened to me very carefully, occasionally asking me a few questions in her soft, gentle manner. She agreed, she said. She thought it would be a good idea to assign me a woman as my therapist.

Meanwhile, I was fighting to stay in focus, to stay with her, and not to accept the invitations from my Voices to follow them into their world. It was taking all my energy to keep the two worlds apart, to keep the Voices away from her, to answer her from the other, objective, real-world part of my brain, to keep my answers to her relating as closely as possible to her questions.

And then it spilled over. I couldn't keep the two worlds apart. My Voices spilled over into my own voice.

"Come to hell with me, Dr. Doller," I shouted, my voice echoing the chant in my own ear.

I was horrified. I had slipped. The Voices were going to punish me. Dr. Doller was going to punish me. Ever since I had first heard those Voices so many years ago, my sole aim had been to keep them hidden. I occasionally had let Dr. Rockland peep at the Voices' world. But when I did so, it was with fear. In the hospital, I resisted speaking of them as best I could, especially with doctors. I never stopped fearing that to let a psychiatrist know that I was hearing Voices was to write myself a one-way ticket to a state hospital, or to death.

I watched Dr. Doller's face for the shock and disgust I was sure she would show.

But nothing changed. She kept right on talking and listening to me with the same tranquil demeanor, the same caring, curious look on her face. I had had many doctors listening to me before. But somehow with Dr. Doller it was different. It seemed to me that she peered right inside of me and sensed what I was feeling.

As we parted, the Voices were still howling, yelling in my ear that Dr. Doller was a witch and that she was trying to kill me. But something deep down inside me—the real, well side of me— told me that the Voices were lying. Deep down inside me I knew that this was a woman I could trust.

Three South was a completely different kind of unit from any I had been on before. For one thing, patients couldn't just come

and go from 3 South. They had to be interviewed, and they had
to be accepted. The patients' families had to be interviewed too
to see how involved they would be in the patients' treatments.

I found the interviewing process incredibly stressful. One day
I came back to my unit in despair after one meeting. I was sure I
was going to be rejected. I had been so nervous that I had lashed
out at the interviewer.

"They aren't going to want me," I told the mental health
worker when I returned to my old unit. "I just told the guy
interviewing me that he was the one who should be on antipsychotics, not me."

When, to my surprise, 3 South accepted me, I still had a long
wait to be admitted. There was very little turnover on the unit,
and it was eight long months after I was admitted before a bed
finally became available.

While I waited, I watched more of my life slide by. I spent my
twenty-eighth birthday in the hospital. While I sat lifeless in the
hospital, I watched the lives of my brothers move on. While I was
in the hospital this time Steven had graduated from college and
Mark and Sally had gotten married. I knew I had agreed to accept
long-term treatment, but when I faced the reality, I retreated into
rage. What did they mean by long-term if eight months waiting
for a bed was short? They were eating my life. My life was being
swallowed up by endless days in the hospital.

Once on 3 South, everything moved at even more of a snail's
pace.

On the other units, the emphasis had seemed to be on getting
better and getting out. I had always felt pressured to show progress. Here it was exactly the opposite. Everyone kept impressing
on me the importance of going slowly, of not expecting too much
of myself.

In the past, I had felt that my problem—when I even accepted
that I had a problem—was like a circuit breaker that had flipped
off. All we needed to do was flip the right switch, find the right
pill, adjust the thoughts in my head, and Presto! the problem
would be solved.

On 3 South, though, the message was different. It wasn't about
flipping switches. It was about understanding your own illness,

and learning to live with it. Everything was geared toward learning to recognize the warning signs before you flipped out, and to get help fast.

We were all supposed to be responsible for our own treatment. On 3 South you couldn't get away—as you could on other units— with breaking the rules and staying in bed when you felt like it. Nor could you lie around on the hall chairs. Everyone had to be out and about, engaged in some activity or socializing.

On other units, group meetings were always supposed to be mandatory, but you could dodge them if you said you weren't feeling well. Here, cutting meetings cost you passes and privileges. It was your responsibility to remember when you were to go to activities, prepare for them and wait at the door if you needed an escort.

What's more, we were all supposed to get involved in not only our own treatment, but in the treatment of other patients as well. On other units decisions about changes in status, or about passes, were made by the doctors, nurses and social workers. On other units, for example, to get a pass we just signed our name to a list on the bulletin board, and the decision was announced at the next community meeting. On 3 South, however, it was other patients who, along with the doctors and nurses, debated their fellow patients' fates.

Before I moved to 3 South, I found this idea appealing. But that was before I arrived and found out who I would be working with. The other patients were all so sick. They were so much sicker than I was!

There we sat in our group meetings, three times a week, nine of us, in a circle in the living room. The doctors and social workers and nurses and mental health workers looked alert and in charge. And the rest of us? It varied by how we felt. Many of us had the diagnosis of schizophrenia. During the meeting on any given day, some might be actively hallucinating. Some might be feeling relatively clear and cogent. Some might be nodding off from the effects of a new medication.

At first I just sat in the group and cried. I didn't want to have anything to do with the other patients. I didn't want to talk about them and I didn't want them talking about me. But the staff wouldn't let me off the hook. If I wanted a pass to go home and see my parents, I had to present my request to the group just as everyone else did.

"I'd like to request a pass this weekend," I mumbled, looking at the floor, arms clenched in front of me.

The social worker spoke up. "I'm meeting with Lori's parents tomorrow evening, and we are going to discuss this issue. We've been afraid that you would run away, Lori."

I flared. "My parents aren't me. What do they have to do with it?"

"We're going to hear from everyone, Lori," said Dr. Doller, who was leading the group. "Then we'll get back to you."

One patient spoke up. "I think Lori should get the pass. You go nuts here being locked up for so long."

"I agree," chimed in another.

Dr. Doller turned to another patient, who was sleeping in her chair. "Claire? Claire? Claire, if you can't stay awake, maybe you should stand up."

Margo, one of the nurses, spoke on my behalf: "Lori seems to be trying very hard to avoid impulsive behavior. I think she should get the pass."

"Lori, how do you feel about what everyone is saying about you?"

Silence.

"Lori?"

"I don't want to talk about it."

"Are you having some feelings about us talking about you, Lori?" asked Dr. Doller.

"I'm having a drug reaction. My throat is all tight and I can't talk."

"Lori, you're a part of this group, and you're expected to participate in it." Dr. Doller's voice was slightly chiding.

My paranoia flared. "You're all ganging up on me. You're all picking on me." And the Voices screamed on: "Maggots. Maggots. They hate you. They hate you. To die! To die! To die!"

Whenever something like this happened, the feelings started to engulf me. The Voices began to flood me with their fury. I didn't want to be here. I didn't want to be anywhere. I wanted out. I wanted to stop the Voices. I wanted to stop everything around me. I wanted to lash out. I'd refuse my medicine. I'd kick the walls. I'd punch the screens. I'd tip over a table and lamp.

The funny thing was though, with this behavior, while people rushed to stop me, no one seemed angry. No one seemed upset. In fact, everyone seemed genuinely interested in trying to figure out how I felt, and what had pushed me toward snapping.

"When you start feeling yourself go out of control, you have to come talk to one of us right way," Margo told me. "You've got to come get help before you're overwhelmed."

Within a few days of my arrival on the unit, Dr. Fischer had come to escort me to her office downstairs on the first floor for our first therapy session. True to her word, Dr. Doller had assigned a woman to be my therapist. It was all just as I had wished, except for one thing. Dr. Diane Fischer, my new therapist, was trying to kill me.

I knew it the moment I saw her. The Voices only confirmed it. Something about this doctor terrified me. All the way down two flights of stairs to the main floor to her office, the Voices warned me against her. All my senses went on alert, as I struggled to stay in control, to watch her, to protect myself against whatever she was trying to do to me. I didn't believe what the Voices told me about Dr. Doller; I did believe everything they said about Dr. Fischer. Everything they said was one hundred percent true. She was going to kill me because she found me so repulsive. I was a fat, disgusting, ugly tub of lard, and I deserved to die. I was frightened. I couldn't take my eyes off her.

By the time we reached her office, the Voices had changed their tune. I was the one to do the killing, they screamed at me. I had to kill Dr. Fischer. I had to do it quickly, before she killed me, they said. If I didn't kill her quickly, they would. I felt my panic mount as the Voices' commands became more insistent.

"Kill her! Kill her! Put your hands around her neck and choke her!" These were more than orders, more than commands. I felt I could not resist them.

I sat bolt upright on a chair in her office, trying hard to answer the routine questions she was asking me, and to warn her that her life was in danger. My body shook all over. I had to warn her in a way that the Voices couldn't hear, or they would kill both of

speak. I couldn't concentrate. There was no way of
without the Voices jumping between us. The orders
growing more and more insistent.

"Kill her! Kill her now!" they commanded.

I couldn't stand it. I leaped from my chair and bolted from the
room. I ran all the way back to the unit where I collapsed, panting
with fear, in the safety of my room.

After that I refused to go to her office again. I refused to meet
anywhere alone with her. I was afraid of what she would do to
me. More than that, I was afraid of what I would do to her. I
was afraid of succumbing to the Voices' charges. I was afraid of
becoming a murderer.

Why did this happen? Why was I so afraid of Dr. Fischer? I had
had many therapists before throughout my hospitalization. I had
often been tense and nervous on meeting a new therapist, or
anxious and depressed when one I was used to left me. But no
one had affected me the way Dr. Fischer did. Dr. Fischer was
special.

All three of us—Dr. Doller, Dr. Fischer and I—were close in
age. Dr. Doller was a few years older; Dr. Fischer was probably
about my age, or maybe a little younger. But Dr. Doller seemed
much older than I, not just in years but in experience and wisdom
and accomplishment. Her manner was motherly and, while she
didn't feel like a mother to me, she did feel like a big sister, the
big sister I never had.

Dr. Fischer, though, seemed much younger. She was petite and
pretty, a perfect size four with long curly black hair. She was chic,
always wearing fashionable clothes. Dr. Fischer wasn't my sister.
She was me. She was the me that I had left behind ten years ago.
She was the me buried deep under these pounds of fat. She was
the me cowering in terror under the Voices' assaults. She was the
me I wanted to reclaim but couldn't. She had everything I wanted
but didn't have. She was everything I wanted to be but couldn't
be. Everything she was, I was the opposite. I couldn't stand her.
I hated her. I loved her. I wanted her to die. I wanted her to like
me. I wanted to kill her. I wanted to be her.

After that first day, I would only meet with her on the unit and
insisted that a comfortably large male mental health worker sit

nearby. I could only feel safe if I knew there were someone nearby to stop her from killing me or me from killing her.

Even so, I couldn't meet with her for the whole forty-five minutes we were assigned. Even sitting next to her was almost more than I could bear. I tried to talk to her, to answer her questions, but the Voices flooded my mind. At the same time, her face began to play tricks on me. I started to talk to her and her face contorted. Her normal face twisted into a leering grin, and then the whole face shifted. Her mouth and nose and eyes all changed positions, and she became a threatening horrible monster.

Then I looked down at my own hands, which were oozing blood and poison. I tried to warn her but I couldn't make my voice heard over the Voices. Once when we were sitting together in the hall of the unit, my anxiety was so great and so painful that I could barely sit still. I leaped to my feet and ran for the bathroom, where I stayed, heaving my guts out, until she left.

For weeks Dr. Fischer and I battled to find a way to meet together. Rather than trying to meet on a conventional schedule, Dr. Fischer had to throw the rulebook out completely for me. She came to the unit twice a day every day to meet with me for five minutes at a time.

Mostly I spent the five minutes we passed together trying to stay in focus, trying to ignore the taunts of the Voices, to rein in my terror, and simply sit still with her nearby.

I knew she was trying hard to help me. I wanted to work hard for her, to do what she wanted me to do. I fought hard. I fought to stay in control. I fought to focus on her face as it twisted and contorted there before me. I fought to concentrate on her words.

After a time, when I had relaxed a bit around her, there would be moments when I was lucid and not quite so frantic. Then I would try to tell her about who I used to be, about the me who would have been her friend if things had been different. I tried to tell her about the me who would have been her peer, not her patient. I tried to tell her about myself in high school, and in college, and about the life I had before I became part of hospital life.

When I began to tremble, and shake with fear, Dr. Fischer gently asked me to tell her what was on my mind.

"Tell me what you are hearing, Lori," she said.

I hated telling anyone about the Voices. They were too terrible, too frightening. They would kill anyone I told about them. They would kill me if I told. I couldn't tell her. But I wanted to tell her. I wanted her to know. I wanted to please her. I wanted to do what was right.

So I decided to write to her. Over one evening I wrote it all down. I wrote down everything that was in my head, all the sounds and noises and meaningless phrases. All the endless repetitions of "To die!" All the hatred, the bile, everything foul the Voices had said to me and about me. The next morning I stuffed into her hands the transcript of my head.

And now she knew. I waited for her to die. I waited for her to laugh. I waited for her to turn on me in disgust. But she didn't. Instead, she was grateful.

"This is wonderful work, Lori. You've put so much effort into this. Thank you," she said.

If I couldn't talk it, then at least I could write it.

All through my various times in the hospital, people had been urging me to keep a journal. This time I decided to listen to them and try. I had always loved writing. Back before I had gotten sick I had been good at it. All through my younger days I had kept journals off and on. I loved the fat spiral notebooks and the feel of the pen in my hand.

This time, though, the journals meant much more to me. In my journals I could tell myself all the scary things I could tell no one else. I could use the journals to keep a record of how I felt from day to day, or even from hour to hour and bring some order to the chaos of my mind.

On May 10, 1988, I began my first journal with a scream of pain and rage:

> *May 10, 1988—I feel like I'd rather kill myself than fight it out here . . . I have come to terms that I'll never lead a normal life again. I'm a crippled loser with no future. I hate everybody. It's everyone's fault that I'm sick and I'm not going to pound my head against the wall blaming myself all the time for my illness.*
>
> *May 11, 8:10 A.M.—Everyone hates me. I'm ignored, made*

fun of, despised by all—patients and staff. I have no one to talk to except Dr. Fischer & even she is getting sick of me.

May 11, *6:05 P.M.—I am feeling very paranoid, very afraid of people especially the staff. I feel that they want to hurt me bad because I am an evil person. The voices give me headaches sometimes.*

May 11, *7:55 P.M.—Please dear God take me. I feel bad again. I wish for relief. Oh boy, I can't breathe.*

May 14*—They started in on me in the night, and now they're bothering me a lot. They say I have to die, that I must die, and that I'm a worthless piece of shit. I'm scared again. It was really quiet and then they exploded. It's hell. HELL!!!*

And then one sunny spring afternoon I ran away.

I had been doing pretty well, actually. I had been allowed to go off the locked ward to visit the library with a group of other patients. When the Voices started urging me to run, I tried to get the attention of the group leader to let her know I needed help.

I guess she didn't understand what I was saying. Or didn't realize that when I started punching the air that I was fighting off the Voices. Or that when I began yelling "Get the fuck out of here!" I was yelling at the Voices—and that I was echoing their commands to me.

I was getting more agitated by the second. The Voices were shouting, egging me on. I couldn't stop them. They took control . . . and I bolted.

Running felt good. For so long I had wanted to run as fast as I could. I didn't know where I was running to but I did know where I was running from. The hospital is laid out in campus-like buildings on fifty acres. I headed through one of the parking lots and out toward the back hospital driveway. I headed away from the main hospital gate that opened out onto the busy Bloomingdale Road. Instead, I headed for the back entrance at the south side of the complex.

When I got off the hospital grounds, I suddenly had no idea where I was. It wasn't a route I normally followed; besides, it had

been so long since I had been out on my own. My heart was
pounding and I could barely hear the screaming Voices over the
sound of my own panting. Still, the sun was strong and the day
warm. That seemed like encouragement.

I was wearing jeans and my blue and white shirt. My suspenders
were hanging down by my sides. I had been given back my shoes
for the trip to the library, so I was wearing my white high-tops.
I just decided to keep walking with no plan in mind, feeling more
and more confused and uncertain. "What the hell do I do now?"
I began to think. The landscape was unfamiliar. I couldn't find
my way. I didn't know what my next step would be. I walked
and walked.

Finally I came to a church I vaguely recognized. Maybe we had
passed it driving when I was younger, or had gone by it without
paying it much notice when my parents came to take me out on
pass. Our Lady of Sorrows Church—a particularly fitting name,
I thought. At least it was a place to sit down. I walked in and
dropped down into a pew.

The Voices were quieter now. I had a chance to think. What
were my options? I could think of three, and I pondered each one:
I could return to the hospital and turn myself in. I could walk to
the nearest overpass and throw myself off. Or I could walk home
and beg Mom and Dad to let me stay there with them. I didn't
know what to do.

I began to pray. I begged God to tell me what to do.

In my childhood I hadn't given God much more thought than
I had hell or the devil. Sometimes I prayed to Him for things I
wanted—like good SAT scores or a date to the prom. But other
than making such utilitarian demands, I didn't see much use for
Him.

That changed the sicker I got. My dad always said that each of
us determined our own destiny. I wasn't sure. I had been tormented for so long, I needed something outside me to believe in,
to guide me and to help me. I began to whisper little prayers in
the hospital, prayers that God would help me fight off the Voices.
God was different from the Voices. The Voices were demons I
heard tormenting me, who spoke to me, who ordered and directed
me. God was something I thought about and felt in my heart.

Sitting in that church, I prayed as I had never prayed before.

Please dear God—help me to make it through
*   this wretchedness in my life.*
I need relief and I'm feeling weak.
I must persevere, but I'm running scared.
I'm so sorry for all the bad I've done in my life.
I've tried to be helpful to others before myself.
I'll try harder—I promise.
I'll never be evil again.
If you want me to listen to the Voices, I will.
If you want me to die, I will.
Just don't send me to hell.
I've been there already.
I'm sorry for all my ugliness, for all my badness.
But please—I want to be saved.
Please dear God, answer my prayers.

I sat in the church for two and a half hours. Somehow the prayers made me feel better. When I left the church, I turned down the road that I thought led toward home.

When I finally arrived after a seven-mile walk, I was trembling big-time. I walked in and surveyed the house where I had once been so happy, and tried to figure out if it was here that I needed to die. I stood in the kitchen looking at the block of knives on the counter, paralyzed with fascination.

Then I saw a car pulling in the driveway. My mother jumped out and came running to me. I ran to her and we embraced. I begged and pleaded with her to let me come home but I knew she couldn't do it.

I knew I had to go back.

22

Lori
New York Hospital, White Plains,
New York, June 3, 1988–June 9, 1988

June 3, 1988, 8:25 P.M.—*I ran away today. I'm back now. And, I feel like a real loser . . . No one will believe me anymore. I made the mistake of not stabbing myself in the stomach 4 times like I thought. I guess I was too chicken—or maybe too tired . . . I'm confused. I'm scared. Scared of myself and what I might do if enraged. The voices bothered me a lot today. They in fact inspired me to run. Next time I run, I'm doing myself in.*

June 4, 3:05 P.M.—*I know now at this moment that when I'm discharged I'll kill myself. So what will they do? Put me in a state hospital. So what will I do? Convince the state hospital that I won't. And upon good-bye to the SH I'll be dead. DEAD DEAD DEAD. No one cares about me anyway except Mom and Dad, and they didn't even rescue me right away . . . I want to cry, like I did in church yesterday. I want relief. Oh, Dr. Fischer, Dr. Doller: Why did you have to be away now?*

June 8, Noon—*I feel that therapy with Dr. Fischer is too slow. At times I feel like murdering her. The voices tell me to strangle her to death. At other times, I wish I could say I love you to her.*

June 9, *3:45 P.M.—I know deep in my heart despite my cries to leave the hospital that I really do want to get better.*

23

Lori

New York Hospital, White Plains, New York, June 1988–December 1988

Over and over I ricocheted from one extreme to another.

Sometimes I felt like a helpless pawn in the real battle that was going on around me and about me. On the one side were Dr. Doller and Dr. Fischer and the rest of the hospital staff. On the other side were the Voices and my own crazy out-of-control emotions. I was in the middle. I was the one they were fighting over. Which way would I go?

Sometimes, though, I felt like a fighter. I would seize control. I would fight the Voices and win. Enough of this bullshit.

The more I tried to reach out to people, the more I found myself caught up in a crazy excess of emotion. I couldn't find a gentle way to let my feelings out. Instead, I damned them up until my strength gave out and they came gushing out in a wild, uncontrolled outpouring.

I even swept my mom and dad up in the flood.

Most days I could barely wait until Mom and Dad arrived. Their visits were the high point in an otherwise bleak day.

Every night just after dinner I waited by the window. From my bedroom window I could see as Dad's car turned off the long curving drive and into a visitors' parking space. I watched the car roll to a stop. Sometimes nothing happened for a long time. Sometimes I would just watch the car sitting there for what seemed like forever, waiting for the door to open and my parents to emerge.

When they finally appeared, I waved to them from behind my safety screen, and shouted down to them. It seemed like the time would never go by as they climbed the stairs to the third floor. Even when they finally arrived at the door to the unit, the wait wasn't over. No one but the nursing staff could unlock the door. Sometimes the staff were so slow in arriving with their jingling keys I felt I was going to jump out of my skin in anticipation, my parents waiting on the other side.

Then they were inside, full of smiles and cheer, and all the energy they brought in from their lives on the outside. They almost always brought something. A new sweat suit. A bagel and cream cheese sandwich with tomatoes and onions, the way I liked it. A rock tape I had requested. Batteries for my Walkman. Cigarettes. A Chinese dinner. Often they brought things not just for me, but for other patients as well. They brought clothes for patients whose families never visited. They brought little gifts for the nursing staff. Once Dad brought a lobster dinner—complete with melted butter, claw crackers and bibs. When they brought food for me, they often brought enough for everyone on the unit.

I loved them so much. I was so proud of them. I was so glad to see them. And I couldn't wait for them to leave. They stirred up in me a whirlwind of violent emotions that I didn't understand, and had to struggle mightily each and every visit to control until they were gone.

Much as I loved my parents, I felt like I was on stage for them too. I fought so hard to seem normal before them. I didn't want them to know how sick I was. I didn't want them to see me out of control. From the moment they arrived my struggle to keep control battled with my fear of losing control. I knew how much my illness hurt them. I knew how much they suffered for me. As much as I could, I wanted to keep the worst of it from them. I wanted them to be proud of me. I didn't want to cause them heartache.

As soon as they arrived, I herded them into my room. I didn't want anyone watching us. Mom and Dad seemed so out of tune with the world I lived in. My mom liked to stretch out on my bed with her shoes off. I lived in dread that someone would come in the room and see her there like that. There weren't any rules against it, but I knew that the staff disapproved of her making herself quite so comfortable. Meanwhile my dad sat on my desk chair facing the center of the room. I paced. I didn't know what to do. I didn't know how to act. They seemed to be expecting something I couldn't give.

Their visits were short, usually no more than half an hour or an hour on weekends. They seemed endless to me. We talked about their friends and the country club and about my playing racquetball once a week, and tie-dying T-shirts in therapeutic activities. We talked about Mark and Steven. Everything they had to say seemed so unimportant to me. The world I lived in— a world of medications, nurses, regulations, passes, Voices and buzzers—seemed so monumental, and the world they lived in seemed so far away. I was so self-involved it was nauseating even to me.

Mostly I struggled to conceal the Voices from them. They each wanted so badly to see me well. If I told my dad about some out-of-control episode, he'd retort immediately: "Well, that was yesterday. Today you're fine. And tomorrow you will be too. And if not tomorrow, then the next day." He was always so positive about everything. I fought to make the picture match. My mother, on the other hand, just couldn't take it. She was always escaping to the smoking room. Sometimes it seemed that the smoking ritual was the only thing I shared with her. I wanted so much to be the daughter she dreamed me to be, but couldn't. It was all I could do to simply put on a normal face for them.

The fire built up inside me. My impatience became anger, my anger became rage. I hated them. I blamed them. My rage bubbled up, then spilled over the walls I had erected. Out it poured with terrifying intensity.

"I hate you! I hate you!" I screamed at my mother. "It's your fault I'm sick. You've done this to me. You're the unbalanced one, not me."

"Get the fuck out of here!" I screamed at my father. "Get away! Get away!" I couldn't breathe. I thought I would explode into a million pieces.

Then they left, my mother in tears, my father white-lipped and shaking. And then I did spin out of control, ranting and shrieking.

Terrible thoughts swamped me, making me feel like a lunatic. I wished them dead. I wished them murdered, or blown to pieces in a plane crash. I wanted to murder them myself. As I looked on helplessly my own raging brain concocted terrible, horrible fantasies. I would stab them. I would shoot them. I would sneak out of the hospital, pour gasoline around their house while they slept and fling out the final match, giving them no way out.

I often spent time in the Quiet Room after their visits. When the rage had finally abated and my sick frenzy had subsided, a new awful emotion would emerge in its place. I would be consumed by guilt and terror. I had killed them. My rage had killed them. They had been killed in a car crash on their way home. Their house was really going to burn down and I would have caused it. I felt terrible, all evil inside, like I was going to crack or break or fall apart and come undone from my own badness.

I wanted to see them. I wanted to hug them. I wanted them to come back. What if they believed me? What if they never came again? What if they really did die?

Whenever I felt myself about to explode, the only thing to do was to hit something, to break something, to punch my hands against the safety screen until they bled, to stab myself with whatever I could find, to strike out in uncontainable rage, fear and pain.

For years, I had felt such rage was beyond my control. But as time went by, I found allies not only in Dr. Fischer and Dr. Doller, but in the nurses and mental health workers too. During my previous hospitalization, I felt the people stationed outside the door of the Quiet Room were hostile jailers. This time, they became more like buddies. During my calm periods I'd stand near the doorway and rap with my keeper about anything that came into my head: Lucky Charms cereal, the weather, clothes, Chinese restaurants. It was just ordinary day-to-day talk, but it helped keep the terrors in check.

Slowly I found myself feeling friendly toward the staff. Debbie was funny. Margo brought me milk and cookies and showed me pictures of her pet ferret. Cathy was my coach. Barbara was somewhere between mother and grandmother. Rose was like an old friend: She had been with me on all three hospitalizations. I talked "girl talk" with all of them. We discussed men's bodies, blind dates and hockey players. Even that simple talk helped to put some order on the chaos of my inner world.

I knew that even this little bit of closeness was helping to keep me from retreating into the world of the Voices. The Voices must have realized it too. They leaped between me and the staff, trying to sow fear and distrust.

"Strangle her!" the Voices shouted about one volunteer who had been particularly kind. "Pick up that towel and strangle her." I tried to warn her of what was going to happen, but all I could manage was an impersonal warning.

"Your life is in danger, Fran," I whispered in a tiny voice.

Still, they didn't seem afraid, and they didn't seem put off. Instead, they kept on working hard to reinforce the doctors' message: that I was not helpless before the onslaught of my Voices. We can't make the Voices go away, they told me. We can't ease the maelstrom of your feelings. But we can teach you ways to feel less out of control when the storm hits. We can even teach you ways to feel the storm before it arrives, and prepare yourself to weather it better.

There was one nurse in particular, an Israeli man named Sorin, who seemed to work especially hard to help me get the upper hand against my Voices and fears. Sorin worked hard at everything. Although he was always putting in sixteen-hour double shifts, I never saw him enough to suit me. He always seemed especially creative in helping me deal with my ugly impulses.

He arranged to have a professional punching bag brought into the unit. When I felt like punching windows and walls or the trees in the courtyard, he encouraged me to do battle with the punching bag instead. I'd pummel the bag until I was hot and perspiring. I boxed the Voices, the sounds. I punched the invisible airwaves that carried the torturers to me. I punched my family. I punched the staff and I punched myself. I punched everything that hurt me, everything that enraged me. I punched until I was exhausted and ready to crawl.

I was also prescribed a once-a-week racquetball game. A staffer from therapeutic activities was assigned to be my partner. She brought me rulebooks, and tried to teach me a kind of yoga to cool back down from the exercise.

Sometimes I really felt I had to destroy things. The staff tried to teach me to channel even those impulses. When the Voices were especially disturbing, the staff would put me in the Quiet Room with a stack of magazines. I'd rip those suckers to bits, venting the violence of my emotions on every page. Then I kicked the piles of shreds like autumn leaves. When I was calmed down, I'd wad them up and play basketball with them, into the garbage can with the remains of the mangled magazines.

The score: Voices 0. Lori 1.

But still the Voices did not want to let me go. The closer I got to confiding in Dr. Fischer, the more the Voices tormented me. The more I trusted her, the more the Voices conspired to drive me away.

I kept on struggling to meet Dr. Fischer, and she kept struggling to get inside my head. From time to time, when the Voices cleared, she tried to coax me to talk about my experiences.

"How's it been going for you?" she said.

"Not so hot," I said.

"What's been happening?"

"I was in a peer group meeting and I found out that they all hate me."

"So everyone hates you? When did you start thinking that?"

"Since yesterday."

"What happened yesterday?"

"I was bringing up a point about the party that we were planning, and no one responded to me, and then the Voices told me to strangle Claire."

Dr. Fischer looked concerned. "It seems like a lot has been happening to you since we last met. Let's try to figure out what's been happening. At the very least it seems like you feel very criticized . . ."

"Yeah, but it was only because Claire was staring in a way that made me realize that she was going to kill me and so I had to _____ ___ first."

_____ little, bit by bit, she probed my mind, gently climbing _____ deeper in. The closer in she got to me, the stranger I _____ el.

Meeting with her on the unit had the advantage of the male staff I could count on to protect both of us. But it had disadvantages too. For one thing, there was no privacy. I was easily distracted by the other patients' wandering by. Some of them didn't wander. They hovered. One guy in particular gravitated toward us. He hung out behind Dr. Fischer so that I could see him and Dr. Fischer could not. I got terribly upset at him. I broke off what I was saying to thrust him away.

"These are private conversations!" I shouted at him and, agitated, dragged Dr. Fischer further down the hall where we could be alone. He'd leave us for a while, but then the next day he'd be right back.

I thought about punching him in the face. But finally I decided to confront him instead.

"What are you doing listening in when I'm talking with my therapist?" I demanded.

He wasn't listening to anything, he said. It was Dr. Fischer's feet he was interested in. He was just sitting there watching them. They were so tiny and pretty in her high heels he couldn't help himself. He just had to stare at them.

His revelation didn't make me feel better. It made me feel worse. The guy was a pervert. I didn't like anyone thinking about Dr. Fischer like that. But the truth was, his behavior rang all kinds of uncomfortable bells for me. I was beginning to like Dr. Fischer. I was beginning to find her attractive myself. From being frightened of her, I had begun to obsess about her. I found myself thinking about her a lot. What was wrong with me? If he was a pervert what did that make me?

The strange feelings I was having for Dr. Fischer frightened and revolted me. I had been locked up inside my own crazy world for so long, I didn't know what it felt like to come out. All my feelings of affection and closeness blew up to gigantic proportions. From hating and fearing her, I grew to think I was in love with her.

I tried to tell my journal about the thoughts that were haunting me:

June 18, 5:40 P.M.—I'm still having thoughts about Dr. Fischer. They scare and upset me . . .

The first time such thoughts popped into my head, I was shocked. I tried to drive the thoughts from my mind, but completely unbidden they kept forcing themselves back.

The Voices jeered at my discomfort.

"You want to touch her, don't you?" they shouted at me while I was trying to stay calm in session. I couldn't look at her face. Sometimes I couldn't look at her at all. I looked at my sneakers, or at the ground, or stared off into space. Sometimes the combination of my own strange thoughts and the Voices' taunting was too much to bear and I would suddenly cut off the session and flee to the safety of my room.

In the mornings I filled my journals with my lovesick yearnings for her, and counted the hours until I could see her again. By afternoon I refused to see her. I couldn't face her with these perverted thoughts circling through my brain. And then I was consumed with guilt and pain. She would hate me. She would leave me. What could I tell her? What could I say to her?

> *June 20, 11:00 P.M.—You know what's the worst part about sitting alone in my room all day? It's sitting alone with my crazy, confused thoughts. I don't write them all down because I can't write when I'm feeling so bizarre and because I'm afraid and paranoid that people will know what kind of world I retreat to.*

> *July 1, 8:00 P.M.—I feel like spattering myself on the [highway] after jumping off the bridge . . . I really feel like having a violent death. Maybe I could use gasoline, pour it over myself, light myself on fire and jump off the bridge onto the highway. I think these thoughts when I'm very angry.*

> *July 2, 2:50 P.M.—Do you know I have to fight to keep from going crazy every day? Who says I don't work at getting better. What should I do, listen to every voice? Act out every impulse? What about my fantasies? Should I make those sick thoughts a reality? I'm working hard, damn hard.*

Whenever I was feeling really bad, I turned to Dr. Doller. Because I somehow trusted her, I felt safe telling her my worst fears. With Dr. Fischer I was experimenting with trust. But instead of feeling better, I felt worse than before. I felt invaded, taken over. I felt I didn't know who I was and I didn't know who she was. I swung back and forth with passionate intensity between feelings of love and caring and feelings of fear and hate. All these feelings I brought to Dr. Doller.

Actually, she came to me. It was late in the evening of one day when I had had a troubling session with Dr. Fischer. I was sitting on the unit and I was shaking. Dr. Doller must have seen something on my face, for she stopped and sat down beside me. There was no shrink talk, no therapeutic silences. Just a plain, straightforward blunt question.

"C'mon Lori, what's up?"

She didn't need to prompt me. It all came pouring out. All my fear and pain and self-loathing for the strange, inexplicable feelings I was having for Dr. Fischer.

Dr. Doller spoke very carefully. What I was feeling wasn't unusual at all, she said. Nor was it wrong or bad. I wasn't sick for feeling that way, and I shouldn't berate myself for it. In fact, my feelings were probably helpful, she said. If I wanted to, I could learn from them. Therapy is like that she said. In the course of therapy, a therapist takes on many different roles to the patient. She can be mother, father, teacher, sister, brother, friend—even lover. The feelings I was feeling were good. They gave me a chance to explore. I should use them, and not feel ashamed of them.

Tension poured out of my body. It was as if she had punctured a terrible boil. Dr. Doller had taken all the badness in me and turned it into good. I was grateful to her, and at the same time pleased with myself for having confided in her.

Sometimes I got angry with Dr. Doller. I found the times she went on vacation especially difficult. While she was gone I would shred money—dollar bills, ten-dollar bills, twenty-dollar bills if I could get my hands on them—using the pun in her name to vent my hostility symbolically.

But sometimes—unlike Dr. Fischer, who kept a therapist's professional detachment—Dr. Doller got mad at me too. Once when I refused to take my medications she lost her cool and hollered at me. She threatened to take away my weekend pass unless I took

the medicine the way I was supposed to. Later on she calmed
down and apologized. I took the medicine.

The Voices reacted differently to Dr. Doller than to anyone
else. They challenged me to destroy her the same way they ordered
me to kill Dr. Fischer. They threatened that if I continued to see
Dr. Doller, they would put both her and me in hell. But somehow
it was different. Somehow I could feel in the Voices a fear that I
had never felt in them before.

While I was sitting with Dr. Doller, I'd be in constant fights
with the Voices. There were two of them in particular who were
my enemies and hers. There they were, the two of them, howling
warnings to me about her. But where the Voices usually yelled at
me to kill someone before that person killed *me*, this time even
though they said Dr. Doller was going to hurt me, I could tell
that the Voices were yelling at me to protect *them*.

> VOICE NO.1: This asshole floods you with lies.
> VOICE NO.2: Eat shit, you excuse for a doctor. Eat shit. Eat
> shit.
> VOICE NO.1: You fuckin' asshole. She's going to hurt you
> for life, shithead.
> VOICE NO.2: She's worth manure, so spit on her goddamn
> brain.
> VOICE NO.1: Give her a good punch and rip open her skull,
> that piece of shit.
> VOICE NO.2: We will not be extinguished by power of M.D.
> BOTH VOICES: By power of M.D. By power of M.D. By
> power of M.D.

They were frightened. The Voices were actually frightened.
She was the doctor with power to destroy them.

Slowly, gradually, I began to be able to confide in her more
and more, and through her to be able to open up more to Dr.
Fischer. After speaking with Dr. Doller, I wrote to Dr. Fischer
telling her how I felt about her. We talked about it, and about
how my fantasies about killing her might really have more to do
with my wanting to kill all those bad feelings.

Meanwhile, I was becoming more and more comfortable telling

Dr. Doller what was really going on inside my head. It was strange. I told her some of the most disgusting, nauseating, horrendous, humiliating and private thoughts and feelings and she didn't seem repulsed. In fact, she always seemed to like me. She was never judgmental, even when I confided my worst secrets and fantasies.

In fact, it was her very matter-of-factness that I found so comforting. Once, after much inner turmoil, I finally confided to her a grisly fantasy that had been torturing me in which I killed and mutilated my father. The fantasy nearly overpowered me with its gruesome detail. But when I poured it all out to Dr. Doller, she didn't seem a bit shocked.

"I'd give that about a seven, Lori," she said. "You can do better than that."

Nor did she shrink from giving me hard messages. Once when I was talking to her of my hopes of being cured, she looked at me soberly. "Lori," she said, "we are going to try to get you better. But you're never going to be able to go all the way back. You're never going to be the girl you were in high school, or even college. You are going to have to learn to work with the person you are now. You're going to have to learn to live with the voices."

When I was feeling up, she taught me to recognize the feeling and savor it. "Remember how good you feel now," she said. "There will be times later on when everything will seem bleak. I don't want to minimize the grim and harsh times. I know how bad you feel then. But they won't last forever. Capture the good moments," she said.

24

Lori
New York Hospital, White Plains,
New York, January 1989

As the new year dawned I tried hard to hold on to those good moments, and on to my hope of a new life.

I tried to understand about the Voices. For years in therapy, Dr. Rockland had told me that the Voices were a part of me, stuff buried deep inside coming out in another, strange way. I had learned to say that when I was asked, but I never really believed it. This time around, I tried hard to understand what my doctors meant when they said the Voices weren't real.

When I heard Voices shouting at me to castrate a male staff member, Dr. Fischer and Dr. Doller explained, there weren't really voices that other people could hear. It was just my own hostile thoughts getting blown up out of proportion inside my brain.

I listened. I thought about it. No way, I thought at first. I don't have horrible thoughts like that. Those thoughts aren't me. It's those Voices who are the crazy demons, not me. Besides, the Voices were so clear, so real, and so vivid. It seemed impossible to me that they were simply figments of my own imagination.

But gradually, with Dr. Fischer and Dr. Doller leading the way, I slowly began to test the waters. If I was hearing Voices cursing me out loud, I'd say nothing, and wait. I'd look around. I'd turn in the direction the Voices were coming from. No one seemed to be disturbed. No one even seemed upset by their vehement words. It was as if they were deaf. I wanted to shake the people around me. You idiots! I thought. Do you think by simply ignoring them they'll go away?

At first I thought I was being tricked. Everyone was simply pretending not to hear the Voices. I didn't know why they were pretending like that but it made me paranoid and suspicious of them. What other things were they plotting against me?

Then the Voices would creep up again. Still no reaction from those around me. I felt a little stirring. Maybe they really couldn't hear them. Quickly I retracted the thought. Of course they were there. I heard them as clearly as "the Star-Spangled Banner" at a baseball game.

Then I started asking Dr. Doller and Dr. Fischer if they heard what I was hearing.

"Do you hear that laughing?" I asked Dr. Fischer in session.

"No," she said.

"Do you hear those people yelling 'To Die!'?" I asked Dr. Doller when I met her on the hall.

"No," she said.

Over and over Dr. Fischer and Dr. Doller told me the same things that Dr. Rockland had said: The Voices were only my own thoughts. The difference was that now I was more ready to hear them. I trusted Dr. Fischer and Dr. Doller. Why would they fool me? Of course I never quite believed them completely. The Voices were too real. But at least I became willing to consider the possibility.

And as I became willing to consider the possibility, I began to be able to see—faintly at first—that the Voices had real emotions behind them. Once I began to be able to tell my doctors what the Voices were saying about them, they began to help me look more closely at what the Voices were saying and why. I would tell Dr. Fischer that the Voices were telling me to strangle her.

"Is it possible that you are feeling angry with me?" she would say. And slowly, gradually, I would begin to be able to realize that I had been angry because she had been late to session, or jealous because I had seen her talking to another patient.

If I couldn't make the Voices go away, then at least I could get to the powerful emotions that were underneath, Dr. Fischer and

Dr. Doller said. So I practiced letting out that anger in different ways, hoping to funnel off some of the fuel that fed the Voices. With the two doctors tutoring me, I tried to learn to identify my anger and express it in words before it turned into a full-blown crisis of Voices.

Sometimes that had led to some strange triumphs. I wrote in my journal:

> *I made progress today. I called Dr. Doller an asshole behind her back and not in the Voices' words. In other words, I got angry on my own.*

As time went on, I tried hard not only to understand, but to make myself understood. I tried to explain as clearly as possible to Dr. Doller about the compartments in my brain. When all the individual compartments were closed, I was safe. When one or more compartment drawers were open even slightly, evil would seep out of one of them and villainous thoughts out of another. Pretty soon my mind would be a mess, everything scrambled together like broken sunny-side up eggs. The chaos of the evil seeping from the compartments would be just too overwhelming for me to bear.

I also made up a system to help Dr. Doller judge the strength of the Voices tormenting me. It was so hard for the doctors to tap into my brain and understand how bad I was feeling. So I came up with a 0 to 3 rating scale. Three was so consumed by Voices that I was overwhelmed. Zero—which hardly ever happened—meant no Voices at all.

Dr. Doller and I would be sitting down on one of the halls on the unit and she would ask me how the Voices were.

"Well, Doc, I'd give it a one." That meant I was feeling relatively okay. When, later in the day, I would report to her that the Voices were climbing into the 2 plus range, and I was beginning to panic and feel suicidal, she would remind me that only a few hours earlier I had been feeling much better, and that I would feel better again.

I even mastered the Quiet Room.

The last time I was in the hospital the Quiet Room had been

such a frightening, terrifying place. Every time I had been sent
there it had seemed like punishment for misbehaving. This time
everyone talked to me over and over again. The Quiet Room isn't
a place for punishment, they said, and it isn't the enemy. If you
can go there on your own you can calm yourself down.

How could I believe them? I had seldom gone there without
being carried. Often I had been in there out of control and screaming until I was dragged out into a cold wet pack. Go to the Quiet
Room voluntarily? Now who was crazy?

But still, they persisted with their almost monotonous chant.
Come for help before you are out of control. Ask for medication.
Use the Quiet Room. Work with us, they said. Work with us.
Gradually I became able to listen to them.

The first time I tried walking into the Quiet Room on my own,
I was trembling. This was it. This was what I had been taught to
do. I could feel the rage and pain building up inside me. "Don't
go! Don't go!" the Voices screamed. "You'll die there! You'll die
there!" they cried. I paused. Was I going to listen to the staff or
the Voices?

Suddenly, I decided. Fuck the Voices. I was going in. At first
it seemed like a whirlwind. There was so much stimulation in my
brain all at once, it seemed I was breaking apart in all different
directions. There were Voices, sights, thoughts, feelings. I wanted
to scream but nothing came out. My heart was out of control in
my body and my hands were shaking. I couldn't swallow. I
couldn't breathe. Too much was happening.

Finally out of mental exhaustion I collapsed. But I relaxed. The
more times I marched myself into the Quiet Room the easier it
was. The Quiet Room became a place to chill out and deescalate,
rather than to be punished. Finally, the Quiet Room really became
quiet.

Nearly everyone agreed I had made real progress. But progress
at what cost? Simply keeping the symptoms in check was sapping
all my energy and exhausting me. And the Voices were still always
with me. Their pummeling talk of hellfire and punishment was
my constant companion. In addition, their crazy crooning had
taken on a sensual, voluptuous quality: "Talk to us, darling little
cunt," they whispered. "Talk to us."

Sounds echoed through my head like thunder. There was a hailstorm in my brain, with tornado winds knocking down telephone poles and trees. I heard bomber planes overhead and braced myself against their destructive roar. I was overwhelmed by every sound I heard around me. I couldn't tune out any noise; each one pounded my brain with equal intensity. Traffic. The wind. Water flowing down a sink's drain. Birds. Windows opening or closing. They all rattled in my head like artillery fire.

But the worst torment these days was not the things I heard, but rather the things I saw. I saw fire, lightning, colored bolts of light. I saw people hanging in the window, and body parts hanging from the trees. I saw fire around people and walls and faces. Sometimes I felt I had projector eyeballs, shooting things and shapes and colors straight ahead of me. Sometimes I saw things as if they were movies floating before my eyes. Sometimes I saw things that looked as real as my bed or my lamp or my tennis shoes.

I couldn't sleep at night because of the creatures in my bed. I sat at my desk writing in my journal one night because I was afraid to go near my bed. "There are four of them sitting on the bed," I wrote.

Usually I saw creatures with faces that were like the scariest Halloween mask ever made or creatures with big blubbery, hairy, slippery green faces. But sometimes I saw people I recognized. I saw the face of my parents' friend Dr. Arnie Maerov melt into a caricature. Why him? Was it simply because he was a psychiatrist, or because he was a friend of my parents? I saw my seventh-grade science teacher, Fred Zaltas. I had had a crush on him when I was thirteen, but I hadn't thought of him in ten years.

I saw my childhood Jerry Mahoney doll. Jerry was like my pal. I played with him, acted out fantasy conversations with him as if we were really friends. We entertained people as I had back in another life so many years ago. We made people laugh. And then he too melted like syrupy wax into a gruesome ghastly figurine, almost like a three-dimensional mind puddle.

And then I saw Charles Manson, staring at me from the walls of my room just as he had once stared at me from the front page of the newspaper back in California when I was a child. He penetrated my entire mind and body with his fierce and frenzied

eyes. Patients in the hospital mocked other patients who seemed
to have a psychotic stare. But no patient that I had ever met had
about him the look that Charles Manson did. His eyes were stilet-
tos piercing through my soul. I couldn't escape his gaze. Every
time I tried to look away he commanded my eyes to stay fixed on
his. I was unable to break his psychotic stare.

I screamed in terror. The staff on the unit came running to
my rescue. I couldn't do this alone. My fists had already begun
pummeling against the wall. I heard sick laughter coming from
everywhere, and realized it was me. The nurse in charge gave me
a pill to swallow. I was out of control. I knocked the cup to the
floor. Time meant nothing. Suddenly I was being held down on
the Quiet Room mattress and given an injection to make the faces
go away. I drifted into sleep and when I awoke Charles Manson
was gone.

I had come to believe that my Voices were just a part of me.
But I still had a terrible time distinguishing them from reality.

On one freezing night in January, I heard a baby crying outside
in the courtyard. It was sobbing away, and wouldn't be still. The
more I heard it, the more upset I became. I went to the nursing
station.

"There's a baby outside," I said frantically. "We've got to go
save it."

The nurse on duty was sympathetic. We went to the window
where I heard the sounds.

"I don't hear anything, Lori. I don't see anything out there
either. You're hearing things, Lori. It's not real."

I got more and more agitated. "It's a baby out there. I can hear
it. Why can't you hear it?" I demanded to be taken outdoors to
look, but the staff refused. It was too dark and cold out there,
they said.

Too cold? Couldn't they understand? That was just the point.
It was ten degrees outside. How could they leave a crying baby
out there in the snow? I decided to take matters into my own
hands. There were pay phones on the units that patients could use
to call home or their friends. I called the police instead. I insisted
they come and investigate the crying baby.

When he heard where I was calling from, the officer on the phone grew skeptical.

"Are you staff or are you a patient?" he asked.

"I'm a patient," I said. "But I'm not one of the crazy patients. I'm completely sane, and I hear a baby crying, and you'd better get down here before it's too late."

He asked to speak to the nurse in charge, who explained that I was hallucinating. When she hung up, she turned to me.

"Lori, there's no baby out there, but if it will make you feel better, we'll get hospital security to come and check around for you."

Of course no one found anything out of the ordinary.

Despite all the progress I had made, how could I go out and live in the world when I couldn't tell what was real from what was not real? How could I face the world locked in a mind that had a life of its own?

What's more, even my body was not my own. For under the influence of the medications I had gone from porky to really obese. At five foot three, I weighed nearly 170 pounds. I felt like a beached whale when my weight had swelled to 130 pounds from my customary 115. At 150 pounds I looked like one. At 170 pounds I refused to peer into the mirror for fear that this blob would look back at me.

I tried to lose weight by starving myself. I didn't eat solid food, and kept myself full by chugging down Diet Cokes. Every Wednesday morning, weigh-in day, I dressed in the lightest clothes I could find and presented myself without shoes on.

But somehow I never lost weight. When I zipped up my jeans, I broke the zipper. My blouses gapped. The sweat suits my mother brought me to wear in lieu of real clothes were great in the winter, but in summer I sweated to death in them. In a family—and a world—that valued thinness and saw fat as a failure of will, how could I explain that the medications had taken over my body the way the Voices had taken over my brain? How could I walk around with this sign of my illness stamped on every line of my body?

How could I go out and live in the world when I had no life?

I knew that in conferences they were talking about halfway

houses for me, ones like Futura House, where I could live under supervision. But increasingly I heard talk of a state hospital. I knew New York Hospital wouldn't keep me forever. My worst fears looked like they were about to come true. The state hospital that everyone had threatened me with when I was "bad" was now looking more and more like a possibility, even though I had done my best to be good.

I couldn't live in a state hospital. I knew if that was my only alternative that sooner or later I would kill myself. For real this time. Others seemed to sense it too. One evening, when I was talking to Sorin about killing myself, he grew very serious.

"If you decide you have to kill yourself," he said, "in the last second before you act, picture my face. Listen to me giving you one last plea not to do it. And know that someone really cares."

> *1-21-89, Sat., 8:25 P.M.—I can't tell from which direction the sounds are coming from. It's eerie, real spooked out, and scary—threatening. I've got to get better already. I need new medication or something. I've got to come up with a prayer for me so I, too, can have a miracle.*

There was only slight hope left.

It was a new medication. I had heard buzzing about it in the hospital for months. It had been used in Europe, but it wasn't yet available in the United States. Two patients in New York Hospital were being offered the drug on an experimental basis. I wanted it too.

I hadn't had much luck with medication so far. I had been on nearly every antipsychotic medication and nearly every antidepressant and nothing seemed to work.

I took pills for psychotic symptoms, pills for mood swings and pills for anxiety. Because nothing had ever really given me long-term relief, the doctors were constantly trying me on something new. I went from one antipsychotic medication to another. Navane. Stelazine. Mellaril. Moban. Haldol. Nothing. Nothing. Nothing.

The same went for the antidepressants. When lithium didn't seem to be effective enough against my depression and my manic highs, the doctors tried attacking the depression alone. They tried

MAO inhibitors. When the MAO inhibitors didn't work they tried tricyclic antidepressants. When the tricyclic antidepressants didn't work, they went back to lithium and tried increasing the doses.

Was the problem the dosage? Raise the dose. Lower the dose. Was it the combination of drugs? Try Prolixin with lithium. Try Thorazine with one of the MAO inhibitors. Maybe one combination or one dose would do the trick. Try Mellaril for psychosis and Xanax for anxiety.

And then there were the minor tranquilizers, dispensed as needed to blunt the anxiety attacks that caused my throat to close, my chest to cave in and my heart to pound so that I couldn't hear myself think. Valium, Xanax, Ativan, Klonopin . . . they all took the edge off, but they were addictive, and so had to be changed all the time.

I knew these medications mainly by their side effects. Some antipsychotic medications made me drowsy. Some blurred my vision. When I took Thorazine I felt like a zombie. My face looked like the frozen mask of someone who had been dead for weeks. I shuffled down the halls and my mind was a shadowy cloud. I was constipated and had terrible trouble with urinary retention. It gave me an appetite like a lumberjack and caused me to gain weight like crazy. My mouth was so dry that my lips would get stuck on my gums. Haldol didn't help the symptoms, and the side effects were horrible and scary. The intense, uncontrollable backward muscle tightening made me feel like my head was being screwed off—like Popeye when Bluto socked him.

Lithium, a mood stabilizer, mellowed out my highs and woke me up out of my depression. It also enlarged my thyroid gland, made me feel thirsty and nauseated and gave me diarrhea. Because lithium was potentially toxic, my blood was drawn as often as three times a week in the hospital to make sure I wasn't being given too much.

The horrible and frustrating thing was that each time my medication was changed, I did feel some relief. For a few days, sometimes even for weeks or months, the Voices would begin to abate. I would begin to feel calmer. My sessions with Dr. Doller and Dr. Fischer would be more productive, and my ability to relate to them would improve. My journal notations would change character too, and optimistic feelings would creep into my private screams of despair. For a short time I would believe Dr. Doller's messages of hope.

And then it would all come crashing down on me again. Had the drug worked briefly before my body got used to it? Had I simply wanted so badly for some medication to relieve my pain that I had willed it to be so?

I didn't know the answer. All I knew was that each time it happened my despair intensified. I felt I was getting worse and worse with each trial of new medication. I felt like a tree being cut down. The more the doctors and medications hacked away at me, the closer I was to falling.

This new medication sounded different. I heard talk that it was helping people that no other medicine had helped before. Some of the things I heard sounded scary too. Some people had died taking it. Here in New York Hospital, one patient had flipped out big-time while preparing to go on this new drug. As part of the preparation, he had had to be taken off all medication for two weeks. Without his usual medication, his psychoses had run wild and he had spent days and days in the Quiet Room.

I didn't care. I had tried everything else. Nothing had worked. If there was a new drug, and someone was being given it, I wanted to be given it too. I didn't see what I had to lose.

I told Dr. Doller I wanted to be started on clozapine.

25

◦══▶·◀══◦

Dr. Jane Doller
New York Hospital, White Plains, New York, January 1989

When Lori asked to be started on clozapine, I had to think about it really carefully. I wasn't sure that it was a good idea. The drug was just becoming available to us on an experimental basis. It was possible that it could offer Lori some relief from the voices and other hallucinations that were tormenting her. It was also possible that it could kill her.

Was the drug worth the risk? I thought back over our work together. When Lori first arrived on the unit two years earlier, I was young. I was single. I loved my work. So I was often on the unit late into the night, chatting with my patients or simply hanging around the nursing station.

One winter evening I was just walking out after a long day, when I passed the unit dining room. Mealtime was long over, and the room should have been empty. But there was Lori, all by herself, pacing around and looking uncomfortable. Some instinct made me stop.

"What's wrong, Lori?" I asked.

"My father's out of town. He's in Chicago," Lori answered.

I waited. That fact in itself didn't seem particularly upsetting to me.

"It's snowing," she continued. It was, indeed, a very bad day, all stormy and blowing. "I'm worried about him."

231

plane will be delayed," I suggested.

began to cry. "His plane is going to crash. It's going to happen because I am going to make it happen. I am going to make it happen because I want it to happen."

It was heartwrenching. She was suffering so. Here was something I could relate to easily. There was nothing bizarre about what she was feeling. She was worried about her father. What's more, she was angry with him, angry because he was away, angry because he wasn't there to visit her, angry because she was worried about him.

In thinking about that she began—as many people do—turning her feelings into fantasies of horrible disasters. And because she was fantasizing disaster, she began to believe she was creating it. It's a very primitive fear, this fear of the power of our own thoughts. It's one of the reasons many cultures have superstitious prohibitions against saying things out loud. Locked away in her own world, Lori just didn't have any way of putting her thoughts and emotions in perspective. This was something I could help her with.

"Of course you're worried," I said. "It's a bad night, and you love your father and you want him to get home safely. You are worried about him, but you are also angry with him."

"I'm not angry with him," she retorted.

"Sure you are," I said. "You have to remember that it's normal to feel angry, but that your thoughts can't harm anyone. Your worry and your anger aren't going to make the plane crash. You don't have that power. But you do have the power to influence the direction of your thoughts. You are saying that you are worried, but it is your own thoughts taking you in the direction of thinking about plane crashes. You can take your thoughts in some other direction if you want."

Then I took her out of the room, out onto the unit, and pulled one of the nurses aside and told her what I had told Lori, so that she could reinforce the message. "Can you spend some time with her, talk to her a little bit for a while."

That was the kind of incident that might have escalated. If I hadn't been walking by, she would have eventually become so tormented inside she would have thrown something or broken something. But it was also something that was pretty easily defused.

As for Lori, she was immensely relieved. I hadn't done much at all, but what I had done had taken away a tremendous amount of suffering from her. She felt like I had done something magical. Simply being able to name and to recognize her feelings had helped her immensely. Something like that happening early on really helped our relationship. She began to believe that I could help her. What's more, I believed I could help her too.

Over the two years she had been with us, I believed we had helped her. I thought over what we had accomplished. She had significantly more insight, and considerably more control over herself. I felt I had developed a relationship with her that was in itself a good thing. It was healthy and sustaining and supportive. I was proud of that, proud of what my own efforts had accomplished.

None of us on the unit wanted to give up on her. We all felt she was someone worth fighting for. When the craziness cleared, she was such an engaging and likable person, witty, thoughtful and fun. And she worked so hard on her own behalf. I had seldom seen someone work as hard as Lori did. She was driven to get well, and used her energy to put into practice every technique we all suggested for her.

But I was constantly faced with the fact that what I was doing wasn't enough. It was all well and good that Lori trusted me, but she was still having psychotic episodes and destructive impulses. She took up a lot of staff time, with meeting after meeting after meeting to discuss what we were going to do with Lori. It was also hard to ignore the fact that she was still in great pain.

A long time ago I realized that, as psychiatrists, we had to have a healthy respect for our own humanness, and our own smallness in the face of what we were dealing with. If a person got better, we could appreciate that we had done a good job, but we also needed to realize that God—or luck—was on our side. If the person got worse and had to go to a state hospital, we had to keep ourselves from feeling that we hadn't done enough. For the truth is, we were powerless in so many of these situations. We did what we could, but sometimes the illness was just bigger than we were.

The feeling at New York Hospital was that because of clozapine's dangers, the drug should be given only to hopeless cases. I wanted to do whatever I could to help Lori. But could I face the fact that there really was no other hope left for her?

A lot of people thought Lori was already a hopeless case back when she came to our unit two years ago. I didn't believe it, though. It wasn't that she wasn't desperately ill. She was. In fact, coming to our unit in itself was like being branded a hopeless wreck. Our unit only took the very sickest patients, the problem patients. We took only the patients everyone else had given up hope on.

And we had a fair amount of success with them. I had some former patients who were living on their own, some living in halfway houses, even a couple who were managing to hold down full-time jobs. We hadn't cured them; these were people for whom no cure seemed possible. What we had done was to help them live more comfortably and function more effectively with the illness that they were probably going to have for the rest of their lives.

That's what I hoped to do for Lori.

Her records hadn't looked promising: Several long hospitalizations. Persistent out-of-control behavior. Suicide attempts. Still, her history looked quite similar to those of other patients on our unit: The normal childhood, followed by a break in her teens. The early inability of her family and of Lori herself to accept the fact that she was seriously ill. The early reluctance of doctors to brand Lori with a diagnosis of schizophrenia, preferring instead to suggest that other illnesses like manic-depression might be responsible.

Then came a middle period when her behavior became more erratic and doctors began considering the possibility that Lori might be suffering from a personality disorder. Her behavior— throwing things, breaking things, and running away—was seen as deliberate and manipulative. It was felt that strong discipline and control were the key.

And then finally, as her illness progressed, she arrived at our doorstep clearly in the grip of severe psychosis. There was no longer much doubt in anyone's mind: In addition to her manic-depression, Lori clearly had full-blown schizophrenia: She was openly psychotic, paranoid and hostile. Her thoughts were disordered; her concentration and her mental ability were impaired.

Looking over the chart, I could see how much effort had been expended on her. Everything that anyone had known how to do they had done, from shock treatments to talk therapy. Practically every known drug had been tried. No effort had been spared, and nothing had worked. No wonder people were on the verge of giving up hope.

Her history didn't scare us here on the long-term unit, though. We didn't see patients like Lori as hopeless. We saw them as a challenge. We felt that we were a different unit, we were a special unit. Part of the esprit of our long-term unit was that we could do things nobody else could do. Just because nothing had worked didn't mean nothing could work. We could take people like Lori whom everyone else had given up on and help make them better.

We didn't believe that medicine was the key. Of course we still kept trying everything in our power to find a drug or combination of drugs that would make sense. Drugs could and did alleviate psychotic symptoms in about two thirds of all schizophrenic patients. But most of the patients who came to us had arrived on a long-term unit precisely because medication hadn't worked. Like Lori, these patients had already been subjected to a bewildering variety of drugs, none of which seemed to do much for them in the long run.

Instead, we concentrated our efforts on getting inside the heads of our patients. Many other treatments focused on using medication to alleviate the psychotic symptoms. These treatments were considered a failure if the patient was still hallucinating. We felt otherwise. We felt that, hallucinations or not, there was a person inside there—and that we could reach that person if we tried.

We spent a lot of time on the unit talking about how to reach our patients. It took a talent, a certain chemistry between two people—and it wasn't always the doctors who had it. Sometimes it was the nurses. Sometimes it was someone completely unexpected like a volunteer, or a cook. It was very much our sense that we could create a bond between our patients and someone who could be their bridge from inside their craziness back to the outside world.

My desire to put my beliefs in this kind of treatment into practice was one of the reasons I chose to come to New York Hospital in the first place. It was one of the few hospitals that had a long-term unit that used these kinds of techniques.

I hadn't always wanted to be a psychiatrist. I had come to psychiatry by a roundabout route. In college I had been an artsy type, interested in cinema, literature and poetry. I saw them all as opening windows into the hidden side of people. In college, too, I had been fascinated with the literature of psychosis. One book in particular, called *Two Accounts of a Journey Through Madness*, intrigued me with its description of a patient's attempts to understand her own illness.

It wasn't until my third year of medical school, though, when we began rotating through different specialties, that I noticed a difference between myself and my classmates. They either liked to run around and do research, or treat sick people. What I liked to do was talk to the people I was treating. I wanted to know what they felt like, what their illness was like for them, and what it was like for them to be in the hospital. I also found out then that people responded well to me. They seemed to want to talk to me.

I decided to become a psychiatrist. And when I arrived at New York Hospital, I asked to be assigned to the long-term unit. I liked the idea of being somewhere where patients were given the time to work through and understand their own illnesses.

My emphasis on psychology, though, didn't mean I was going back to the old days of blaming schizophrenia on flawed parenting—the old model of the schizophrenogenic mother. We weren't looking for a psychological cause of the illness. None of us disputed the biological cause of schizophrenia. We were, instead, looking to understand the *experience* of schizophrenia, and to try to help our patients learn to tolerate that experience better.

I felt that it was one thing to talk about impaired dopamine pathways, or atrophied frontal lobes—explanations that make up the scientific underpinnings of what we know or surmise about the causes of schizophrenia. It was quite another to understand just what it was like to live with a broken brain. For that is what the experience of schizophrenia is like. A person is walking calmly through a normal life when suddenly and without warning, something terrible occurs, something she has no words to explain. Something actually does break inside the brain.

What is there in any human being's experience to prepare him or her to cope with a broken brain? Who can understand what a catastrophe this break is for the human soul? For the thing that has broken is the person's ability to relate to another person. The thing that breaks is whatever it is that connects people to their environment, that allows them to recognize another person as someone outside of themselves.

It is hard for any of us who have not experienced it to understand the internal desolation such a break must cause. It must be worse than the worst experience of solitary confinement. People with schizophrenia are locked out of the outside world, and locked inside their heads with nothing but these wild, out-of-control thoughts banging about inside. For what has also broken is the brain's ability to process emotion and thoughts. In people with schizophrenia the normal emotions—that we all every day categorize, process and either accept into our consciousness or push back into the recesses of our minds—run amok. Emotions that would normally be comfortably catalogued as unacceptable take on a life of their own as voices that seem more real than the real world outside.

We felt that by trying to understand what patients were feeling, we could help them to understand too. And by helping them to understand, we could help them feel less overpowered and less terrified by their symptoms. We could help them understand what had happened to them, and we could help them learn to manage their condition.

Take Lori's out-of-control behavior. Her record suggested that earlier doctors had believed she was breaking things, smashing walls and running away on purpose. They believed her behavior was under her control. They believed she was manipulative, attention-getting, and locked in a power struggle with staff that could be handled only through strict discipline.

I chose to believe otherwise. I saw her behavior as an understandable—if troublesome—response to her scary inner world. As I observed her, I could see how she would get. If we were around as she was accelerating into an out-of-control incident, we could see it happening. As she spiraled out of control, we could talk to her. We could say, "Lori, get away from that window." But she couldn't hear. I could see the look of terror, the trembling. This woman wasn't playing mind games. This woman was in genuine distress.

And how would she have any idea how to handle that distress without being taught?

I saw the job of the long-term unit as teaching her to recognize her symptoms as phenomena, and to seek help immediately from those around her before they became too much for her to bear.

First though, we had to help her develop relationships with people around her.

People with schizophrenia are filled with an essential longing. They have a longing to explain what is happening to themselves. And they have a longing for a connection, for some relationship that will give them a pathway back toward the world they have lost.

It is precisely this kind of relationship, though, that Lori, and people like her, found most scary and difficult to accept. Because they have difficulty distinguishing what is "me" from what is "not me," anyone who comes too close threatens the very core of their beings. They run from the love and care of their family; they distance themselves from the rest of the world. It isn't unusual to find people with schizophrenia who have almost no romantic or sexual experience. If your ego is a fragile thing, and you are afraid of being disrupted, or being invaded, then the idea of an intimate relationship is very frightening.

That's why Diane Fischer's relationship with Lori was so stormy. As Lori's therapist, it was Diane's job to get into the deepest recesses of her mind—which was a place Lori was afraid for her to go. Lori knew that Diane was trying to get inside her head, to probe her darkest, most secret feelings. That terrified her. She was constantly running away from Diane, or firing her, leaving messages in her box that she didn't want her to be her therapist anymore. Behind her flight were her own fears that Diane would reject her first.

My relationship with Lori, on the other hand, could be far more relaxed. I handled her medications, her passes, her statuses. Our interactions could be much more casual and informal. I was always available to chat.

What I did with Lori wasn't therapy. The therapist's job wasn't to say, "Oh, everyone feels that way." The therapist's job was to say: "What does this mean to you? What do you feel about it?" But by saying to Lori, "Don't worry about it, we're going to make everything all right," I was also building a therapeutic relationship.

Because her relationship with me was so concrete, we could break through her reluctance to let anyone know what was going on in her mind. She could say to me, "I'm afraid to tell you, I'm afraid to tell you," and I would say, "Oh Lori, how bad could it be?" Each time she broke through the reluctance it got a little easier, and a sense of trust began to grow.

Eventually, she began to show me some of her journal entries. When it came to the one about the voices wanting to kill me, I was worried. I wasn't worried because I was afraid Lori was actually going to kill me. I was worried because I could tell from her voices' comments that Lori herself was really beginning to believe in me. She thought I was powerful enough to get rid of the voices, and she was using the voices to let me know that.

I was worried because I was afraid I was going to let her down. I knew I could help her, but I knew that relief and control were all that my help could offer her—not an end to the voices. I could teach her to live with the voices, but I couldn't make them go away. I didn't think there was anything that could do that. That needed stronger medicine than I was able to offer. I didn't think there was a medicine in the universe that could do that.

And then came clozapine.

By early 1989, clozapine had become a big deal on our unit. Clozapine was the first entirely new antipsychotic drug to be introduced since Thorazine in the 1950s. We knew that the drug helped people who hadn't been helped before by medications. We just didn't know which people it would help, or why.

What we did know was that clozapine was a dangerous drug. While it had been used in Europe and experimentally in the United

States for years, it hadn't yet been approved for general use here. We had just gotten access to clozapine under a compassionate-use protocol. It wasn't as rigorous as a research program, but the drug's use had to be carefully monitored. Sandoz, the manufacturer of the drug, was collecting data to present to the Food and Drug Administration as part of its application to market the drug in the United States.

The protocol we were to use in dispensing the drug on an experimental basis was complex and a little bit scary. That's because a number of patients in Europe had died from complications caused by the drug. In some cases, clozapine caused a condition called agranulocytosis, a suppression of the white blood cells that was potentially fatal. Before we picked the patients to start on clozapine, we all went to seminars to discuss the drug, the paperwork that would have to be done, the consent forms and who would have to sign them, the rigorous blood testing and monitoring that would be required, and the process of stopping the patient's existing medications and switching them to clozapine.

During the seminars we learned that one in three people would do better on clozapine than on other antipsychotic drugs. Those people who suffered from the most severe types of side effects of antipsychotics—the stiff and twitching limbs—would also get relief from those symptoms. No one was claiming to us that clozapine was a miracle drug. At the same time, they were emphasizing its dangers: About one in one hundred people who took it risked dying from it.

We hesitated. At first we weren't sure who to offer it to. One obvious case was a woman on our unit who suffered badly from side effects. But I wasn't sure about giving it to Lori. No one was promising that it would definitely help people like her, and I hesitated to risk her life on a bet.

In psychiatry there have over the years been many new drugs that have been touted, but which in the end proved to be not much different from the old ones. So I was always skeptical.

Still, by the time the first person had been on clozapine for about a month, I was convinced that it was worth a try for Lori. We had begun to see dramatic results with this other woman.

From a stiff, withdrawn, catatonic person, she had become more open, conversational and insightful. Lori was desperate to start a new medication, any new medication, and I agreed to go along. All we needed to do was get her parents' consent.

26

Nancy Schiller
Scarsdale, New York, February 1989

The longer Lori was in the hospital, the harder I found it to visit her there.

As soon as our car pulled in through the front gate, I would begin: "I'm not going in, Marvin. I'm going to stay in the car." Marvin was stolid.

"You're going in," was all he said. He realized, I think, how badly I needed to vent my anxieties.

"I'm not going in, Marvin. I just can't take it anymore."

When we pulled into a visitor's parking spot, and Marvin turned the engine off, I would sit crying in the cold, dark car. Over and over I sobbed that I was not going in, that I couldn't go in. Marvin didn't say much. He just kept repeating that I was going in, until finally some of my tensions and fears dissipated. I dried my eyes and reached for the car door.

As I walked from the car to the hospital, I kept repeating to Marvin over and over again that I couldn't go through the door. On the landing I said I wasn't going up another floor. Outside the locked door of her unit, I said I was turning back.

I was so tense that the littlest thing irritated me. The wait outside the door for someone to let us in seemed interminable. When the door finally opened, I resented the routine they put us through. We felt like two dummies standing there while they searched through my purse and the bags we brought looking for dangerous materials.

"I know all this already," I wanted to shout. I knew not to bring in anything glass, or any plastic bags, or wire hangers, or anything made of sharp metal. Especially when the staff member was new, I just wanted to scream: "I've been doing this for years, don't you understand. Years. I know all this better than you do."

Once we were inside, the visit itself was so painful for all of us.

Sometimes Lori would seem almost well, and it would be the most eerie and frustrating thing. She could carry on a conversation. She seemed like she was with us. Those days, Marvin and I would leave, half seriously discussing with each other the possibility that she was right, perhaps she did not belong here.

But in some ways, those near-well days were the most frustrating for us. She looked so normal that we kept forgetting she was not. When she told us how she had hit a screen, or knocked over furniture, we would yell at her to express our frustration. When we looked at her hands and realized she had been punching things or destroying things, we would yell at her as we would have yelled at our normal daughter.

"How can you do this to yourself?" I shouted at her, when she told me she had refused her medication again. "You're sabotaging yourself. How can you do this after everything you've been through?" I was furious, and let her know it.

Then the very next time, she would be hallucinating and out of it, and I would be filled with such guilt and sorrow. She looked right through us, listening to some inner cacophony. I would grab her face in my hands and pull her right up to mine.

"Look at me, Lori!" I shouted, "listen to me." But on her face would be the look, the same look that I had seen on my mother's face—the same look we had been seeing on Lori's face all these many years. Would it never go away?

When she herself became angry and enraged I tried to tell myself that she was ill, that it was her illness talking and not my Lori. But when her fury began to spill out of bounds and we had to leave, it cut to my heart. I had to slink out through the unit, with the screams of my daughter shouting "I hate you! I hate you!" following me out into the stairwell.

Coming to visit Lori was hard, but leaving was harder. As Marvin and I walked down to the car we would look up, and there she would be, her white face looking down at us from behind the safety screen. And I would drive down the long drive, crying as I had come, leaving her there locked up behind me.

What was to happen to Lori?

We had grown more and more pessimistic. The roller-coaster ride of dashed hopes over the past few years had been so hard to bear. Every time they tried some new medicine or some new technique, we would see a brief period of improvement. Maybe this was it, we thought. Maybe she's getting better. But every time her body would seem to adapt to the change, and her illness would come crashing back, sometimes even harder than before.

What made it worse was that, unlike earlier in her illness, this time we really felt that Lori was getting the best possible care. Lori was connecting to Dr. Doller and Dr. Fischer as she had never connected with anyone before. What's more, we could see that everyone genuinely cared about her. There seemed to be a real partnership there. When we visited, Rose, one of the mental health workers, would say: "We know how you care about her and we care too."

"Lori is such an unusual girl," Sorin would pull me aside to say. "She has such fighting spirit. She is going to get well. We can't let her down." Yet more and more I felt that we had let her down. She was getting tired and discouraged, I could see that. We were getting tired and discouraged. These days when people we didn't know well asked us about Lori, I was simply evasive. "She's trying to find herself," I said. "You know how they are at that age." We weren't trying to hide it anymore, it was just that we couldn't face talking about it more than we had to.

By the time the social worker called Marvin and me in for a joint meeting with Lori and Dr. Doller, we knew that Lori was near the end of the line. We knew they had kept Lori in the hospital longer than they were really supposed to. They had bent rules and cut corners because they were really convinced they could help her.

And they had helped her. She was better, but still not well enough to live alone. We all needed to talk about what she was going to do next. She couldn't come home, that was certain. Dr. Doller and the social worker, both recommended against that. They felt that at home she would drop back into passivity and dependency and never make any further progress toward being her own person.

Marvin and I agreed. What's more, I knew that for my own sake I couldn't have her at home. I remembered the two and a half years she lived at home after her first hospitalization as the most stressful, awful time I have ever lived through. I was always walking on eggshells, always afraid I was going to do something or say something that would set her off. Should we take her out for dinner? Should we let her stay in her room? She was trying so hard to please us, nothing was normal or natural.

I never slept well. I got up every night to see if she was still breathing. I would come home in the evening to find the garage doors closed and I'd be afraid to open them. What would I find inside? I never was sure when it would be for real.

All along the staff at the hospital had been encouraging Lori to enter a halfway house and to join a day program at the hospital. I knew Lori would never do it. She had been there before. She had seen people locked in what seemed to be unending cycles, in and out of hospitals and halfway houses. She didn't want that kind of a life. "I'm not going to keep going through the revolving door," she said.

So what were our other options?

We could send her to a state hospital, they suggested, adding hopefully that some of them weren't all that bad. Marvin and I just stared. Or we could send her to a nice custodial facility. There was one, a farm in New Hampshire . . .

So we were supposed to send Lori away to graze like cattle? I remembered the very first doctor we had dealt with, way back at Payne Whitney, who suggested that we put her away immediately. Was this what it had come to after all these years?

They said she had improved. They said she was better. But they hadn't known Lori when she was well. I looked at Lori. She weighed 170 pounds. She was enormous. She was unkempt. Her expression was flat and her eyes were glazed. She bore no resemblance at all to the real Lori. Cousin Sylvia flashed into my mind.

"My God," I thought. "She'll be sitting on a park bench feeding pigeons."

It was unthinkable. We had to consider not just where to put Lori, but of how Lori herself would live. For I knew that Lori would not accept for long the bare existence that was her life now, and that these suggestions were offering her.

I could already feel how frantic she was becoming watching her life slip away from her. The reminders were everywhere. I felt them myself. Every time I saw an announcement of one of her classmates' weddings, I felt sad for what she was missing: Why had this happened to Lori? I thought. When her university held its reunions and annual alumni dinners, I answered for her. "She won't be able to attend. She's out of the country," I lied. From time to time one of the men she had dated during her first time out of the hospital would call looking for her. "She's not here," I simply said, and wondered when or if she ever would be.

When we talked about it with her when she was home on leave, she seemed depressed and pessimistic. "I don't have a job. I don't have a boyfriend. I don't have any friends," she said. Every so often when she was out on leave she would hear about one of her friends from the hospital, or from the halfway house who had killed herself. I knew she was thinking about herself.

When Dr. Doller and the social worker explained the possibility of trying the new medicine clozapine on Lori, they seemed pessimistic. They said it had dangerous side effects. They told us it could kill her. They gave us reprints from scientific journals. Marvin looked them over. It appeared that it was the very sickest patients who got the most benefit from clozapine. There were examples given of near catatonic patients who had responded to the drug.

How many times over the past few years had I wondered why we had fought so hard to keep Lori alive. She was so miserable. She was so unhappy. She was only staying alive to please us. When she ran away and came home, I took her back.

"Why did you run, Lori?" I asked.

"Because there is no hope," she said.

I took her back. I told her there was hope. But in my heart, I thought there was none. I considered our options. I didn't want

Lori to have to live her life the way she was. Was this girl who was so achieving and bright and creative to be doomed to just existing? That was death already.

"You've tried everything else known to man and nothing has worked," I told them.

"You've got no choice but to try this drug," Marvin chimed in. "If it kills her—well, maybe she's better off dead."

When I heard what we had said, I was horrified. How could any parents say that about their child? But I thought about it and realized we meant it. If this drug didn't work, then maybe she really was better off dead.

27

Lori
New York Hospital,
White Plains, New York,
March 15, 1989–November 6, 1989

The first day I took clozapine, I felt like I was stoned. An obscure feeling entered my body.

I had been waiting for this for so long. This was my last hope. Was this it? Was this the cure I had been waiting for? Anxiously I watched myself. Puzzling sensations were surging through me.

I started out on a very low dose, 25 milligrams in one small yellow tablet at bedtime. As the days went by, gradually, very gradually, the dosage was increased. Twenty-five milligrams. Fifty milligrams. Two pills at bedtime. Then one in the morning and two at night. Up and up I went, 100 milligrams, 150, 200, 250 . . . all the way up to 700 milligrams.

I could barely bring myself to acknowledge any changes that might be occurring. My own emotions were warring within me. I wanted desperately for this medicine to work. I was almost willing it to do its job and free me from my tormenting Voices. Yet I was terrified at the same time. For all I knew, these pills were placebos, and the effects I was feeling were only the product of my own fierce desire to be well.

What's more, I wasn't actually sure I was feeling better. Different, maybe, but not altogether better. In fact, in a lot of ways I felt much, much worse. One of the patients who was supposed to get clozapine before me had been taken off all his other medications, and had flipped out. Dr. Doller didn't want that to happen to me, and so she got permission to start me on clozapine before I had stopped taking the Prolixin I was on. So at the same time as I was increasing my clozapine dose, I was decreasing the Prolixin. The two medications dueled in my body and gave me strange, unpleasant feelings. My chest and throat were tight. I felt like I was smothering.

My emotions too were unchained. In preparation for the clozapine, Dr. Doller had taken me off lithium, my mood stabilizer. Without its help in blunting the swings of my feelings, I plunged into a deeper depression than I had felt in a long time. I felt tearful and weepy, out of sorts and remote.

Something about my depression, my anticipation, my anxiety, my hope, my anguished fears for the future combined to overload all the restraints that Dr. Doller, Dr. Fischer and I had so painstakingly built over the years.

Some of my actions became wild, the kind of out-of-control acting out that I had renounced while working with them. As the Voices chanted, "Four stabs to the abdomen!" I tried to stab myself. I only used a plastic fork, but it made a nasty puncture wound, and got my status lowered in the bargain.

Some of my actions were whimsical, as I acted out little private jokes. When Dr. Fischer went on vacation, she gave me a handful of pennies, one for each day she would be gone to mark off the time—for me to think of her thinking of me. Instead of carefully laying them aside, each day I swallowed one. It made me feel closer to her. That got me multiple trips to the hospital medical clinic for X-rays and nasty-tasting medicines.

But slowly, behind all the depression, the conflicting medications and the outrageous behavior, the new medication was doing its work. Gradually, subtly, changes began creeping up on me. People began remarking on my changed demeanor. I was less impulsive, they said, and more thoughtful. I was looking brighter, more alive, they said. My parents said they saw beginnings of the sparkle back in my eyes again.

Even I could not ignore it. The most striking thing I felt was a new sense of calm. For the first time in years, I slept. I slept not only through the night, but for part of the next afternoon. No medication on earth had given me that feeling of relaxation before. I felt less restless too. The feeling that I was going to crawl out of my skin began to abate.

My head felt strange. It was as if it were draining out from the inside. My head had been filled with sticky stuff, like melted rubber or motor oil. Now all that sticky stuff was dripping out, leaving only my brain behind. Slowly I was beginning to think more clearly.

And the Voices? The Voices were growing softer. Were the Voices growing softer? They were growing softer! They began moving around, from outside my skull, to inside, to outside again. But their decibel level was definitely falling.

It was happening. I was being set free. I had prayed to find some peace, and my prayers were finally being answered.

April 20
I want to live.
I want to live.
I want to live.
I want to live.
I want to live.
I want to live.
I want to live.
I want to live.
I want to live.
I want to live.
I want to live.
I want to live.
I want to live.
I want to live.
I want to live.
I want to live.
I want to live.
I want to live.
I want to live.
I want to live.
I want to live.
I want to live.
I want to live.

April 26 Wednesday, 6:20 P.M.
My birthday. 30 years old. Never felt better. I'm hanging in there real tough thinking of PACE (Positive Attitude Changes Everything). I'm going to have a great, great life fulfilled with warmth and love and happiness and health, and consistent growth. HAPPY BIRTHDAY, ME.

The thing that frightened me most was the possibility that the clozapine's effects would wear off. After all, that's what had happened with each other new medication I had tried. A brief flurry of improvement, then a crash. Anxiously I waited.

My head kept clearing. Thinking was less of an effort. The scrambled-eggs unscrambled, the mixed-up spaghetti strands of thoughts unraveled. The compartments that had come unhinged, flinging their contents into a wild unruly heap in my brain, creaked shut. Thoughts presented themselves to me one at a time in more or less logical order.

When the Voices reared up and roared, it was as if they hit a glass shield, crashed and fell away. I could hear their cries and complaints. But now I was hearing them as if from far away. Their noises were muffled and remote. They were shouting, clamoring, angrily protesting their own demise. But dying they were. Clozapine was standing between them and my brain. Denied the nourishment of my thoughts, they were perishing.

Even my body kept on coming alive. Increasingly people were remarking on the way I looked. Animated, they said. Alive, they said. My face began taking on expressions other people said they had not seen in years. Emotions—subtle human emotions, like curiosity, interest, sympathy, humor—began registering again. My dad said even my walk was different. When I was sickest, I had a walk he called my zombie walk, my motionless arms at my sides, my feet shuffling down the hall. Now I was actually walking like a real person, arms swinging, head up, my body relaxed and a jauntiness in my step.

But the biggest change was in the return of something I hadn't realized was missing: I began to feel connected to other people.

For as long as I could remember, it had been the Voices who had seemed real to me. Other people had seemed far away, distant, as if they inhabited another planet. Their very presence frightened me. I felt alienated from other people, alone. I could never quite decipher other people's meaning or intent. When they intruded on my space I backed off, disturbed by their encroachments. I was suspicious or afraid of people who said they were trying to help me.

For most of my time in the hospital, I had done my very best to isolate myself from the other patients. I had spent as much time as possible at the far end of the long hall where the stereo was. I wanted to be near nothing but my music. When another patient came down the hall toward me, it was as if an enemy were invading my territory. Immediately, without even a word, I would pack up my tapes and leave the area, feeling that some peace had been taken from me.

As I got better, I began to share my stereo space more willingly. Other people ceased to feel like intruders. Something in me was growing that enabled me to reach across the air that separated us, and feel that we were all just people. I even began to be able to lend out some of my most precious possessions—my Walkman, my tapes, pretty pieces of clothing. Something in my brain was reaching outside itself, stretching away from the inner world of Voices and faces and toward the outer world of friends and family.

And gradually, I did begin to recognize other people as friends. As I got better and my status went up I was allowed to go to activities. I was offered a choice: I could go with a staff person, with an escorted group, with a fellow patient or by myself. These days I would wait for ten minutes for another patient to get ready so that we could both walk over together. I wasn't afraid to call other patients my friends.

I was even starting to take a more active role in the unit. I was elected secretary of patient government for 3 South. It wasn't a big deal. All the patient government did was handle things like plans for outings, or tie-dying T-shirts, or raising money for our activities. But to me it meant everything. Not only did it mean that I was taking on more responsibility, but it also meant something I never would have believed possible: People liked me and respected me.

I even switched roles a bit. No more running away for me. When one of my fellow patients confided in me that she planned to run, I tried to talk her out of it. When she did take advantage of an open door and tried to bolt, I ran after her, grabbed her and brought her back.

Slowly, old feelings began to unlock. My mind began to be able to distinguish myriad complex emotions where none had existed before. All the powerful feelings had always been there in my heart; it was as if there had been no spot in my brain to register them. My mind had been a slippery surface that only the most violent of emotions—fear, anger, hatred, fearsome love—could puncture. Now that rock-hard glacial surface was melting, leaving scrabbly little footholds where feelings could take hold and grow.

For years I had swung between powerful poles of emotions. I had hated Dr. Fischer. I had loved her. I feared her. I craved her. Torturing swings between two equally unacceptable poles. Only the work we had done together had kept me from being torn apart in those currents.

Now I was beginning to feel other things. My heart could feel other possibilities, and my mind could see that those other possibilities existed. I might like Dr. Fischer. I might look forward to seeing her. I might be annoyed with her. I might disagree with her. The gunk draining from my brain was unclogging whole areas of me that been petrified in poisonous resin for so long that I had forgotten they had ever existed. Our work together took on whole new possibilities.

But before we could take advantage of these possibilities, something happened. Dr. Fischer announced that she was leaving the hospital.

Leaving the hospital? All I heard was that she was leaving me. I knew she had been a postdoctoral fellow. I knew that it was her training she had been doing at New York Hospital, and that it wasn't a permanent post. But I had never realized that she would leave the hospital before I would. I had never thought of her leaving at all. She was so important to me. I needed her. How could she leave me?

We kept on meeting, kept on talking. She kept on advising me on my recovery.

"Go slow, Lori, go slow," she said. She worried that I was growing too impatient to be well, too impatient to show progress.

"We're moving at a snail's pace," I complained.

"Then move like a wounded snail," she said. "You'll only cause yourself problems if you try to move on to the next level before you've gotten used to this level."

We talked about her departure. We talked about what it meant to me. All the old feelings came flooding back. She was leaving me because I was no good. She had finally gotten sick of me, just as everyone else had gotten sick of me. She was turning her back on me because I was a loser who would never leave the hospital. We talked about my feelings about myself, about her, about being abandoned, about—eventually—being on my own.

For the most part, we managed. She tried to get me to focus on the emerging subtle feelings, rather than the powerful, terrifying ones that used to engulf me. Don't turn those feelings back onto yourself, she said. Feel them. Feel the real feelings underneath. Feel that I would miss her. Feel that I would remember her. Feel that I would feel sad that she was gone.

But the closer and closer we came to her date of departure, the harder it became to hold on to the new feelings, and the more seductive the old ones became. The old feelings and patterns were still stronger than the new. I began avoiding her, refusing to come to sessions. Dodging her when I saw her. When I did manage to come to sessions, I would sit in stony-faced silence. I knew that one day we would say goodbye and that would be it. I didn't want that day to come. I wouldn't let her leave me. I would leave her first.

The thought gave me an idea. I would kill myself in honor of her leaving. I wanted to be special to her. How better to make myself special in her memory. If I killed myself just as she was leaving, she would never be able to forget me.

Proudly I brought my idea to Dr. Doller. She looked at me with a half smile on her face, her head tilted in her quizzical, listening pose.

"Lori," she said. "No one could ever forget you—just the way you are."

And for the first time, something in me heard her, and was proud. Maybe there was another way. Maybe I could make Dr. Fischer remember me by living, not by dying. Maybe I could make her remember me by being the best patient she ever had. By taking everything she had taught me and putting it into practice.

Maybe I could make her not only remember me, but be proud of me.

Still, I faced the end of June with dread. I couldn't bear to see her go. And when, finally, we sat in her office—the office I had struggled so hard to be able even to enter—I couldn't picture never being able to come here again. She had been such a big part of my life for so long. She had come so close to me, done so much to save me. I didn't want to die for her anymore, but how could I live without her? We agreed that we would exchange letters for as long as I wanted to. Finally I could no longer hold on, and tears spilled out over my cheeks. This was it.

We walked back to the unit in silence. As we approached the door where we would finally part, she turned to me.

"Would you like a goodbye hug or a goodbye handshake?"

Before she could offer her hand I grabbed her. I gave her the biggest, most heartwarming hug I could muster. It was nothing at all like all the fantasies that had been brewing in my mind all these years. It was nothing like the kinds of hugs the torturing Voices had urged on me in sessions. It was normal. It was friendly. It was a warm, kindly, enveloping bear hug. And then she was gone.

Who would fill the place in my life that Dr. Diane Fischer had left behind? Even Dr. Doller somehow didn't seem enough. But still, where else would I turn? I was hurting so badly I had to talk with someone. Later on that afternoon I met with Dr. Doller. I cried out my pain and loss, trying to explain to her just how big a hole in my long days Dr. Fischer was leaving behind. But as I spoke I realized that while I had lost a friend, I had not lost my only friend. I looked up at Dr. Doller and saw that she had tears in her eyes too.

Gradually my daily life in the hospital changed. My room had furniture in it again. They had taken it away to reduce my stimulation. Now it was back. I could put my things in my dresser and offer a chair to my guests just like any other patient. The bodyguards were gone. No one was stationed outside my room. No one accompanied me to the bathroom. No more room-care plans, eating solitary meals on solitary trays in my solitary room.

I was getting up, getting dressed and going down to the cafeteria to eat with everyone else.

There was no discussion of my being discharged immediately. I was doing well, but no one wanted to jeopardize it by letting me go too soon. I needed to make sure my medication was at a therapeutic level before I left. I still needed other medication for my other symptoms. After I had been on clozapine for a while, Dr. Doller put me back on lithium and slowly my moods began to stabilize.

Many times I got frustrated by the slow pace. "I want to get out of here now!" I announced to Dr. Doller over and over again. "I'll go live with Steven," I announced. "I don't care if Mom and Dad are mad. I'll get a job delivering flyers in the city. I'll make it on my own." But the feeling passed. The clozapine continued its work.

I had no idea how the medication worked. Was it plugging up some hole in my brain that had let all my normal thoughts leak out? Was it going in there like a drill, drilling out some boulder, clearing a path for my real, hidden self to emerge? Was it evaporating the food in my brain that the Voices had lived on? Was it starving the Voices out, leaving nothing but me behind? I didn't know a thing. All I knew was that whatever it was doing, it was helping me feel like a real human being again, a human being who existed in the world with other human beings.

I didn't need to strike out as much anymore. Now, instead of smashing windows, I wrote in my journals a list of the things I found stressful:

> *pass for a haircut*
> *weekend passes*
> *Dr. Doller on vacation*
> *activities*
> *Dr. Fischer leaving*
> *new therapist?*
> *weight*
> *discharge pending*

As much as I hated the slow pace of the discharge, I welcomed it too. As much as I wanted to be discharged, I found the prospect

frightening. I knew I was getting better, but I was afraid to test
it. I was afraid of being expected to act normal. I was afraid of
becoming too stressed out and relapsing.

Still, I stayed with the program. Underneath all the fear I
wanted desperately to be better. I wanted desperately to be free.
I wanted desperately to begin the life that had been denied to me
for so long. There was so much to do before that could happen.

For one thing, I needed a therapist. After Dr. Fischer left, people
made a number of suggestions. There was a private practitioner
in White Plains who might do. There was a doctor Dr. Doller
knew. But there was only one person I wanted. When Dr. Doller
agreed to be my therapist, I knew I was going to make it.

Next task was to find somewhere to live. Earlier I had rejected
a halfway house when my parents and Dr. Doller suggested it.
After clozapine it was different. I began to believe that a normal
life was possible. And so I agreed to enter a halfway house. In
September I had an interview at Search for Change. The last time
I had left the hospital I had rejected Search for Change because
there was a rumor of a mouse there. This time I wasn't going to
let a rodent stop me. This was the place that was going to help
me get back into the world again.

Even more than in my last hospitalization, I needed to adjust
to doing things on my own. It had been over two years since I
last had walked around freely.

Little by little I ventured further and further afield. I walked by
myself to the dentist on Mamaroneck Avenue in White Plains. I
took another trip into town to get my hair cut. I went with another
patient to eat Chinese food. Each trip out caused me anxiety. Just
keeping a good hold on myself was an effort. Sometimes I had to
take some medication to keep the jittery feelings under control.
But each time I went out, I got a little more used to it, and it
became a little easier.

I was also coming home regularly, staying with my parents,
going shopping with my mom, going out to eat with my dad. I
was also getting my things ready for my big move. On one
weekend home with my mother, I was going through all my
things stored in the attic of our house. Among my old books and
papers, my college records and memorabilia, I found my old copy

of *Helter Skelter*, the story of Charles Manson's murderous cult. I threw it straight in the wastebasket. His evil eyes would never torture me again.

In the hospital, keys made the sounds of freedom and control. When I was at my sickest, I heard the sound of keys coming down the hall and knew to stop whatever it was I was doing. If I was ripping up dollar bills, I would stop immediately. If I was fiddling with something to use later to hurt myself, I would hide it.

The best key of all was the 9925 key. It was the universal passkey to all the doors on and off the units, to the nursing station, the pantry, the therapeutic activities building—even the Quiet Room. It was the key that Dr. Rockland and Dr. Doller and Dr. Fischer and all the staffers used to come and go from the unit. Patients never touched that key. That key was power. It was the key that opened the locked doors that stood between me and freedom.

Freedom meant loss. In a strange way I had even become fond of this seemingly terrible place. After all, it had been my home for—altogether—nearly four years. I knew the way my bed felt. I knew when the heat came on, and how the place felt in the morning. I knew the times of day when you woke up. I knew when and where to line up for my medication.

I thought about leaving behind all this security. The rules and procedures that had been so foreign to me so many years ago when I had first entered the hospital were second-nature to me now. I was used to community meetings, used to the system of asking for passes. I knew what food was served in the dining room, and how to get seconds and find secret hiding places for the things I liked best.

I knew I was going to miss the staff. Some of them had followed me through all three of my hospitalizations. I thought about the staff who had stood by me, encouraging me. I thought about J.J. and Margo and Jean, who had been with me through the worst. I thought about Rose, who had been my pal. I thought about Barbara, who had given me poems and notes urging me not to give up. Most of all, I thought about Sorin. How was I going to make it without Sorin there behind me? I had a fleeting moment of fear. It passed. I would make it. I would make them all proud of me. I would show them all what I had learned. I would show them all I could make it.

On my last day I was quiet, withdrawn. All the feelings inside me were so hard to control. Quietly and without much comment, I said goodbye to each one, giving each a little gift to remember me by. And then they gave me a gift too. They handed me the 9925 key.

On November 6, 1989, I opened the door to the outside world all by myself, and left the hospital forever.

Epilogue

Lori
Hartsdale, New York, 1994

Today when I walk through the doors of New York Hospital, I do so not as a patient but as a teacher. When I walk through the entrance, I might be wearing a stylish linen jacket, slacks, boots and hoop earrings—not baggy warmup suits.

On weekends I work part-time in a gift shop. This isn't a hospital gift shop selling newspapers, candy, gum and flowers for patients. It's a funky place called What's What, selling everything from stuffed animals to designer handbags to mirrors that laugh when you look at them. I enjoy helping people pick out gifts and making neat corners when wrapping packages. I've even worked full-time as a counselor in a halfway house—the same kind of place I lived myself just a few short years ago.

These days I don't live in a bare room with the furniture removed, or even in a community residence anymore. I remember well the day just over a year ago when I moved into my own apartment. After my friends from the halfway house had lugged up the last box and left me alone in my new home, I sat down on the parquet floors. I just looked around me in dazed happiness. I couldn't quite believe I was here at last.

The apartment I live in today is a beautiful place, filled with furniture I picked out by myself, and with food I like in the refrigerator. All kinds of little things about my new life please me. My desk. My floor lamp from South Africa. My fax machine. The fancy tea kettle I keep ready for company. The shower curtain covered with bright-colored fishes. My limited edition animated cartoon art. It's all mine. If I break a mug, it's my mug. I can keep everything neat and clean just as I want it. I can walk around the house in my underwear if I want. The message on my answering machine is my own.

And of course, there's the door. A regular, ordinary front door that opens and closes with a key I keep in my purse. Anytime I want to leave, I do. Anytime I want to go someplace, I drive myself there. I don't need to ask anyone's permission, I don't need to sign out. At last, my life is my own.

I teach three classes at New York Hospital each month. One is for patients and their families on what it feels like to experience schizophrenia. The other is about clozapine. The third is on how to stay well after discharge.

Who would better know than I? For today, four plus years after I left the hospital for the last time, it is I who am in control of my illness and not the other way around.

It's been a long road here.

I spent three and a half years in a halfway house called Search for Change. I had a lot to change. I had a lot of learning to do. After a total of three and a half years in the hospital, I had learned well how to be a patient. I had to learn to be a functioning person out in the real world. Every day I went back to New York Hospital to the day program, which was designed to help former patients make the transition between the hospital and real life. We showed up there as if to a regular job, signed in, took a lunch break and went home at the end of the day. Attendance was mandatory. We had three personal days off and two weeks' vacation.

We used one another and our counselors to practice behaving normally. At times these groups were so intense that people stormed out in tears. I sometimes was so confused and threatened that I came across as hostile. Gradually, I began taking account of the feedback people were giving me, and started modifying my behavior.

Pretty soon I began to get more used to life on the outside. Following the rules at Search for Change wasn't so difficult. It wasn't such a big deal to make my bed every day before I went out. Doing my chores twice a week became routine. Cooking for nine residents and two or three counselors became a fun challenge.

And at day hospital I began to learn one important lesson: how to live without the Voices.

For as the Voices began to recede, something startling happened within me. After years of begging them to go, to leave me in peace with my own thoughts, when they finally did leave, I found to my surprise that I missed them. They had, over time, dissipated into a kind of background static, only occasionally coming back with their full-force chants. I should have been happy. Instead, I felt like there was a neon vacancy sign flashing. My head felt so empty. Without them, I felt lonely.

I began to reminisce about them, to think about them wistfully as one might an old friend who has died. Now that they were mostly gone, I wanted them back. So I brought them back: I willed them back into my life. I turned my mind inward, searching in its dark recesses to find where the Voices lurked and imagined their presence. Hiding among the static I found them. By focusing my attention on them I was able to coax them out. I welcomed them like lost friends. They were horrible, cruel and profane, but at least they were familiar.

This went on for a long time before I realized what I was doing. I wanted to get well. I wanted to live normally. I wanted to relate to normal people as an equal. Yet here I was walking backward, down the road to sickness and madness again. I was choosing my sick Voices over a healthy reality. I must really be crazy!

After that, I began to turn outward more. Part of the problem was that, once the Voices left, there was nothing in my head to think about. The Voices had dominated my brain for so long that they had left no room for any other thoughts. What brain space I had left over all those years was devoted to fighting off the Voices' overpowering attacks. What's more, as a full-time patient on a locked ward, even if I had had more space to think, I had nothing much to think about. The dreary sameness of my daily life gave no foothold for thoughts to grow and take root.

Obviously what I needed was a life.

So I began to devote my energy to building one. I used every tool they offered me at day hospital. I met with a counselor, usually every week, and together we worked on an elaborate goal sheet.

I had trouble articulating myself verbally in sessions with the other patients and counselors so I practiced giving one piece of feedback per session, and kept up with my writing, which was a helpful form of self-expression. If I overloaded myself with activities and became too stressed, then I set specific hours for each activity and worked on not obsessively exceeding those limits. If I heard the Voices lurking in the background or if the temptation, to follow them back into their world became too strong, I fought them any way I could. I would listen to my Walkman, talk to my friends, take a shower, take a walk, ask for help.

I had been isolated for so long I had to work hard at reconnecting. I was still paranoid, fearful of people, down on myself for my perceived failures. I set myself the goal of deliberately thinking good thoughts about myself, and of checking with other people if I thought they were angry with me.

I had been out of the world for so long that I had no network of friends to fall back on. So onto my goal sheet it went: I will initiate two telephone calls each week to someone outside my family. I also joined the other patients in a social group, going out to eat, going to the movies, going to the beach. I had to practice all over again what it meant to go out and have fun.

For years someone else had taken the responsibility for managing my life. My medications were doled out four times a day. My meals were ready at regular hours. The only money I was responsible for was the pocket money my father gave me. If I was going to make it on my own, I had to relearn how to do things on my own. I got the job as meal planner at the halfway house. I learned how to plan meals and shop. I learned how to put aluminum foil in the bottom of a pan when cooking steak or chicken to make cleaning up easier. I learned how to budget, and to plan how I was going to spend my money. I relearned how to balance a checkbook, something that had once been easy for me. I began to learn how to structure my time myself, without depending on the hospital's routine of medication times and meetings to rule my life. When I arrived at day hospital I was given a pocket calender and began to write down all my appointments and obligations. I even began to take responsibility for my medications for myself. Starting with one day's medications, and gradually working up by adding a day at a time, I learned at Search for Change how to count-out the doses into a multi-compartment box the size of a fat paperback I carry, and to remember to take them religiously four times a day.

The responsibility was scary. Before every big change, I found myself growing anxious. I was afraid of failure, afraid of finding out that I could not do a task, afraid of each step that took me further away from the security of the hospital. But I also reveled in my accomplishments. I was taking big steps back toward having a life of my own.

To my great delight, too, my weight began to drop. It had begun dropping in my last months in the hospital, from 170 to 166 to 164 . . . slowly, steadily, a pound at a time, the layers of fat that had encased the old me began to fall off. Lower and lower my weight dropped—160 to 158 to 155 to 150, to 147 to 143. By my thirty-first birthday, less than six months after I had left the hospital, I was under 140 pounds. Out shopping with my mother one day, I bumped into someone. When I turned around to apologize, I realized it was a mirror.

I didn't recognize the stranger looking back.

At first, I was very self-conscious about approaching my old friends. They had all gone on to accomplish such impressive things. They had good jobs, nice families. It was like they were the grown-ups and I was still a little kid. I felt inferior to them, and afraid they would scorn me. When I overcame my fears and called them, I discovered that, although our lives had taken very different paths, they are still the very oldest friends I have, and that I need that connection. Lori Winters, Tara and I all got together in Connecticut for lunch and laughed like the old friends we were. Tara and I met once in Florida where we were both spending a brief vacation with our families, and she's always asking me to come to Washington to visit. Lori and I get together once in a while for lunch and gossip. I even spent one Christmas with Lori and her husband and two little boys.

Gail Kobre Lazarus tickled me with her response to the new, improved me. "She's baaaaacck! Lori's baaaaaack," she said, mimicking a horror movie—only this time not *Carrie*, the movie that haunted me so.

I've been reaching out, trying hard to make new friends. I've rekindled friendships with buddies from high school. When I have friends over, I cook dinners of chicken and pasta and make brunches of bagels and lox. I've tackled the bar scene. I attend singles dances and discussion groups. Sometimes I'll go by myself, sometimes with a friend. The goal is to meet other people; and it's fun. It sure beats being in the hospital.

At first the only thing I knew was my illness, my medications and the halfway house, which didn't make me a very interesting conversationalist. But as time has gone on, I've become more adept at talking about more general things—about family, and friends, and relationships, and things in the news, and vacations and movies.

Nothing about dating is easy these days for any thirty-ish single woman. But I've even come to think it's fun. Now that I'm back to my college weight—118 pounds—I feel chic and pretty again. I dress casually in jeans and a sweater, spray on my favorite Calvin Klein Escape perfume and head for local hangouts. Since I don't drink, I usually sit at the bar and order some food, to keep myself looking busy while I scout for a good-looking guy who's alone. I've met a hot dog peddler, a fax machine salesman who owns his own company, an IBM computer programmer, a General Motors plant supervisor and a cemetery executive.

I very badly want to get married and have kids. But with all the medications I take, I think I would probably be better off trying to find a ready-made family. So I'm looking for a nice divorced or widowed man with kids of his own. It's going to take a very special guy to realize how much I have to offer him. But I know when I find him, he won't be disappointed. (That's a glimpse of my personal ad.)

When we're making small talk at the outset of a date, it isn't always easy when the moment arrives to come clean about my past. A lot of guys just can't take it. In retrospect, some of their reactions are even funny. For quite some time I dated a guy I met who worked where I was having my car repaired. We got along well and had a pretty good time together, so finally I decided to tell him. I took him to my apartment and showed him an article I had written about my history.

He finished reading the article, then looked at me in disgust.

"You don't have schizophrenia," he said.

"Yes, I'm afraid I do," I replied.

"No you don't. You're just making it all up," he said. "Why did you write that?"

When I showed him the box of all the medications I take, he became angry and threatened to call my parents.

We kept on meeting for several weeks after that, but he never became convinced. I decided I couldn't continue seeing someone who had such a hard time accepting me for who I really am, so we broke off. I never saw him again.

As for drugs, real drugs, street drugs, I have never taken up the offer to get high with anyone since the cocaine incident at Futura House years ago. I've come too far and accomplished too much to waste it all by sliding back into the shadowy world of drugs.

I meet with Dr. Doller twice a week. She helps me monitor my medication. I take twenty-six pills a day for my psychotic symptoms, my mood swings, for anxiety and for the side effects that the drugs cause.

We have a great partnership these days. I carry a little tape recorder with me wherever I go, to record anything that happens during the week that I feel I need to pay attention to. With Dr. Doller's help I have learned not to be overwhelmed by the emotional swings I am subject to. I have learned to weather the low points and to realize that good times will return. I have also learned not to let myself follow too enthusiastically the manic highs.

Dr. Fischer and I kept in touch with each other for about a year after she left the hospital. Then one day I received a letter telling me she was about to have a baby. I couldn't take it. I destroyed all the letters she had sent me, and never wrote her another one.

I'm sorry we lost touch. I want her to know me as I am today, and see how well I am doing. I want her to see what her work has helped me to achieve. I want her to be proud of me, and proud of herself as well. Just recently she wrote me a letter. I know that one day I am going to be able to summon up the courage to write back.

I'm still very close to my parents. We spend a lot of time

together. I love them and respect them. I'm grateful for all their help. At the same time, I've learned I can also get angry at them. But when I do, I can express it without getting out of control or worrying that I'm driving them away. I now understand how powerful an emotion love is.

I've even suffered a bit of a relapse and recovered.

It happened over the summer when I was working on this book, dredging up old memories of the time between my first two hospitalizations. It was a particularly difficult period in my life and very painful to recall. At the same time, other stressful things were going on in my life: My brother Steven had married and moved with his wife Ann to South Africa. I missed him and was anticipating missing Mom and Dad, who were retiring and moving to Florida. I was feeling abandoned by my other two strong supports as well: Dr. Doller was taking a maternity leave, and my caseworker Jacquie was returning to school. At the same time, Dr. Doller and I were experimenting with lowering my medication. It was all too much for me.

Within a week I began to feel strange, all buzzy and unstable inside. Within two weeks, I was having a full-blown attack. Amanda, my writing partner, was climbing into my brain. She had seized control of my thoughts. What's more, she wanted me dead. For over a year we had been talking with each other several times a day, laughing and joking and enjoying each other's company. Suddenly I was terrified of her. I fled from her. I stopped answering the phone. Even the sound of her voice on the answering machine sent tremors through me. She was trying to control me, to ruin my life. Days went by.

Such a psychotic episode could have easily spun out of control. It didn't. What stopped it? I did. I knew something was wrong. The illness had seized a portion of my brain, but it hadn't seized all of it. I knew I needed help. I raised my medication back up to its normal level. I called Dr. Doller. I talked to my parents. At first I scorned what they said. My Voices and I knew better. But I never became completely consumed. Over the years I had learned to trust Dr. Doller. So if she said I was experiencing a psychotic episode, then I probably was, no matter what the Voices told me.

Soon the medication took hold again, and my fears subsided. I picked up the phone myself to call Amanda on her birthday. A few days later, we met in the city. When I treated us both to two huge bowls of steamed clams and melted butter at the Oyster Bar at Grand Central Station it was more than just her birthday we were celebrating.

I still hear the Voices from time to time. I try to take my own advice. I distract myself, lecture myself, and focus on the outside world. I have taught myself to use a little mantra when they reappear: "These Voices are not real. Don't be frightened. Don't get upset. They are not real. Don't let them overcome you. Try to think of what happened just before you heard them. Is there some emotion you can isolate that will help explain why they are here now? They are not real. It's okay. Don't be afraid."

When I hear the Voices, I shake myself back to reality by using all my senses. If I'm riding the train to Manhattan, for example, I concentrate on the taste of the Diet Coke and the smell of the perfume I am wearing. I look out the window at the changing view, and listen carefully to the sound of the conductor collecting tickets. I feel my own ticket flipping back and forth between my fingers.

Some people can tell when I'm hearing Voices. I wish they couldn't. I don't mind talking about the Voices, but knowing that their presence is evident to others feels like an invasion of my privacy. If people let on that they know I am hearing Voices, I sometimes think it's because they've heard them too, and not because a particular expression has flitted across my face.

Nonetheless I find talking and joking about my symptoms helps keep them in their place. So I do it all the time. Like the time Anne Schiff, my father's secretary, questioned me about a current news item.

"What do you hear, Lori?" she asked.

"Oh you know me," I said. "I hear all kinds of things."

When Amanda lost manuscript pages or forgot to return phone calls, I would chide her: "I'm supposed to be the daffy one, not you." When she needed to impress someone important, I offered to lend a hand: "I'll have the Voices write you a letter of recommendation," I said.

For years I tried to hide the Voices because I assumed they would horrify people. As I have found out recently, that is not always the case.

When one of the mailmen who serve our complex expressed an interest, I showed him an article about me and my history. He was a young guy and I watched him carefully as he read through it. At the end, he looked up.

"You hear voices?" he asked incredulously.

"Yes, sometimes I do," I said, and waited for the look of horror to cross his face.

The look was, instead, one of pure admiration.

"Coooooool!" he said, with tremendous enthusiasm.

I wanted to hug him.

★ ★ ★

Writing this book has been painful and exhilarating. It was painful to force myself to remember things that I would just as soon forget. But it's been exhilarating to see how far I've come.

Dr. Doller told me once when I was in the hospital that I could never go back. I could never again be the girl I was before that dark night at summer camp. Looking over my life, I know now that I don't want to go back. I want to go ahead. I look forward to a future filled with accomplishment, learning and the love of my family and friends.

Many people helped me get to where I am now. Now it is my turn. Painful as it has been, I've written this book hoping that my story can help others the way I was helped. If my life and my experiences can help other people find their own ways out of darkness, I will know that I have not wasted the great gift I have been given: the chance to begin life again.